1 MONTH OF
FREE
READING

at
www.ForgottenBooks.com

By purchasing this book you are eligible for one month membership to ForgottenBooks.com, giving you unlimited access to our entire collection of over 1,000,000 titles via our web site and mobile apps.

To claim your free month visit:
www.forgottenbooks.com/free981615

ISBN 978-0-260-88754-2
PIBN 10981615

This book is a reproduction of an important historical work. Forgotten Books uses state-of-the-art technology to digitally reconstruct the work, preserving the original format whilst repairing imperfections present in the aged copy. In rare cases, an imperfection in the original, such as a blemish or missing page, may be replicated in our edition. We do, however, repair the vast majority of imperfections successfully; any imperfections that remain are intentionally left to preserve the state of such historical works.

LASELL LEAVES

"DUX FEMINA FACTI."

VOL. XXVI.   LASELL SEMINARY, AUBURNDALE, MASS., OCTOBER, 1900.   NUMBER 1

Published monthly during the School year by the Lasell Publishing Association.

EDITOR-IN-CHIEF.
GEORGIE M. DUNCAN, '02.

ASSOCIATE EDITORS.
ANNA M. PINKHAM, '02.   BESSIE Y. FULLER, '02.   IDA M. MALLORY, '03

LOCAL EDITOR.   SUBSCRIPTION AGENT.   EXCHANGE EDITOR.
RUTH M. TALCOTT.   ETHEL M. GALLAGHER, 'or.   MABEL MARTIN, 'or.

BUSINESS MANAGER.   ASST. BUSINESS MANAGER.
ETHLYN F. BARBER, 'or.   JOANNA F. DEERING, '02.

TERMS, in Advance: One copy, one year (including Postage), $1.00.   Single copies, 15 cents.

Editorials.

ONE more summer vacation has come and gone, and we are again settling down to the work of another school year.   It is with great pleasure that we welcome the new girls this year, and hope that they will have here a very pleasant and profitable time.

The weather this fall has been especially beautiful, and has made possible to us all many enjoyable hours of exercise and pleasure in the open air.   Although we have had a few unpleasant days since school began, these have not much interferred with our outdoor exercise.   We are glad to see that the new girls are making good use of the tennis court and golf-links.

We realize that the new girls feel that "There's no place like home;" we all felt that way ourselves when we first came; but it ought to be some comfort to think how much more fortunate we are here than are those poor people in Texas and other parts of the world, to whom so much disaster has come of late.   How thankful we should be that our homes and dear ones are spared to us even though we may not be permitted to be with them just at present.

Several changes in our faculty have been made this year.   Miss Carpenter, who for a number of years past has taught the literature and history classes, has added to her duties this year, that of preceptress. Miss C. M. Austin assists Miss Witherbee with the English, and Miss Kendrick with the Latin, besides having charge of the library. She is a graduate of Smith, class of '99' and made a specialty of English and the classic languages. ⁄ Miss Edith Lynwood Winn is the instructor in violin, mandolin and guitar. She is a pupil of Julius Eichberg, of the New England Conservatory of Music, and in addition to this, has studied several years under Johanne Kense, of Berlin. A woman of wide culture, she has won distinction in the various capacities of teacher, soloist, essayist, and lecturer.

This year every girl is required to take chorus, which is divided into three classes, according to the girls' ability to read music —the beginners, those a little more advanced, and those who can read readily. This last constitutes the Orphean Club, and consists of about twenty members. Mr. A. E. French, our teacher, was for a number of years instructor of music in the Boston public schools. Last year the chorus classes were not very large, as it was altogether optional, and too many of the girls neglected to take advantage of the fine opportunity given. We feel sure that the work will do us a great deal of good.

Mrs. Miriam Loomis of Marietta, Ohio, takes this year the places of Miss Barrows, Mrs. Norton and Mrs. Perry, as Director of Household Economics.

A Suggestive Editorial.

INSTEAD of "boy" put "girl" in this editorial extract from the *New York Christian Advocate*, and it will be just as true:

Choose "Chums" Carefully.

When boys go from home to school or college they learn the meaning of the word "chum" by experience. "Girls," says a writer, "are more 'chummy' than boys." Perhaps they are; at least they are likely to spend more time indoors than boys, and so may be together more. But when a boy really likes his chum they may be as happy as any girls can be, and help each other as much. The best friendships in life often start in this way and last till death.

This is the bright side of the picture.

Sometimes there is a dark side;—black as a starless midnight.

Many a boy has been ruined by his roommate. We could tell some truthful and awful tales of what we saw in boarding school and college, but it is not necessary, for similar things are going on all the time. Last week four of a gang of the worst criminals in this country were arrested, and are now in prison. One of them has been a banker and a State senator, and was once reputed to be wealthy; but for many years he has been a swindler, robbing, forging. This man and another arrested with him were "chums in college," and were known then as gamblers. It is probable that one led the other astray, and it is possible that if one had been a firm, moral, Christian young man the other might have been led into the right path. Choose your chums with care; drop your best friend if you find him morally rotten, and drop him at once.

These two men belonged to the best families, and had the finest chance to do well in the world.

Choose your acquaintances and, above all, your chums with care, and avoid those whom on further acquaintance you find unworthy. No other way is safe.

The sorrow of yesterday is as nothing; that of to-day is bearable; but that of to-morrow is gigantic, because indistinct.— *Euripides.*

Queen Louise.

THE name Queen Louise, and the picture of a very beautiful woman descending a staircase, are closely associated in the thoughts of most of us school-girls, because somewhere in our rooms, on wall or dresser or in art album, we have this picture, which we count one of our treasures. There may be other pictures of this royal beauty, but this of Rechter's is best known and most admired. For this reason, some account of this noble woman may be of interest.

Louise of Prussia was born in 1776. Her early training was received from very pious and conscientious people, and thus acquired a certain religious tone, and it was, furthermore, for the most part carried on in French instead of in German, for which she expressed a regret in after years. Her generosity and loving thoughtfulness for others, a life-long characteristic, was evident when she was but a child. One day when out walking, she gave all her money to a poor widow, who begged for bread for her starving children, and at another time she was found reading to the sick child of one of the castle servants.

At the age of seventeen, Louise met the Crown Prince of Prussia, to whom not long after, she was married. The Princess much preferred the quiet of home life to the court, and was never so happy as when looking after her husband's comfort, in the fashion of a true German housewife. She had three children, two sons and a daughter, to whom she was devoted, and gave a great share of her time and attention. When the Prince ascended the throne at his father's death, she left her quiet life for the more public one of the court with regret. One thing about her new position that pleased her, however, was the fact that now she could give as much to the poor as she wished.

Up to the time of Napoleon's evil ascendency, the Queen's life was a happy one, but now Prussia was drawn into her disasterous war with France. The King, of course, had to go to the front; her people were in dire distress, which she was unable to relieve; and the news of defeat came daily to her ears. When negotiations for peace were being made, Napoleon requested an interview with the Queen, who strongly impressed him with her beauty and her royal bearing, but was unable to influence him sufficiently to make the terms of peace more favorable for Prussia.

The death of the Queen occurred in 1810 at her father's home. It was like her gentle nature, that during her illness, she should regret the anxiety she caused her relatives. She was but thirty-four when she died, yet all Prussia mourned the death of the good and beautiful Queen. Her gracious influence long survived her in the hearts of her people. She cherished to her dying day the hope that Germany would one day be a united people, and it seems a pity she was not allowed to see the establishment of that German unity she so much desired, or to know that her own sons it was who were eventually to fulfill, this, her dearest hope.

Loving Words.

Loving words will cost but little,
Journeying up the hill of life;
But they make the weak and weary
Stronger, braver for the strife.
Do you count them only trifles?
What to earth are sun and rain?
Never was a kind word wasted;
Never one was said in vain.

—*Anon.*

He only can enrich me who can recommend to me the space between sun and sun. —*Emerson.*

Habit is habit, and not to be flung out of the window by any man, but coaxed down stairs a step at a time.—*Mark Twain.*

The Modern Department Store.

IT is only within the last few years that the large city department stores have existed. Until Mr. Macy of New York conceived the idea of having numerous departments under one roof, instead of under twenty, the city store had in general some one special line of goods which it sold to the exclusion of all else. But in the department store of today you can find almost every desired luxury and necessity. Here you can completely furnish your house, from cellar to attic; can buy even the books for the library, as well as the kitchen utensils and groceries; can stock your wardrobe extravagantly or otherwise; can purchase your bicycle, and indeed, any kind of outfit for out-door sport; and when wearied by shopping, can take your luncheon at the cafe on the tenth floor, or in the Japanese tea-room. If you wish you can rest in the ladies' waiting room, read the new magazines, or write your letters. You can also have your hair dressed in the latest fashion by expert hairdressers, or your nails manicured.

The shopper little realizes how gigantic is the organization, and how complex the system necessary to run this immense store, the management which delivers her purchases at her home before she arrives; or how perfect service must be in order to prevent anyone of the hundreds of packages daily sent out from being lost, or left at the wrong place. Under Wanamaker's immense roof are over two thousand employees. The firm, the gentlemen who own the store, have not only to sit in their office and receive the profits; they must know how the business is progressing; how each department is working, and must approve the special sales. Their chief assistant, the superintendent, who is in charge of all the departments, receives the applications of all those desiring any position in the store; makes the rules for the employees; sees to the special sales; and approves the choice of the buyers.

The heads of each department, the floorwalkers, are next in importance. They see that the articles in their departments are attractively arranged; that the clerks obey the rules; that the customers are promptly waited on; and that the shoppers who go for information, or to make complaints, are attended to in either case.

Then comes the army of clerks. In all the best department stores, the clerks are required to be respectful and obliging to customers; they must be neat in appearance, too, and it is generally required of them to dress in black. There seems to be no preference in respect of sex, both men and women being employed. In order that the stores may be able to employ the nicer class of clerks, they must treat them with respect and consideration. Wanamaker has erected for his clerks a compartment house, which is built with regard to comfort, health, and economy. Another large store has provided a cafe where the employees may eat their luncheon, paying only the actual cost of the provisions. Most stores encourage their clerks to form reading clubs, or other societies, in which they may become better acquainted with one another.

The next on the list of employees are the cash boys and girls. If a store employes only cash boys, they are generally required to dress in uniform; but if girls also are employed, uniforms are not used. The cash boys must be quiet and quick in fulfilling their duties. In most stores electric bells are used to call the "cash," and are less trying and disagreeable than the rasping call of "cash!" by the clerks.

Part of the basement floor is used in some stores for the crockery department, the groceries, and sometimes for the cheaper articles of dress goods; but there is one division not open to the public, and that is where the packages are brought from all parts of the store, sorted for delivery according to the different parts of the city where they are to go, and taken away by the delivery wagons. Every driver has his special route which he always follows.

Another department not accessible to the public, is that where the buyers are stationed. There they interview drummers and examine samples. These buyers have control over the purchase of articles for the store, subject, of course, to the approval of the superintendent, and they must see well to the quality and assortment of the goods for the department which is in their hands. Every department has a special buyer, but there is generally more than one buyer for each department, one traveling abroad, another traveling in this country, and still another remaining at the store to meet the drummers who come there. Even the notion counter has its buyer who, when he sees any taking new invention in hair-pins, say, must find the best maker of these, and purchase a supply. There seems to be no choice as to whether the buyers should be men or women, indeed women are considered better in some departments.

In the ready-made clothing department models are usually employed, whose whole duty is to try on the garments so that the prospective buyer may see for herself how others would see her in that particular robe. These models must look stylish in any garment, be it ball dress, walking suit, or bicycle skirt; consequently they must possess that indefinable thing called "style," or they could never show off these dresses to advantage. There are also dressing rooms, with courteous attendants, where ladies from out of the city can dress for reception or ball.

During the holidays, the stores are tastefully decorated as a means of advertisement. Each firm has its own opinion as to the best means of advertising. Most stores try to attract public attention by their beautifully decorated windows, but the windows of some stores are more artistically decorated than others; the store which should not decorate windows would be considered far behind the times, so that it behooves the stores to decorate in some way or other. It is the decorated windows that show the prevailing fashion in the making of dresses, as well as the fashion in dress goods for the present and the coming season.

During the Christmas holidays, the windows are filled with Christmas bargains and toys for the children, and the store which Santa Claus honors with his presence is the children's favorite. At Easter time the windows are filled with Easter bonnets and dresses, of which the prevailing color is violet. Another store, perhaps, expects its immense advertisements in the morning papers, to attract shoppers.

Department stores are of much greater advantage, in various ways, than the type of store in which but one sort of goods is kept, or a small variety of commodities. To the beauty and imposing effect of the business portion of the city, for example, these large and handsome buildings add greatly. Their exquisite window displays of attractive goods draw many customers from places outside the city, as well as from the city itself; hence large sums of money are realized because of the greatness of the tide of custom. This brings more business to the city at large, as may easily be seen, and thus materially contributes to its prosperity. Moreover, in the purchasing of such great amounts of various kinds of goods, as must be got to replenish the stock of so large a business, large discounts are made so that it is possible for the firm to sell them cheaper, and yet make a fair profit, which is of direct advantage to the shopper, and equally so to the manufacturer. Since, then, these large establishments are of such decided advantage and profit to manufacturer, the firm, and the shopper, is it not idle and uncalled for to cry them down as is the fashion with a certain class of people?   L. K. W.

PERSONALS.

—Mr. Bragdon attended the Smith College celebration of its twenty-fifth anniversary, at Northampton, October first and second, and much enjoyed being present at the interesting exercises of that occasion.

—It will interest Lasell pupils to know that the great grandmother of our new teacher, Mr. French, was Laura, sister of Benjamin Franklin. Mr. French has been much employed in public school work, and is now in charge of the singing in the schools of Dover, N. H.

—Kittie Totman Brownell of old days, sends an interesting letter. The destructive tidal wave that destroyed so much life and property at Galveston, did not reach LaPorte, where she lives, and the town was but slightly damaged by wind. This is good news.

—Mr. Stowe of Galveston, father of Willie and Virginia, writes of the dreadful work of clearing away the debris of the flood, disposing of the bodies of the poor unfortunates found, and of the great business losses suffered by so many in the city, himself one. His home, and that of Virginia and her family, next door, withstood the storm, though put to an awful test. Virginia and her children are at present away from the city, as is Willie, also. None of their relatives were lost in the great disaster.

—Mary Roberts and Agnes Batchelder Wylie, with her husband, called in July.

—Margie Schuberth and Blanche Kelley, ('96), made us a short visit.

—Nellie Briggs of Somerville drove over with her father.

—Among others who have recently called are: Cara Sawin, ('96), Troy, N. Y.; Mary B. Cruikshank, ('96), Newton, Mass.; Elsie Burdick, ('99), Hartford, Conn.; Alice Conant, Camden, N. Y.; Helen Ramsdell, ('00), Woburn; Bertha Metcalf, Plainville; Elise Scott, ('99), Chestnut Hill; Elsie Reynolds, ('00), E. Haddam, Conn.; Ella B. Cotton, ('00), Omaha, Neb.

—Mr. A. F. Miller of Fremont, Ohio, father of our Julia Miller, made us a too brief call.

—Rosa Best of Malden gave us a delightful call the other day.

—Belle Bragdon, '95, reports the following notes of her Omaha visit on her way east from Pasadena. Mr. and Mrs. Bragdon returned via Canadian Pacific R. R., as his notes elsewhere tell.

—Mabel Taylor, ('95,) is happy in her new home at Omaha. Grace Allen, ('95), and Elizabeth Allen, ('98), as well as Mabel Taylor, are "golf girls," and spend much time at the beautiful Omaha Country Club, of which they are all members. Elizabeth still keeps up her violin a bit.

—Martha Stone Adams is living with her parents since her husband is travelling so much of the time.

—Ella Cotton, ('00), is enjoying herself at the "Country Club and everywhere."

—Margie Schuberth, ('96), spent a few days last August at Wilmington, Vermont, where Gertrude Clarke, ('97), Dorothy Manning, ('95), and Miss Newton of Holyoke, were keeping house during August and September.

—Dorothy Manning has been East the greater part of the summer, visiting Blanche Kelley, ('96), Gertrude Clarke, and friends in Holyoke and Nantucket. She starts for Dayton, O., about the first of October.

—Nell Quirk, ('97), spent a while with Gertrude Clarke before returning to her home in Minneapolis, Minn.

—Rose Best is keeping house for her father and mother at Linden, a suburb of Malden, Mass.

—Belle Bragdon has gone to New York to take a course of convalescent nursing.

—We hear thro' a new pupil that Alice Conant has developed a very sweet and capable voice. Glad.

—Laura Conger, the daughter of the United States Minister to China, is our Laura Conger, and has been through the siege with her father and mother in Pekin. Mr. Bragdon saw her last in Pasadena in the spring of '99.

—The opening of school this fall brought a gratifying number of our old friends to see us once more, and though by force of circumstances their stay was all too short, it was none the less a pleasure to have them with us again. Elizabeth Kiser Irwin, ('77), came from Keokuk, Ia., to bring us her two pleasant daughters; Lucy Curtis, of Rockland, came with her niece, and Myrtle Hewson, her sister, Lotta. Of our new pupils Edith Sisson is Maritta Sisson's sister, and Charlotte Massey is the daughter of Belle Jones Massey. Clara Robbins was here awhile when school began, to help launch the new girls comfortably—nice of her to do so.

—Carita Curtis sent us word of herself in a pleasant August letter. She was at New Rochelle, N. Y., with her mother and sister, and Mrs. Avery, a friend of her sister's. She was having, of course, a delightful time, and spoke, furthermore, of the pleasure she had here with us at Commencement time. She mentions Ethel Smith as a loyal Lasell daughter, which Carita herself claims also to be. Ethel is with her sick brother, she says, making his life brighter. There is a plan afoot for a great reunion of Lasell girls in Omaha this coming year. Evelyn Ebert was expected shortly, at the time Carita wrote, for a day's visit, being only so far away as Glen Ridge. Besides these pleasures, she mentions a class in literature each morning. Truly, her summer must have been very pleasantly spent.

—From Alice Fuller was received, in June, an invitation to her Commencement exercises at Pratt Institute.

—Among our summer callers was Mrs. Henry B. Glover, mother of our Carrie, of loved memory.

—The advertising agent of the *Boston Transcript,* Mr. William F. Rogers, is the husband of our Mabel Sawyer Rogers, ('95).

—Maudie L. Stone, ('88), brought her friend, Miss Gridley, a teacher of art at Emporia, out to Lasell to spend a Sunday in July. Maudie was taking work in the Summer school, and wished Miss Gridley to meet Mr. Bragdon, see Lasell, and enjoy the pictures here.

—Clara Eads, ('93), speaks a good word for Nell Jones, with us this year, and a dear friend of hers. In May and June Clara visited Harriet and Alice Noble, and from their home went to her brother's college graduation. Besides this, she speaks, too, of a delightful visit to friends in Garland Dell, Indiana.

—Edith Bailey, ('oo), says some pleasant things about Caroline LeSeure who is now one of us, Edith has a new address: 205 High street.

—Among our summer visitors were our new pupil, Miss Maud Campbell, her mother and younger sister, from San Jose, California, who are trying the virtues of the Atlantic coast.

—Principal Bragdon's brother, George E. Bragdon of Pueblo, Colo., was much urged to accept the Republican nomination for Lieut. Governor of that state, but steadfastly refused. The Bragdon's don't "take to" politics, as a livelihood.

—"I saw the Fowler girls, Della, Etta and Nora. Della has a new baby girl, which is 'the only baby.' Della and Etta are so well they each refuse to be weighed." So writes Katie Gibbons Ashenden, who came from Texas to have Dr. Will Haskell mend her eyes (when did Katie's eyes ever look as if they needed mending?) and of course called at Lasell. She reports Mr. Ashenden as making a fine place for himself in Dallas, as voice teacher and singer. We all knew he would.

—Flo. Gardner, ('93), has spent most of her time since graduation in traveling. Her sisters, Al and Lucie, she says, are very happy in their homes. The former has two children, eight and four, respectively, and Lucie one, almost three now. Nellie Davis's, ('93), father, she tells us, is dead. Nellie is very sad and lonely, and finds it hard to rally from so severe a blow. Anna Staley, ('92), who was to have been married to Sue Richards' ('91), brother in June, has also met with deep sorrow. Mr. Richards was taken suddenly ill, and died before Anna could reach him. Ava Rawleigh is happily married, and has a dear little home. The Rowe girls, Alice Platt Durand and Bess Crawford Hawxhurst are all in Evanston.

—Laura Conger, here some years ago, is the daughter of Minister Conger at Pekin, about whom there has been so much said recently, because of the Chinese troubles, and the imminent peril of the foreigners in that city.

—Helen Ramsdell's, ('oo), father wrote us in August, that Helen's health was all right now. They had just returned from a Canadian trip. Since then Helen has been here to see us, and be her own evidence that she is no longer ailing. We are glad.

—Lina Morgan Jones, whose stay with us was cut short by illness, writes us after the lapse of twenty years, and tells us of herself and experiences since then. Like so many others, she has lost the dear father and mother; two brothers also have gone on before. She is married, and has a fifteen year old boy. Not long since, she had a visit from Lottie Snell Simms, ('82), who has three children, and lives in Herkimer, N. Y. She mentions especially, of the teachers, Miss Carpenter and Miss Blaisdell.

—Martha Ladd Burton sends new address: 271 No. Willow street, Waterbury, Conn.

—Georgie Lord sends best wishes for the new school year. Thanks.

—Ella Huestis, we hear, enters Smith this year. Our best wishes to her. We heard from her once during vacation.

—Julia Cox adds her good wishes for the coming year, to those of other good friends. She was ill during the summer, she says, wherefore she cannot return to us this fall. We wish her speedy and complete recovery.

—A newspaper clipping of more than ordinary interest to us tells us, that Annie Kirkwood, here in ('85), has gained for herself a very comfortable business position as a life insurance agent, though the early stages of her work were beset by difficulties. Her courage and resolution, however, together with perseverance and devotion to business, won the battle and gave her a signal victory. We rejoice in her success.

—Annie Young's, ('97), father wrote us, recently, that Annie had been seriously ill during the summer, though when he wrote she was well again, and enjoying her trip to Colorado with him. They expected to return east at about the last of this month.

—Sara Bond Goldsmith, ('95), of whose recent sorrow another column tells, gives 128 Commonwealth avenue as her permanent home address. Just now she is in Denver, with her sister-in-law, expecting to spend the winter there.

—That Emma C. Hackett, Jennie Lyons and Julia A. Norris, in the Woman's Medical School, Northwestern University, received honorable mention on the occasion of the June graduation of students from that institution, is the welcome news brought us by a little clipping from the *Chicago Tribune* of June 15.

—The grief occasioned Mabel Case Viot, ('94), by the loss of her mother in the summer, was cruelly aggravated, by the fact that she was unable to reach home before her mother's death. Mabel and Mr. Viot had gone to Europe on their wedding trip, and in Switzerland, received news of Mrs. Case's dangerous illness. A second cable message received in England gave hope of her recovery, but this was presently followed by a third announcing the fatal termination of her illness, on receiving which the young couple immediately sailed for home. How sadly different the return from the departure! Mrs. Case was a lady of marked social and intellectual gifts, and was greatly esteemed in Highland Park, where she was a prominent figure in social and church circles.

—Sue Brown Brill, (88), and her husband, called to see Mr. Bragdon during the summer. Sue seemed to thrive on married life, he says.

—Mrs. Dr. Bragdon of Evanston (our Principal's brother Mett's wife), and her children, Carl and Sarah F., were here during the summer.

—Hazel North brings us welcome news of Beulah Smith, who has just returned from an enjoyable European trip. Beulah is well, and gives a glowing report of her summer's pleasure.

—Myrtle Davis, ('97), so one of her friends tells us, is to be married in October to a gentleman from Boston, Mr. Durell Gage.

—Roe Porter, ('00), writes that her family expect to move to Detroit for the following school year, her sister expecting to continue her lessons on the violin, and Roe to study piano and art.

—Lena Josselyn, ('97), writes, "We are all busy getting ready for Marion's wedding in October. Katharine Bucknum, ('96) is coming on to be one of her bridesmaids. Marion and her husband will live in Boston." Grace Ordway, it appears, is a cousin to this gentleman, Mr. Young. Mary Johnson Whitney, ('98), she says, likes St. Louis very much. Alice Burnham Carpenter, ('98), is very proud of her dear little girl. Lena's engagement to Mr. Frank Lamson was announced sometime during the summer. She encloses in her letter a program of her club, the Nineteenth Century Club. It is a well chosen one, and has been given an artistic form in this tasteful, little pamphlet.

—Nora Burroughs, ('97), we regret to hear, has had a trying experience; La Grippe last January, a relapse, and ever since that a long, slow struggle back to health. She spent her summer in the North, endeavoring to regain lost ground, and at the end of it was feeling very much improved, indeed.

We hope she is quite well again by now. She visited Lucia Shumway Suffel, ('97), for awhile, "the same dear Lucia, as of old," and while there saw Fan Fairchild, who "looks ten years younger than when at Lasell," and Flo Joannes, also. At Madison, Wis., Nora met Ellen Sanborn and Marie Griswold. She had had Paris letters from Grace Washburn, who was one of Mr. Shepherd's European party in the summer. Julia Aldrich, who she tells us, is to be married in October, gave a tea to her prospective bridesmaids in May, and Nora was present, meeting there Annie Young. Annie, who as we all know, is a literary person these days, makes children's stories her specialty, and seems to be doing well at this work.

—Julia Anderson writes, September 21, that she is again in the hospital, which we are sorry, indeed, to hear of her. She speaks of her sister's little daughter, born in July; and of Myrna Lamson, who has grown stouter since we saw her. Julia thinks her greatly improved.

—We were all so glad to see Evie Harris the other day. She, and a cousin of hers, came in towards evening, partly, as Evie confessed, because she greatly wished to be present at evening chapel again, and she felt rather disappointed that our newly arranged hours put chapel at noon on school days, instead of in the evening. She was looking exceedingly well, and evidently felt as well as she looked. Through her we learned, to our deep regret, of the recent death of one of Bessie Risser's brothers. Bessie and her sister were expecting to enter Smith this fall, but this sad occurrence may cause a change of plan.

—Theodora Bratten, too, came from Belmont, where she now is, with her mother, to see us one day during the last week of September. She is pushing on her preparation for Tech, and looks well and hearty. Had

a fine summer, part of which she spent in study.

—Ella Ampt expects to be married in October, we hear, to Dr. Hamann, a surgeon, professor of anatomy in Western Reserve University, and on the staff at several hospitals. They are to live in Cleveland—"on Prospect St.," she says.

—Lester Hibberd Saxton writes that at her wedding Ella Wilson, Marie, Edith Blair, and Katherine McDowell were bridesmaids; that she has not yet gone to housekeeping, Mr. Saxton's business necessitating much travel, which for the present she is sharing with him; that her address is still Richmond, and that she saw Julia Hammond in Chicago, and learned that Elizabeth Stephenson had been visiting her but a short time before.

—Josephine West tells of a call from Mr. Ryder, formerly art teacher here, with whom she enjoyed a chat about Lasell. Her brother was home all summer, and they had a fine time together.

—Several of our old girls have sent in their subscription to the LEAVES for this year. More should do so, it seems to us, if they are at all interested in the doings and happenings at Lasell, and in their old mates of whom the Personals have much to say.

—Mrs. Symns, Effie's mother, whose recent death is noticed elsewhere in this issue, was greatly respected and beloved in the community where she lived, and her death is felt as a personal loss by many not connected with the family by any ties of relationship. Her funeral services were attended by a noticeably large gathering, and in this and other ways proved how strong a hold she had upon those among whom she had lived.

—Our Dorothy Manning ('95) and Gertrude Clarke ('97) called one day not long ago, for about ten minutes—all they thought Lasell deserved(?)

—Florence Ray, ('96), we hear, is to be Belle Bronson's only bridesmaid—the wedding is to be a quiet one. Dorothy Manning is to visit Florence, and will likely be there for the wedding.

—Elsie Doepke is soon to be married. Her father is building her a pretty house in Mt. Auburn, near Cincinnati.

—Clara Lewis was .visiting Worcester during the Music Festival. Blanche Kelley ('96) and Margie Schuberth ('96) saw and spoke with her frequently. They also saw Irene Wellington recently.

—Katherine Mason has been at home the greater part of the time since last March, with her father and mother. . Her brother and sister are away this year. She writes of finding content and happiness in her home life, although at first she missed the society of other young people, having at school had so many of these about her.

—A most welcome, tho' too brief, call was made in October by Frances Barbour Sonntag, who now lives in Buena Park, Ill., near Lulu Orrell Eddy. She still sings and much regretted not seeing Prof. Davis, to whom she acknowledges herself in large debt.

—Mlle. Le Royer reports a fairly pleasant trip across the ocean in June. While they were in Paris, she and Joe Milliken saw Fan White. Fan was on top of an omnibus, as were also our travelers, so that all they could do was merely to greet each other as they passed. They did not meet again, and consequently had no chance to exchange experiences for our benefit in these columns.

—Through Nelly Packard Draper ('84) who had a day's visit in July from Gussie Lowe Brownback ('84), we learn that the latter is living in the old Lowe homestead in Norristown, and that Blanche ('87) and her family, and Ava's husband and children

live near. Gussie's husband and two boys were in Boston at the time of her visit to Mrs. Draper. It has been thirteen years since these two old schoolmates had seen each other.

—A nice letter from June Hoyt Waite, now living in Seattle. Her little boy is five and a half years old, and his mother's joy. June had a call some time since from Ruth Sankey Ripley.

—Nellie Carnahan, here in ('95), wrote a good letter from Superior, Wis., where she was visiting her sister. She expects to enter the State Normal School next fall.

—Katherine White (1900) has had a very pleasant summer at home, "trying to be useful," and succeeding admirably, we feel sure, knowing her as we do. She sends her dollar for LEAVE's subscription, and adds sundry items of interest to readers of the Personals. Alice Ashley, ('00), visited during the summer both Mabel Martin and Mabel Coffin, the latter of whom has now gone to Europe for the winter. Avila Grubbs ('99) and her mother have had a delightful summer abroad, traveling through France, Switzerland, and Germany. Annie Ives has been enjoying the summer delights of the seashore, camping out in a cottage at Branford, Conn. Mary Houghton ('00) made her a visit there in July. Alice Jenckes ('99) has had several fine trips on board their yacht "Millie." They took a cruise of several weeks up Long Island Sound. When at Watch Hill, R. I., they took Ruth Talcott aboard for a trip, which was a great pleasure to both girls. Alice Ashley, Agnes Flaherty, and Mabel Stilson were with "Peggie" for several weeks after the close of school. Emily Kothe ('00) spent her summer at Lake Maxinkuckee, in Northern Indiana, boating, swimming, and sailing to her heart's content. Louise Gurley spent part of August with Katherine.—Thanks, Katherine! That's a fine budget of news.

—Mabel Englehart Dudley sends for our Album a picture of her cute little daughter, Mabel Irene Dudley, a year old in April, we believe. Her mother assures us that wee Irene is one of the best and sweetest of babies, and indeed she looks it. The family spent part of the summer with Mabel's people in East Orange, N. J. Mabel speaks of seeing very often Bessie Prescott White, and wonders what has become of Margaret Coon Brown, who, when last she had news of her, was living in Oak Park, Illinois.

—Mary Smith writes of a pleasant visit, after school closed, at Belle Robinson's home; and of another no less pleasant when Belle spent some seven weeks with her in her Virginia home. She had seen the Hubbard girls a short time previous to the date of her letter, and had a long Lasell chat with them. They are well.

—Louise Peycke tells us of a visit made by Flora Taft to Janette Knights, and of a prospective one that she and Flora were each expecting from Janette shortly. She saw Helen Harris and Ella Cotton in Omaha during the summer, and also Alice Andreesen Kountze, whose home has recently been brightened by the advent of a little boy.

—Rena Fellows' ('99) engagement to Mr. Frank Drummond Hight, of Bangor, was announced not long since. Rena spent nearly all her summer at home. Florence Pooler and Maude Mayo, ('98), paid her each a visit, and at the time she wrote she was expecting visits from Gertrude May and Alice Conant. She had, furthermore, heard several times directly from Avila Grubbs, who was enjoying the summer exceedingly. Of Francis Allen ('99) she had heard through Bangor acquaintances who visit at the place where Frances spends her summers.

—Emma Goll Dacy ('98), whose sad loss

in the death of her dear mother is elsewhere noticed in this issue, writes of the circumstances attending Mrs. Goll's last illness. Blanche and George were with her, and Mr. Dacy. The other brother is already a business man on his own account and doing well. Their mother's death was a severe shock to them, following as it did so soon upon her being taken ill.

—Carrie Manning Dexter ('95) sends best wishes for a good school year. So like her kindly thoughtfulness!

—Florence Ray ('96) has had an ideally pleasant European trip. Was gone five months and a half, and found everything delightful, even to "a smooth passage home with six meals a day and never a minute's illness." She chanced to find Bess Shepherd aboard and enjoyed several good Lasell chats with her. She was looking forward at the time of her letter to a visit from Belle, who is to be married early in October. Florence promises us a visit when next she comes to Boston. We shall be glad to see her.

—Josephine Steel Warrens sends cunning snapshot of her small mannie, who in his long trousers looks the "middy" to perfection. The dear little mite!

—Sadie Everlyn Eldredge to George Harris Wilder, on Wednesday, October 24, at Portsmouth, New Hampshire. Home address, after January 1: The Cascade, corner Central Park, West, and 87th street, New York, N. Y.

—Clara Slade Cameron to Benjamin Brayton Read, Jr., on Wednesday, October 24, at Fall River, Mass. Home address, after Feburary 1: 707 Highland avenue, Fall River, Mass.

—Katharine Morgan to Gilbert Pomeroy Drew, on Tuesday, June 19, at Oshkosh, Wisconsin. Their address: The Hotel Palms, Los Angeles, Cal.

—Mary Whitmore Peck to Thomas Walter Butcher, on Tuesday, July 3, at Wellington, Kan.

—Ellen Almeda Chase to Edwin Willis Rich, on Thursday, July 15, Dedham, Mass.

—Lottie Appel to Samuel W. Levey, on Tuesday, July 31, Denver, Colo. Their address: 169 N. 93d street, N. Y. City.

—Emily Angell Eaton to Orville Verner Thomas, on Wednesday, August 1, Denver, Colo. Address: 125½ South Broadway, Denver.

—Edith May Nickerson to Louis Stanhope Brigham, on Wednesday, August 8, at Newton Highlands, Mass. Address, after November 1: 56 Hartford street, Newton Highlands.

—Lestra Morrisson Hibberd, ('96), to Samuel Stanker Saxton, on Wednesday, August 8, Richmond, Indiana.

—Eva Lillian Ferris to George Franklin Foote, Wednesday, September 5, So. Norwalk, Conn. Address, after November 1: 6 Taylor avenue, So. Norwalk, Conn.

—Margaret C. Duncan to Chester H. Aldrich, Saturday, September 15, Lowell, Mass.

—Heléne Kate Little to Harry Mayo Peck, on Wednesday, October 3, Glens Falls, N. Y.

—Louise Thatcher to James Elmer Ayres, on Wednesday, October 3, Bennington, Vermont. Home address, after December 1: 19 Park avenue, Oneida, N. Y.

—Isabel Editha Bronson, ('96), to Robert Angus Alister Johnston, on Wednesday, October 10, Ottawa, Ontario.

—Edith Howe, ('97), to Irving DeForest Kip, on Friday, October 12, Passaic, N. J. Address, after November 15: 194 Pennington avenue, Passaic, N. J.

—Mary Bourne Hathaway, ('88), to Onsville Macpherson Farnham, on Wednesday, August 29, New Bedford, Mass. Their address is 11 Kearsage street, Roxbury, Mass.

—Laura Chapman to Lewis Nostrand Anderson, on Wednesday, October 17, Elmira, N. Y. Address, after December 1: 513 Bedford avenue, Brooklyn, N. Y.

—Julia Ann Aldrich to Robert Thompson Williams, on Wednesday, October 17, St. Louis, Mo. Home address: 510 Whittier street, St. Louis.

—Marion Ednah Josselyn to Charles Nicholas Young, on Wednesday, October 24, at Manchester, N. H.

September 11.—All day Tuesday came the new girls, some with their parents, some with old girls, and others alone. Most of them spent the afternoon and evening in being registered, meeting their room-mates, and planning the fitting up of their rooms; a few of the more fortunate ones were engaged in unpacking their trunks, while others were interested in looking about the place, which was to be their home for so many months. Welcome to you, new girls!

We old girls hope you will enjoy Lasell as much as we have.

September 12.—How good it was to see our last year's friends come flocking in, all apearing so glad to be back; but we missed from among them many faces that were dear, and longed for the girls who would not be with us again this year.. In the evening a Boston orchestra played during the dinner hour, and afterwards in the gymnasium, where there was dancing until nine o'clock.

September 13.—All the classes met as usual during the day, and in the evening Col. H. B. Sprague lectured on Shakespeare's "Julius Cæsar." Those who heard him give "Macbeth" last year were pleased with the opportunity of listening to him again, and enjoyed this play equally well.

September 15.—During the Saturday afternoon lecture Miss Carpenter invited the new girls to a reception to be given that evening by the Faculty and the old girls in the gymnasium, from half past seven until nine o'clock, and in order to get acquainted more easily, she proposed that every girl should wear a card with her name and address upon it. The Misses Barber Howes, E. Harris and Lum received. After an hour of pleasant chatting, refreshments were served, Miss Kendrick presiding over the coffee table, Miss Nutt serving the chocolate, and Miss Ransom, the lemonade. Then some one played for such as wished to dance, and the rest continued the pleasant pastime of getting acquainted, until it was time to disperse.

September 16.—Instead of the regular Christian Endeavor meeting on Sunday evening, Dr. F. E. Clark, who has so recently returned from his trip around the world, talked upon "The Broad Way, and the Narrow Way," commenting on the appropriateness of such a subject for us, who were just starting out upon a new sea-

son of work, expressing a hope that we would all choose "that better part."

September 17.—Soon after lunch Mr. Bragdon, with all those who had expressed a desire to see Boston sights under his guidance, left the Seminary for a trip to Bunker Hill and the Navy Yard. The former place of interest was first visited, most of the party climbing the 294 steps to the top of the famous monument on Breed's Hill. From this height an excellent view was obtained of the city and vicinity. Next the party hastened to the Navy Yard, first visiting the rope factory, and after this the foundries, where iron is beaten into all sorts of shapes for use upon the ships, proved interesting, as did also the old ship sheds. Moored near by was Dewey's flagship, the Olympia, and very fitting it seemed that "Old Ironsides" lay anchored not far off. Although entrance to the former was denied, all went on board the latter. The training ship Wabash was next visited, after which a few of the party entered the Navy Yard Museum, while the more musically inclined stayed outside to listen to a marine band. It was now time to hasten homeward, and all left Boston feeling well satisfied with their "little journey in the world."

September 23.—The Monthly Missionary meeting took the place of the Christian Endeavor, as Mrs. Waterbury, a former missionary to India, who was to speak to the girls, could not conveniently come at any other time. She took for her text, "Lift up your eyes, and look on the fields," and then gave a most interesting talk upon the mission work done in the principal Eastern countries. In closing she mentioned three things that each one of us could do now to help on missions: 1, Learn about the work; 2, Give to the work; 3, Pray for the work. Every one was much interested in what she said, and felt a greater desire to help than in past days.

September 24.—A party of fourteen, with Mr. Bragdon as conductor, took a delightful trip to Nantasket. The ride by rail, through South Boston, Weymouth and other places, was very picturesque, and gave a clear idea of the surrounding country. Nantasket, although quiet, seemed no less delightful to many who had never before been to the coast. After a hearty dinner the party climbed over the rocks, saw many interesting points along the coast, and walked on the sand. The ride back on the boat was very enjoyable, and especially interesting because of the numerous noted points to be seen en route.

September 25.—Rev. Charles M. Sheldon, the author of "In His Steps," was a guest of the Newton Christian Endeavor Union, at the Eliot Church, Newton, and all those who cared to hear him went over with Mr. Bragdon. Taking for his subject "The Open Door," Mr. Sheldon went on to speak of the many opportunities to be faced today. "This," he said, "is the greatest age the world has ever seen, not because of its money making power, not because of its inventions, not because of the knowledge of natural sciences, but because there never before was an age that provided such great opportunity for us to serve God and man."

October 1.—The annual trip to Lexington and Concord, taken on this day, was, if such a thing were possible, more enjoyable than last year's excursion. Four barges of enthusiastic sight-seers left the Seminary at a little after nine. It was about an hour's ride to Lexington, the first stopping place. Here was seen the famous Buckran Tavern. On the common is the site of the three meeting houses behind which the British formed, and a granite slab near by marks the line of the Minute Men. The Hancock House was especially interesting with its relics of 1775. The patriotism of the girls was aroused as they gazed at the home of Jonathan Harrington and heard again the story of how he died on the doorstep, faithful to his country's cause. On the road to Concord is the well at which James Hayward was killed, and the bluff used as a rallying place by the British was pointed out. There were other objects of interest also, not of an historical nature at all, one being a box of apples which Mr. Bragdon unexpectedly produced, and which were much appreciated by all. Concord is very interesting, both in an historic and in a literary way. "The Wayside," the home of Hawthorne, and, for a time, also that of Louisa May Alcott, was the first stopping place of the party. Here is the magnificent grove of pines in which Hawthorne took his daily walks. Emerson's home came next, then the Alcott residence; the party did not stop here, however, but going farther, saw in Sleepy Hollow cemetery the graves of all these famous people. The lunches were eaten near the old North Bridge, on the other side of which is French's famous statue of the Minute Man, a remarkable work of art on account of the character expressed in the face. On the way home all stopped at the Hill burying grounds, visited the place where Thoreau's hut formerly stood, and took a look at Malden Pond. The party arrived home at about a quarter of six, well satisfied with their day's outing.

The fine excursion wagons were furnished by Mr. G. E. Keyes, who has for many years managed the excursions of this sort for Lasell.

October 8.—At 12.30 on Monday, two barges left the Seminary on an excursion to Cambridge. The first object of interest shown us was Paul Revere's house, where he printed a paper and some Continental money. Near by, in a corner of an old graveyard, was a slab which marked the site of the meeting house in which was held the first provincial congress. At Mount Auburn we visited the graves of Philipps Brooks, the great preacher; Fanny Fern, the noted writer for children; Rufus Choate, the great Boston lawyer, and the business partner of Mr. Durant, the founder to Wellesley; Edwin Booth, the actor; Jean Louis Agassiz, the Gernman scientist; Oliver Wendell Holmes, and James Russell Lowell. We also went to see the crematory of Mount Auburn Cemetery, formerly the old chapel, and visited also Outlook Tower. Not far from the chapel, we read the inscription on the large stone sphinx erected in 1872 in commemoration of the emancipation of the slaves. It reads thus: "American Union preserved, African slavery destroyed by the uprising of a great people, by the blood of fallen heroes." Soon after we had left the cemetery we came in sight of "Elmwood," Lowell's birthplace, and a little farther on saw the home of Longfellow. We stopped at the Washington Elm, marked by this inscription: "Under this tree, July 3, 1775, Washington first took command of the American Army." Next came Memorial Hall, and from there we went to the Agassiz Museum of Harvard. We spent much time admiring the glass flowers. A placard says of them, "These glass models illustrate vegetable structures, and are part of a collection as yet unarranged, presented to Harvard University by Miss Elizabeth C. Ware and Mary S. Ware in memory of the late Dr. Charles E. Ware, class of 1834." The models are the work of Leopold and Rudolph Blaschka of Germany. We reached the Seminary again at about 5.30, well pleased with our journey.

—The Lasell students recently sent $40.00 to the Galveston Fund. There are five pupils from Texas at Lasell this year.

Too Late.

Some painful things have happened this year in the necessary turning away of the overflow. Four of last year's girls, for good reason, doubtless, on their part, retained their applications until too late. This we felt very sorry about, for it seems a pity to interrupt. Several new ones, thinking there was no hurry, came to the door with friends and trunks. But hardest of all was to turn from our door, our own Bettie Morris, now Mrs. John Shearn, who came with four children and nurse, all the way from Houston, Texas, to leave the oldest, Cora, a charming girl, in the old school where the mother spent five years. This *did* moisten our eyes. We hope for earlier application next year. Mrs. Shearn looks almost our own Bettie, who made us all love her in the earlier days. If I were a girl, I'd say she hadn't changed a bit in looks. We have since heard, through Bettie's mother, that Cora was placed in Mr. Williard's school, at Wollaston, before the family returned to Texas.

PASSED AWAY.

—Always side by side with the joy of reunion of friends in the fall, when schools reopen and business is resumed, comes news from one and another of our dear friends or valued acquaintances, that grief has invaded their homes, and that precious faces are missing from the family circle. To the LEAVES comes tidings of the death of Mrs. Emma A. Goll, mother of Emma and Blanche; of Mr. George R. Davis, father of our Nellie Davis; of Mrs. Willard Case, mother of Mabel Case Viot; of Mrs. Elizabeth Tiffany Symns, mother of Effie Symns, Tiffany Symns, mother of Effie Symns, who many of us remember; and Mr. Delos E. Goldsmith, husband of Sara Bond Goldsmith.

—Just as we go to press, word comes of the death of a beloved cousin of Sadie Hollingsworth Thompson, Miss Leila Hollingsworth, of Evansville, Ind., corresponding secretary of the Woman's Board of Missions, and a woman of fine abilities and noteworthy graces of character.

—To all those whom the departure of these has left desolate and sorrow-stricken, we wish to express sincerest sympathy and deep regret.

You Will Never Be Sorry.

For using gentle words.
For doing your best.
For being kind to the poor.
For looking before leaping.
For hearing before judging.
For thinking before speaking.
For harboring clean thoughts.
For standing by your principles.
For asking pardon when in error.
For being generous to an enemy.
For showing courtesy to your seniors.
For making others happy.
For being kind to animals.

LASELL LEAVES

"DUX FEMINA FACTI."

VOL. XXVI.   LASELL SEMINARY, AUBURNDALE, MASS., NOVEMBER, 1900.   NUMBER 2

Published monthly during the School year by the Lasell Publishing Association.

EDITOR-IN-CHIEF.
GEORGIE M. DUNCAN, '02.

ASSOCIATE EDITORS.
ANNA M. PINKHAM, '02.   BESSIE Y. FULLER, '02.   IDA M. MALLORY, '03

LOCAL EDITOR.   SUBSCRIPTION AGENT.   EXCHANGE EDITOR.
RUTH M. TALCOTT.   ETHEL M. GALLAGHER, 'OI.   MABEL MARTIN, 'OI.

BUSINESS MANAGER.   ASST. BUSINESS MANAGER.
ETHLYN F. BARBER, 'OI.   JOANNA F. DEERING, '02.

TERMS, in Advance: One copy, one year (including Postage), $1.00.   Single copies, 15 cents.

ADVERTISING RATES.

SPACE.	3 months	6 months	9 months	SPACE.	3 months	6 months	9 months
1-8 Column, ...	$2.00	$3.75	$5.00	1-2 Column, ...	$6.50	$11.00	$15.00
1-6 "	3.00	5.00	6.50	3-4 "	9.00	15.00	20.00
1-4 "	4.00	6.50	9.00	1 "	12.00	19.00	25.00

The Editors will be glad to receive from the students and Alumnæ any communications and items of interest to the school.

Editorials.

WE were glad to see our girls show such great interest in politics in general, and especially in the presidential election of this year. During the last few days before the election they became very enthusiastic, and many tried to make themselves more familiar with the main points of the different political platforms, that they might better judge their respective merits. The principal topic of conversation at the table, at the walking time, on the golf links, in fact everywhere the girls were, was the coming election. We were all delighted to be allowed to cast our votes in the gymnasium on Tuesday afternoon, and waited somewhat impatiently for our own returns, which were very satisfactory, of course, to the majority. The votes cast were as follows: For Woolley, 6; for Bryan 12; for McKinley, 130. From this it may be inferred that we have practically a Republican school this year.

It has been known for some time that the election would be close this year, and everyone has watched the indications anxiously, and when election day at last arrived the country was at the highest pitch of excitement. It is the more surprising, then, and the more gratifying that our people, so great in numbers and so diverse in sentiments and interests, should so quietly accept the decision made at the polls, and show so little desire to indulge in any violent expression of dissatisfaction. This shows that the law-abiding spirit is more general and more deeply-rooted than many would have us believe.

Now that the welfare of our country is once more assured, our interest centres upon the state elections for governors and senators, for a time eclipsed by the more important election of the president. Of course each girl is especially interested in the welfare of her own state. We sincerely hope that the young men are as earnest and enthusiastic in politics, as the girls seem to be; they could hardly be more so than some of us.

GYMNASIUM and drill have begun earlier, it seems to us, than last year, owing probably to the chilly weather we have had. We are glad to see Miss Adams once more in the gymnasium, and on the whole are not sorry to resume our vigorous exercise there, though we were a little dissatisfied at first, perhaps, that it began so early. We hope that the zeal of the new girls in this work will not slacken as the year advances, for it is one of the best and most beneficial of the school, if we take it in the right way. Another very helpful exercise is our military drill. It seems to us that the new girls are not so enthusiastic over it as they would be, if they were fully awake to its value. The work of the junior companies is the same as in former years, but the senior company has in place of bayonet drill, the Butt's Rifle Calisthenics, which we think is going to prove more graceful and interesting than the bayonet drill. This we shall have later in the year.

Happiness is not perfected until it is shared.

Address of Welcome.

By mistake in calculating space, the welcome of Mrs. Martin to the students was omitted in our last issue. So great was the disappointment of our readers that we are glad to publish it even at this late day.

Notes from Mrs. Blanche C. Martin's address to the pupils of Lasell Seminary.

Once again it is my happy privilege to extend, for the Faculty, a cordial welcome to the pupils of Lasell Seminary,—a name awakening pleasurable emotions in every state in the Union, and one that has become known as the synonym for high ideals, honest endeavor, and impregnable courage—ideals, which keep one alert with noble discontent, and provide a motive for noble life,—honesty of purpose, which, having raised its ideals and progressive standards, strives up to them,—courage, which stamps its armor with Lowell's behest:

"Greatly begin, though thou have time,
But for a line, be that sublime.
Not failure, but low aim, is crime."

With heart, as with voice, we welcome those dear familiar ones, who have returned to help us with the light of their presence, and their confidence; and we recall with tenderness those who have left us to enter the larger realm of study. With no less sincerity and love, we welcome to our halls and hearts those strange young faces, where curiosity and inquiry reveal the corner-stone of a mutual interest.

We meet here as pupils and teachers, but throughout that intercourse must be the influence which binds those positions into a unity of purpose and action—the bond of friendship—a friendship that means more than that social friendliness and pleasurable attraction, which make people seek each other for the pleasure it gives. Right friendship is that heart-touch of sympathy and understanding which makes it possible for one person to seek another in trouble or difficulty in any of the deeper experiences of life. The heart-touch of compassion lasts always, and is far beyond the common friendship, which is based upon approval or admiration.

We do not seek to educate you in what you are sometime to be. Life and its meaning is already here. Eternity is now. Our requirement is not merely the compression of many facts in the gray matter of your brain, but the complete expansion of yourself. Here in this school, all we ask is the obvious effort of each pupil to do her best. Nature has fixed no boundaries to human endeavor. The courage and the will of the individual alone are responsible for limited results.

As you will learn later on, education does not mean the mere attainment of certain facts, but the broadening of the individual to increase the power of life and elevate the quality of character, and make the intellect a power for good, and the will capable of enforcing it.

Lasell means more than text-book knowledge. It means a thorough appreciation of things, books and people. It means a sympathetic and noble recognition of the excellence of beauty, truth and good. It means susceptibility and adaptability, those qualities which enable one to live in harmony with environment, and draw from the treasures of life, as well as contribute to them.

Adaptability is the spirit of the age in education. Adaptability is the result of an all round development of power. An all round development of power means a well balanced intellect,—an intellect that can swing on its swivel without tipping, and adjust each particle of knowledge to the demands life may make upon it. Adaptability means the recognition of every opportunity and the courage to attack it.

Opportunity exists everywhere; in the home, in the school, and in the world; and its greatness is only measured by the power of the individual to meet it. The individual who is awake to the virtue of the immediate present compels opportunity, because he is able to "recognize the hint of every incident."

Ralph Waldo Emerson says: "Man goes along with his head over his shoulder, lamenting the past, or, stands on tiptoe to foresee the future, unheeding the riches that surround him, and shall never find peace until he, too, learns to live with Nature in the present, above time." Comparatively few truly live. The majority mope through a kind of existence without ever realizing their own greatness and power to overcome all undesirable conditions. We should learn early in life that the secret of success and the mastery of situations lie in alertness and self-confidence. Edward Rowland Sill gives a most convincing illustration of this truth in a poem he has well named

"OPPORTUNITY."

This I beheld, or dreamed it in a dream:—
There spread a cloud of dust along a plain;
And underneath the cloud, or in it, raged
A furious battle, and men yelled, and swords
Shocked upon swords and shields. A Prince's banner
Wavered, then, staggered backward, hemmed by foes.

A craven hung along the battle's edge,
And thought, "Had I a sword of keener steel,—
That blue blade that the King's son bears,—but this
Blunt thing—!" he snapped and flung it from his hand,
And lowering crept away and left the field.

Then came the King's son, wounded, sore bestead
And weaponless, and saw the broken sword
Hilt buried in the dry and trodden sand,
And ran and snatched it, and with battle shout
Lifted afresh he hewed his enemy down,
And saved a great cause that heroic day."

To my mind, this poem contains one of the greatest of life's lessons—the immediate recognition of opportunity, and the courage to attack it. Rarely, indeed, are we permitted to hold the blue blade of opportunity, but it makes little difference whether the blade be blue and keen, or blunted and broken, if it is firmly grasped in the strong right hand of courage. Whatever our life work, it is always more or less a struggle, where we meet and conquer circumstance, in proportion to our courage and desire. This you will find capable of constant demonstration in your Seminary career, and these demonstrations are born of the virtues of cheerfulness, helpfulness, faithfulness and responsibility. Character grows from the cheerful acceptance of responsibility.

Lasell is a school of varied opportunities, with teachers of specific personalities. Professor Bragdon, awake to the necessities of each generation, has selected his educational staff with a view to present each branch in the school curriculum in its most forceful and convincing manner. His desire, recognized by his co-laborers, stimulates each, not from a spirit of rivalry, but from true emulation to create a perfect whole; yet in every branch the attitude of your minds determines the result. It is for you to realize that in order to receive the greatest benefit from the school, every lesson must mean to you life and personal development. You must have faith not only in yourself, but in others. You must have courage which is born of high purpose, you must carry with you an atmosphere of hope and good cheer, and make an effort each day to live that which you are ambitious to become.

Set your ideals high, for "the height of the ideal which you follow is the measure of your character and the index of your achievements." Try each day to idealize the commonplace by looking for the best. "Seek and ye shall find." Seek for the ideal in your school, in your teachers, and in your companions, and, finding, let nothing separate you. Do not let disenchantment appear to you as wisdom. Yourself may be responsibile for your disappointment.

However, it is not the discovery of ideals, but the search for them, that elevates. No honest endeavor was yet lost. Although a person may fail of the supposed object toward which he is striving, the greatness of soul which he realizes by the effort is, after all, the true reality. Greatness is not in what a man has, or attains, but what he becomes, or is. The soul is bound on a mystic quest, which is so far beyond the judgment of the brain we use, that we must needs place before us temporary aims to lure us on to renewed endeavor. Attainment satisfies but for a moment. That moment is the one in which we look out from the high platform which we have attained, and perceive a greater. Then the divine discontent comes upon us, and we strive again. The lesson of it all is, that we must not gaze with longing eyes upon the past, but with its wealth of meaning well garnered in the soul, advance with gladness in the conviction that the world is better and greater than we thought. Emerson says: "The voice of the Almighty saith, 'Up and onward forever more,'" and years of experience and wisdom gives the following tribute to such pursuit:

IDEALS.

My boyhood chased the butterfly,
  And when the shower was gone,
Sought treasure at the rainbow's end,
  That lured me wond'ring on.
I caught no bow or butterfly,
  Though eagerly I ran,
But in the chase I found myself
  And grew to be a man.
In later years I chased the good,
  The beautiful and true,
Mirage-like forms that take no shape,
  They flit as I pursue.
But while the endless chase I run,
  I grow in life divine.
I miss the ideals that I seek,
  But God Himself is mine!

This my friends is the message of Ideals, "As a man thinketh, so is he." Place yourself continually in the atmosphere of purest thought, and it will be rewarded in your completion of character. Tomorrow our duties begin; tonight we welcome you with loving tenderness, and desire to plant firmly in your hearts the thought that your growth, welfare and happiness, are our deepest consideration.

CLASS OFFICERS.

Senior.—President, Ethlyn Barber; vice-president, Edith Dustin; Secretary, Isabella Clemens; treasurer, Bessie Lum.

Junior.—President, Ellen Chase; vice-president, Florence Hayden; secretary and treasurer, Edith Harris.

Sophomore.—President, Frances Leavitt; vice-president, Joel Lapowski; secretary, Marie Biddle; treasurer, Isabel Blackstock.

The following have been favored with calls from members of their family: Misses Brewer, Dwinell, Walter, Tarbox, S. Lawrence, Mower, Bullock, Nelson, Tirrell, Whitney, Scoville, Goodwin, Talcott, J. Austin, Barker, Lockwood, Douglass, Upham, Day, Zeller, Bowers, Davis, Sisson, George E. and F. Toole, Hazelton, Pearson, A. Smith.

Former Pupils.—Helen Abbott, LaVerne Reynolds, Jessie Macmillan, Maud Conklin, Mabel Lutes, Grace and Ethel Loud, Bessie Roper, Marion Harrower, Helen Ramsdell, Ida Trowbridge, Laura Birdsey, Elizabeth Starks, Marietta Sisson, Emeroy Ginn, Elsie Reynolds, Mildred Faxon, Elise Scott, Mrs. Belle Jones Massey, Mrs. Alice Mayo Hicks, Helen and Ruth Rishell, Margie Schuberth, and Edith Atwood.

Don't forget to be gentle and respectful to the aged, even when they are fussy and tiresome.

A Tidy Bedroom.

There is no place in which a girl's character and individuality may be more clearly displayed than in her own room. If she is orderly and neat, careful of her belongings, or careless, destructive and extravagant in their use, her bedroom reflects traits and peculiarities. If she loves books and pictures, one will find them in her room; if her tastes are trival and uncultivated, her surroundings will show her need in culture. If she regards her room merely as a transient spot in which to sleep and dress, and not a place to read and think in, or where she may sometimes enjoy the companionship of her girl friends, she does not know the pleasure of having a room of her own.

I know a girl who said: "I have tried to make my room a sort of cast to mold me in; to make it, in other words, represent the ideal girl I wish to make myself. In that way I have a room to grow up to, as well as to grow up in. I used to be very spasmodic about keeping my room in order, going at the task with such energy at rare intervals that I quite exhausted my orderly powers. But in my experience of trying to improve myself I find that one is helped infinitely by the simple habit of putting one's room in order, and by the harder task of keeping it so. I think one is sooner able to rule one's self, to sort out one's good thoughts and hurtful thoughts, and keep the character in order if one has proved able to manage all the little trifling, external belongings."

This girl's room, then, reflects her determination to conquer carelessness in habit and thought. With unconscious force she is training herself in method, accuracy and thoroughness, and these qualities are invaluable in life.

Her room also shows the refinement of her taste. A bookrack on a table contains

volumes by some of her favorite authors.
Ruskin's "Sesame and Lilies," Tennyson's
and Longfellow's poems, Grimm's "Life of
Michælangelo," and Dickens' "Old Curiosity Shop" are among them.   Beside her bed
is a small table with a Bible and other de-
votional books.   Two photographs repro-
ducing the original paintings by the old mas-
ters, now in the Dresden gallery, hang on
the wall—Raphael's "Sistine Madonna,"
and Leonardo da Vinci's head of Christ.
Because she loves the associations attached
to the celebrated buildings of the world there
are photographs of the great cathedral of
Canterbury, England, with its history of
thirteen centuries; Westminster Abbey,
London, where are the tombs of kings,
queens, royal children, poets and statesmen;
Holyrood palace, Edinburgh, where Mary
Queen of Scots, lived.   The owner of this
room loves romance, as all girls do, and has
a photograph of Anne Hathaway's pretty
little thatched and vine-covered cottage at
Shottery, near Stratford-on-Avon, in England—the cottage to which Shakespeare often walked across the fields in the days of
his courtship of the one who became his
wife.—*The Delineator.*

Young Women's Christian Association.

Religion is not a matter of prayer meetings only.   On coming to college a new girl
at the Woman's hall asked an older one why
a certain senior was so popular.   "Oh, she
is so full of fun, and she always has time
for everybody's troubles, but never has any
of her own."   This senior had learned that
religion develops every side of a person's
nature, making one quick to understand the
trials of others, and teaching him how to
comfort.   She was not a careless student,
in fact, her work was always promptly and
thoroughly done, but she never worried
about her studies, because she felt that re-

ligion would carry that load for her.   She
had realized to some extent the truth of
what President Eliot said here—that the only true use of knowledge was that of serving
one's fellow men.

Religion offers the highest example of
noble living that can be found, and everyone
should remember that he can attain no more
than what he strives for.   Moreover, to one
who is touched by the soft influence of the
Christ-love, the world is many times more
beautiful, friends many times dearer, and
life is much more worth living.

The Young Women's Christian Association is trying to bring these blessings of religion to every girl in college.   Perhaps it
is not what it should be, but perhaps it needs
your help.   It is never too late to begin,
and surely every little counts.   The association is the only circle in which all the
girls can mingle, with their common aims
and desires.   Every Christian girl, the one
who was interested in church matters before
she came here, and the one who was not,
should stop and ask herself seriously whether
it would not be better simply to join the association, if nothing more, than to say when
she has finished her course—"Not one thing
did I do in college to share with anyone the
happiness that came to be from above."—
Elizabeth Bragdon in The Northwestern.

A WORD TO LASELL SHOPPERS.

The importance of trading with the firms
who advertise in the LASELL LEAVES cannot be overestimated.   We should not expect their patronage if we do not give them
our support in return.   Another way for
Lasell girls to be loyal!

Any ordinarily bright woman can write
an essay on Ibsen or mathematical astronomy if she tries hard enough, but it takes a
genius to keep the cook good-natured.—
Chicago Times-Herald.

A Choice Blend.

NEWSPAPERS sometimes mix their matter in the rush to get to press. Here is an item that recently appeared in an Eastern daily:

"The church was finely decorated with holly and evergreen and the altar was hidden in a wealth of flowers. Out of the recesses rose rare tropical plants, and from the ceiling hung fifteen Western veals, which at this time of year are scarce and correspondingly dear at 6 and 8 1-2 cents per lb. There was also an active demand for choice lambs, and farmers east of the Mississippi River can profitably turn to sheep raising and take the bride, who wore a gown of white corded silk, a creation of Worth's, with pearl ornaments.

Then came the maid of honor, the cousin of the bride, Miss Henrietta Blower, of Chicago, wearing a dress of white tulle, with diamond ornaments, and she was followed by a small bunch of Montana sheep, which bleated most piteously, as they were driven on board and shipped to the winter hotels in Bermuda. They will there be cut en traine and slightly decollete, and after the rest of the party had reached the rail, the minister turned and said impressively, 'I cannot bid more than 6 1-2 cents for state veals, but cablegrams from London quote refrigerated beef at a price that will enable me to pay $4.90 for a car of choice Indian beeves, and hearing this there was a rush for the young married couple, and the bride fell into the arms of her father, who is known to bear a striking resemblance to a Connecticut ox, weighing 1,875 pounds. The market here took an upward turn and advanced 1 to 2 cents, and the guests, who numbered about 200, were served with a sumptuous dinner at the house of the bride."

Needless to say, the item created a sensation.—*Exchange.*

Painting Her Portrait.

"IF I could be such an old lady as that, so beautiful, serene, sweet and lovable, I shouldn't mind growing old," said a young girl the other day, speaking of a white-haired visitor who had just departed.

"Well, if you want to be that kind of an old lady, you'd better begin making her right now," laughed a keen-witted companion. "She doesn't strike me as a piece of work that was done in a hurry; it has taken a long time to make her what she is. If you are going to paint that sort of portrait of yourself to leave to the world, you'd better be mixing your colors now."

The merry words were true; and, whether she willed it or not, the girl was already "mixing the colors" for her portrait and drawing day by day the outlines of her mature womanhood which shall yet brighten or darken the lives round her. Many a careless, selfish girl has in her inmost heart no higher ideal than "to be like mother" when she shall have reached mother's years; but in the meanwhile she is content to be as unlike her as possible. She has an idea that age brings its graces with it, and that a beautiful character comes like silver hair, naturally and without effort.

Girls, you are outlining your future and choosing its coloring now. The woman you wish to be must begin in the girl.—*Forward.*

The Long Skirt and Its Danger.

A SCIENTIFIC man in Rome has just been conducting a very practical experiment.

All this time, since the long skirt came into fashion, doctors have been talking microbes, and warning women of the evil of their ways. But has any one thought to put a gown under the microscope and give visible proof of the truth of what he has been saying? Not a soul, except this learned scientist in Rome.

He employed three young women to take their long skirts out on a microbe-collecting expedition. When they returned, after doing their duty thoroughly and well, he took the three garments to his laboratory and gave them a searching investigation. .

He found all the microbes of the streets. The result was horrible to relate. Allied in force, the microbes of those three skirts were found to be sufficient to contaminate the whole population of China, and that is more than four hundred and fifty millions.

Yet the number of these microbes was probably no greater than each one of us brings into the house every time we go out in that article of attire with death in its train. The wonder is that we manage to live at all!
—*Philadelphia Press.*

DROPPED STITCHES.

I dropped a stitch in my knitting
    As I sat at work one day
And it seemed such a little matter
    I sang as I worked away.
But lo, when my work my finished,
    I saw with infinite pain
The stitch I had missed in the morning
    Had rendered it all in vain!
That all of my perfect stitches
    Were useless because of one;
That one little flaw had cost me
    The loss of my heart's "Well done!"
Just so it is in our lives, dear,
    But the stitches dropped, ah me!
Are part of the soul's own garment
    We weave for eternity.
The stitch of unbridled passions,
    Of an evil, bitter thought,
The stitch of neglected duties
    Are into the pattern wrought!
The stitch of the first cigar, lad,
    The stitch of your first strong drink,
And the work of your life is ruined—
    Does it pay, dear, do you think?
Alas! for the stitch unheeded,
    Ah me, for the mischief done,
For the glad hopes of the morning,
    For heartache at set of sun!
            —Selected.

Diversity of Growth.

Although the rate of increase of population for the last decade is about four per cent. less than the one immediately preceding it, the actual increase of population exceeds that shown by the census of 1890 by 266,726. Again, while the average rate is 21 per cent., Idaho shows a gain of 92 per cent., Montana 84 per cent., and North Dakota 75 per cent.; while Maine has only gained 5 per cent., Kansas 3 per cent., Nebraska 1 per cent., and Nevada shows a decrease of population. The Territory of Oklahoma shows the most astonishing growth, having increased its population from 61.834 in 1890, to 398,245 in 1900—a gain of 550 per cent. New York is still the Empire State, with a population of 7,268,009; Pennsylvania, Illinois, Ohio, Missouri, are second, third, fourth and fifth in order. Texas has passed Massachusetts, and is now the sixth State in the Union in point of population. The results of the latest enumeration have been reached so quickly because of the improvement in tabulating machines. The work is nearly a full year ahead of that of the preceding census.

The Centre of Population.

One curious revelation of the new census is that the centre of population has moved but slightly since ten years ago, and it will require a nicer calculation than is yet possible to determine whether it has moved westward or eastward. For a long period it had been steadily moving westward, and by the last census it was found to be a little west of south of Greensburg in Indiana. By this census it appears that the states wholly west of the longitude of that point have increased almost precisely the same as the states lying wholly east of it, about 6,000,000 each. The remaining 1,325,000 increase is in states which the meridan passes through, and not until the increases in the east and west parts of these are determined will it be known what and in what direction the change is. The eastern and western halves of the nation appear to be increasing in population with remarkable evenness. It is possible that the northern or southern movement of the centre may be greater than the eastern or western movement, and perhaps it will be found that the movement is really farther from the centre of ten years ago than is now thought probable.

Taken from the editorial in *School Life:*
Everyone born into the world is destined to belong to one of two classes: either he will be a leader, or he will be led. It is the large majority, we shall find, that are led; it is the very few who lead. Yet to those few who are called to leadership is given an influence so great, that they control and shape the characteristics of all.

Leadership is a necessity. When right and efficient, it stimulates growth and "makes the world go round." When incompetent and bad, it militates inestimably for evil. What a responsibility, therefore, rests upon those into whose hands are placed such agencies of might for right or wrong, and how time reviews their every act and judges them!—*From the Editorial of School Life.*

Taken from *R. M. T. S. Register,* Scientific Notes:
The Smithsonian Institute at Washington will shortly possess the most rapid camera in the world. It is designed to take a successful negative with an exposure of one six-hundredth of a second, and it is hoped that this may be increased so that a negative may be obtained in one one-thousandth of a second.

EXPANSION.

Met a feller t'other mornin'—
  Most amusin' sort o' cuss;
He'd a curus style about him—
  Cert'n'y couldn't well be wuss.
I says: "Where you hail f'm pardner?"
  An' he smiles in knowin' way
An' replies in forren lingo:
  "Porto Rico, U. S. A."

Seen a feller down on Broadway
  With a shockin' head o' hair,
An' a lot o' tropic garments,
  An' a most outlandish air.
"Where's he frum?" a feller shouted,
  But before we'd time to say,
This yere heathen turned an' answered:
  "Honolulu, U. S. A."

Met a feller down at Olive
  With a somber-ero on,
Had a lot o' shaggy whiskers,
  Nearly all his clothin' gone.
Stopped and asked me for a quarter;
  Says: "My home is fur away."
"Where you frum?" The varmint answered:
  "Santiago, U. S. A."

Seen a feller at the Southern,
  With a heavy iron box;
Overcoat was lined with bearskin;
  Wore a dozen pair o' sox.
Sized him up to be a miner,
  Judging by his aw'ard way;
Seen him write in big characters:
  "Dawson City, U. S. A."

Seen a saddle-colored heathen,
  Wearin' earrings in his nose,
Linen cuffs around his ankles;
  Most indecent lack o' close.
"Where'd this heathen guy yere spring frum?"
  I inquired in lofty way;
An' he had the nerve to answer:
  "Frum Manila, U. S. A."

Gee! I says, I never heard of
  These yer cannybuls before!
Are these heathens yere all voters,
  Will we stan' fur any more?
Next you know you ask a feller
  Where he's frum an' he will say,
With a lordly kind o' flourish:
  "All creation, U. S. A."
      —*Ed. Sabin, in the Saddlery News.*

PERSONALS.

—Emma Goll Dacy, ('98), sends clipping stating that the suit brought by her mother against the Metropolitan West Side Elevated Road of Chicago, to secure damages for depreciation of the value of her property due to the extension of that road across Ashland Boulevard, has been decided in her favor, the amount of damages awarded being $7,750. Mr. Dacy was the prosecuting attorney, and it was due to his skilful conduct of the suit that it was not lost, as has been the case in all other similar suits, excepting only that of St. Jarlath's Church, and F. Samuel Whitowski, in which liability of the company was affirmed, and damages exacted to the amount of $10,000, and $3,000, respectively. Grace Allen, ('95), Emma tells us, was in the city (Chicago) in October, to attend the wedding of Alice Drake, an old Omaha friend of hers. Emma expected to see her during her stay.

—Laura Birdsey and Elizabeth Starks called to see us one day towards the end of October. They looked unusually well, and were very evidently in the best of spirits. Laura is at home this fall—she was here only on a short visit—and is devoting herself to music, in which she hopes to do something really worth while. Elizabeth is taking a course in physical culture, in Boston, and it seems as if this were the one thing she has been needing to make her good and strong, for she hardly looks like the same girl. Rosy and well, too, is Ida Trowbridge now.

She paid us a flying visit at about the same time. She regrets her inability to graduate this year with her class, but is so much better in health than she was, that she finds ample consolation in that fact. At a recent entertainment in her home city, Ida contributed to the evening's enjoyment by giving several readings, which were appreciatively received. Bessie Roper came one day, and Grace and Ethel Loud with her. We were glad to have them with us again, even though but for so short a time.

—Clara Robbins sends subscription for LEAVES, and speaks of being very busy at home this fall.

—Bessie Phelps Yocum sends news of the arrival at her home, on October 12, of a very little boy, Ezra Phelps Yocum. Our congratulations.

—Jessie Kemp writes that her mother is now well on the way to complete recovery from her illness of last August. Her little brother, William, they have recently placed in the Curtis School for Boys, Brookfield Centre, Conn., and Jessie feels quite content, feeling convinced that it is just the place for him. She says she is still hoping to return to us and finish her course.

—Corinne Salisbury also sends LEAVES subscription, being anxious to keep track of us all.

—Isabel Bronson Johnston was here with her new husband, who seems to be a manly fellow. We think they will be happy and useful. They will not go to housekeeping until a new house is built.

—LaVerne Reynolds and Helen Abbott are teaching music in their respective homes, and doing well at it, too. We were glad to see their bright faces one day in October.

—Marion Gage is to begin to study the science and art of nursing, in February, she tells us, here at the Newton Hospital. We wish her all success. Cecile, she further says, is teaching a small private class in Brookline.

—Grace Etherington, of the New York Lasell Club, sends good wishes for this school year. She has the interests of the club very much at heart, and is working in her usual energetic way for its success.

—Annie Hackett is librarian of the High School in her town. Frank Bowman, she says, has had a fine trip to the Yellowstone. Annie sends LEAVES subscription.

—Edith Atwood is at Melrose, Mass., for the winter.

—Olive Smith has been teaching at Ashland, Maine, and is considered a very successful teacher. She is to enter the Emerson College of Oratory this year, so we learn from a timely newspaper clipping.

—Anna Howe Shipley, whose daughter Alice is now at National Park Seminary, under care of our old friends, Mr. and Mrs. Cassedy, writes us of the birth, on June 15, of a third daughter, whom they call Helen Virginia, "the most welcome little girl in all the world."

—May Hayward, here last year, is teaching this year, we learn, and likes the work very much.

—Through a recent letter from the principal of Quincy Mansion School, we hear that Bettie Morris Shearn's young daughter Cora, whose application to enter Lasell this fall came to our regret too late, is winning golden opinions there. Evidently she is Bettie's own daughter.

—Grace Richardson regrets not being with us again this year, but is on the whole contented and happy as her father's housekeeper, and has a very appreciative word to say about the value of her cooking lessons here. The knowledge gained stands her in good stead now.

—Mrs. Mara L. Pratt Chadwick, who in former years taught physiological psychol-

ogy here, is at Malden for the winter. Her marriage occurred last spring, and the loss of her husband by appendicitis but a short time after.

—A pleasant letter from Isabel Ginn and Emeroy tells us that they are both at home now with their father, busy with home duties, yet remembering very kindly Lasell and Lasell friends, to keep in touch with whom they send subscription to the LEAVES. Claire Beebe and Helen Holman, they have heard, are both to be married this month.

—Mr. Bragdon regrets that through inadvertence, the notice of Jane Myrick's marriage did not receive notice in the October LEAVES.

—Ethel Walton ('99) is boarding at Mrs. Parker's ('58) and enjoys it while pursuing her law course.

—Alice Mayo Hicks, here years ago, sends us a program of what must have been a very diverting German entertainment, given on Monday evening, October 29, in High School Hall, Needham. An amusing little German drama, "English Spoken Here," was presented, in which Alice took the part of "Frau Kaufmann."

—An interesting clipping has been sent us giving an account of Eva Ferris Foote's wedding, on the fifth of September. It was a church wedding, and "the largest ever held in the South Norwalk Congregational Church," by report. Of beautiful decorations, and all the other accompaniments of a fashionable wedding, there was no lack; a reception followed at the bride's home. Her father's gift to Eva was a pretty residence at 6 Taylor avenue, South Norwalk.

—Carita Curtis, ('99) we learn through Ella Cotton, is in Omaha now. She expects to make her début soon.

—Alice Kimball ('98) is in Boston for the winter.

—Agnes Flaherty ('00), is in Cambridge,

studying vocal music under Miss White.

—Elizabeth Hitchcock, they say, is engaged to a Chicago gentleman.

—Sallie Ellwood Wirt is to make New York her home shortly.

—Eva Kennard Wallace is keeping house in London, England.

—Genevieve Slayton is also in London, and expects soon to go to Germany to study art.

—Inez Hill Staples has a dear little daughter born recently. She lives at Biddeford, Maine.

—Albert E. Dacy, Emma Goll Dacy's husband, is quoted in one of the Chicago papers as having put a question to Mr. Bryan at a certain recent political meeting in that city, to which the Democratic candidate did not reply, but cautiously took refuge in beating about the bush instead. Mr. Bryan was talking about "the consent of the governed," when Mr. Dacy asked, "How about North Carolina?" At another meeting, Mr. Dacy discussed the issues of the late political campaign, with Mr. Dobyns, in the presence of the largest crowd gathered at the City Hall during the whole campaign.

—Minnie Buchrach announces her engagement to Mr. Benjamin Deutsch.

—Nellie LaSelle writes of having seen Mae Burr and Lil Tukey Morrison recently. Mae took part in a flower parade in Lincoln the other day, riding in a trap decorated with pink and white chrysanthemums, and showering confetti on her Lasell friends (among others) "for dear old Lasell." A certain lady of Nellie's acquaintance said to her on one occasion, "I've known a great many girls from Lasell, and I've never heard one unpleasant thing about it." Nell says, "I felt real proud."

—Alice Mayo Hicks called to see us one day early this month. It was such a pleasure!

—We are genuinely sorry that Grace Tirrell's health will not permit her continuing her school course. The doctor advises a change of climate. Our best wishes go with her.

—Mabel Lutes was expecting soon to go to St. Louis at last accounts.

—Mr. Bragdon's brother, Mr. George E. Bragdon, and his wife, recently entertained at their home in Pueblo, Colo., Secretary of the Navy, John D. Long. In the course of a speech made by the Secretary at that time he said, "The best argument that the various departments of the government have been well administered, is the fact that they are not brought into the campaign as issues."

—Flossy Stedman Richards is now in her own home in Needham, and thinks her baby boy, born August 9, is the greatest boy in the world.

—Mr. Bragdon has a comfortable reason to know that apples from Manistee, Michigan are *very*, VERY good.

—Bess Shepherd ('94) is teaching Modern Languages in Simpson College, Indianola, Iowa. She reports it a wide-awake school of over four hundred students, coeducational. She will be glad to hear from and see some of the old girls who live in that region, and sends greetings.

—Bessie Towle Waters of Somerville, Nina Burr Day of Newark, N. J.; Millie Swan Hall and Emma Gass Moody of Cambridge, called to see Mr. Bragdon in October. Bessie Waters and Emma Moody have each three beautiful children. They report Theresa Hollander Wrightington living in Longwood.

—WHEELING, W. VA., Nov. 7, 1900.— West Virginia has gone Republican by from 12,000 to 15,000 majority. The entire state ticket is elected. The congressional delegation is solidly Republican. This means that our Katherine White's father is Governor.

—Jane Myrick, ('98), to George Slocomb Gibbs, on Thursday, August 30, at Jamaica Plain, Mass.   Address, Aldworth street, Jamaica Plain.

—Gertrude Amelia Jones, ('97), to Thomas Martin James, on Thursday, October 11, at Kansas City, Mo.

—Alma Avis Claflin to Harry Dunning Banta, on Tuesday, October 16, at Boston, Mass.   Address after December 1: Rockview, Rockview street, Jamaica Plain, Mass.

—Jennie Miller Arnold, ('93), to George Ropes Felt, on Wednesday, October 31, at Peabody, Mass.

—Ella Fredonia Ampt, ('96), to Carl A. Hamann, on Wednesday, October 31, at Wyoming, Ohio.   Address after January 1: 744 Prospect street, Cleveland, Ohio.

—Mary Brownell Davis to Alfred Douglas Flinn, on Thursday, November 1, at Boston, Mass.   Address after January 1: 984 Beacon street, Newton Centre, Mass.

—Edna Mae Makepeace to Aldro Amos French, on Wednesday, November 7, at Attleboro, Mass.

—Edna Mary Dice, to Charles Maxwell Robertson, on Tuesday, Nov. 17, at Crawfordsville, Indiana.   Address after December 18: The Wallingford, Indianapolis.

Lasell Song.

Why must Lasell forever lack a song? There are musical people enough, and people enough who can make a simple rhyme, such as that ought to be.   Some have made some very respectable Lasell Songs, but the one that has struck the popular fancy, the singable Lasell Song, has yet to be written. A good deal of name in Lasell history is waiting for the teacher or pupil who shall bring this to pass.   Sentiment that is overwrought, or too elaborately worked out, will not meet the case.   It wants some simple, sensible words, set to a music that sings itself.   C. C. B.

October 11.—The dinner hour was enlivened by the music of a very good orchestra, and during the evening the music was continued in the gymnasium until study hour, the girls enjoying several good dances meanwhile.   The party of fifteen girls who went on this same evening with Mr. Bragdon to see Sothern in "Hamlet," regretted doubtless that they must miss this good music, but felt that to see the great tragedy well played would compensate amply for this loss.   The party was rather smaller than Lasell theatre parties usually are, for many thought that on account of the length of the play, it would be necessary to leave before the last act, and hence concluded not to go.   Those who went, however, were able to stay through even the last scene.   The part of Hamlet was admirably acted, although all who had seen Irving admitted that Sothern was not so successful as that actor in interpreting this great character.   All the girls, nevertheless, enjoyed the play immensely, and came away with heightened interest in that great author whose plays are as enthusiastically received today as they were when first presented.

October 13.—After all recitations were over, Mr. Bragdon took a large party of girls to the Yale-Dartmouth foot ball game at the Newton Athletic Grounds. Although the teams were very unevenly matched, the Yale men being stronger and in better condition than the Dartmouth, the latter fought bravely and kept the score below twenty, though few thought they would do so, the result being 17-0. After the game a special car brought our Lasell party back. All were much pleased with the afternoon, and even the Dartmouth girls admitted having had a good time.

On the evening of this day occurred the golf dance, given by the seniors to the juniors. It was the most "informal" affair of the year, thus far. The girls appeared in the gymnasium in their golf skirts, their shirt waists turned in at the necks and rolled up at the elbows, and with their warm golf capes thrown about them. The reason for this careful wrapping up was not obvious, even though some of them had come as far as from the third floor. The gentlemen, who were naturally the escorts, and who were easily distinguished by the handkerchiefs tied around their right arms, gallantly hung the numerous capes on the chestweight machines, and began filling out the programs, which were decorated with designs of golf clubs and balls, the work of an artistic senior. Aside from the brilliant display of golf capes, the gymnasium was artistically adorned with golf bags and clubs, which decorations were admired during the leisure moments by the young ladies who reclined on the numerous divans, evolved from convenient steps, and classroom benches, by means of sundry rugs and pillows. After the first grand march and circle, and between the various dances, lanciers, waltzs, and twosteps, the corner of the gymnasium where the lemonade was to be had, was the most

frequented spot in the room. At 9.15 the gentlemen and ladies left as promptly as they had come, and in each corridor, before the final good nights were said, each expressed great enjoyment of the evening.

October 15.—A party of girls from the school went on an all day's trip to Salem. They first stopped at the Peabody Academy of Science, which contains collections of animals, minerals, rocks and various kinds of wood. After which they visited in turn the Essex Institute, what remains of the first church in Salem; the home of Mr. Peabody, a noted English merchant; and, while driving around the town, saw the house where Hawthorne was born, and also the supposed "House of Seven Gables." Then the Salem Court House, the home of Roger Williams, the "Witchcraft House," and the Old Bakery were also visited. It was time to return home after seeing these, and all felt well repaid for their day's excursion.

Tuesday evening, October 16, brought a treat to a party of the music-loving ones among us, in the shape of a fine organ recital at Shawmut Congregational church, by Mr. Henry M. Dunham, our teacher of organ, assisted by his brother, Mr. William H. Dunham, tenor. Miss Alice Siever was the accompanist. The program follows:

Guilmant,	*Sonata in C. minor (No. 5).*
	Adagio. Finale.
Wagner,	*"Liebeslied" from "Die Walkure"*
Bach,	*Prelude in C minor*
Rheinberger,	*"Provincalisch"*
Dunham,	*a. Preludio*
	b. Intermezzo
(17th Century),	*a. "Drink to me only"*
Dibdin,	*b. "Tom Bowling"*
Widor,	*Adagio (from Symphony No. 6)*
Marty,	*Pastorale*
Whiting,	*Sonata in A minor (first movement)*

October 22.—In the afternoon Mr. Bragdon took those who wished to go, on an excursion to historic Boston. Our party, consisting of seventeen, left the Seminary

directly after lunch, and returned in time for dinner. Among the interesting places visited may be mentioned the Old South Church, Faneuil Hall, the Boston Museum, King's Chapel, and Hancock Tavern. An object of especial interest was the Old North Church, in the belfry of which the lanterns were hung out as a signal for Paul Revere.

October 25.—Friday evening a few went into Boston to hear Leland T. Powers give selections from "The Taming of the Shrew." The recital closed with "David Copperfield's Courtship of Dora." Mr. Powers is one of the best impersonators of the day, and recites in a very attractive manner. All who went felt well repaid by so enjoyable an evening.

October 27.—As Hallowe'en came in the middle of the week this year, the seniors chose the previous Saturday evening for their "Hallowe'en Poverty Party," to which all the school were invited. At seven o'clock a long line of girls danced into the gymnasium, which was lighted only by sundry pumpkin lanterns, a hurdy-gurdy playing the march. All wore black masks, and wierd, indeed, they looked in the dim light of the grinning lanterns. Upon the stage was a gypsy tent, in front of which sat Marinette Ramsdell, dressed as an old witch, and armed with a small broom to dust away the cobwebs, according to Mother Goose. Close by was her kettle, suspended from a tripod, in which magic potions were doubtless brewing! Over by the open fireplace the fire upon the hearth burned vigorously, and on either side of the chimney were apples, chestnuts and pop-corn in abundance, while other apples were suspended by strings here and there around the gymnasium, and some were alluringly floating in a tub of water, where anyone who wished might "bob" for them. Pretty soon the electric lights were turned on, and all joined in the grand march, after which the girls unmasked. The evening was spent in dancing, popping corn, roasting chestnuts, hearing futures from the old witch, and playing the usual hallowe'en games. Just before we all dispersed, Dr. Winslow took several flashlight pictures of the girls grouped about the stage.

October 30.—A joint recital which some of us attended, escorted by Mr. Bragdon, was given in Symphony Hall, by Mrs. Katharine Fisk, contralto; Miss Leonora Jackson, violinist, and Mr. Clarence Eddy, organist. Miss Jackson, a violinist of some note, played charmingly.

October 31.—As Hallowe'en was celebrated the Saturday before by the poverty party, not much of special interest occurred on this evening. At dinner each table had a Hallowe'en cake, containing either a ring or a thimble, which afforded a great deal of amusement. Just as the clock struck ten, all the doors began to slam, as though a powerful gust of wind had swept down the corridors. This was succeeded by a great calm, which lasted until twelve o'clock, when some stray ghost, wishing to celebrate more than the others, rang the Chinese gong, to welcome in the first of November, the month of Thanksgiving.

A Notable Anniversary.

Of especial interest to Lasell was the fiftieth wedding anniversary, celebrated in August, of Rev. and Mrs. Charles W. Cushing, of Rochester, N. Y. Mr. Cushing was the third principal of Lasell, holding that position from 1863 to 1874, at which time, retiring from the management of the school he was succeeded by Mr. Bragdon. The celebration took place on the fourteenth of August, Mr. Bragdon and family being invited, as also Miss Carpenter and Miss Blaisdell, who were here during Mr. Cushing's principalship.

FRENCH.

A young man would like to teach a class in conversational French. Is well recommended, and uses best method. Class of beginners or more advanced pupils, $1.00 per hour for four persons or less; .25 for each additional member. Please address C. Carpouthian, Needham, Mass.

Our former pupil, Mrs. Alice Mayo Hicks, vouches for Mr. Carpouthian in every way, and on her word we commend him to those desiring a teacher who can come to a home.

PUPILS BY STATES.

Massachusetts,	41	Indiana,	3
New York,	12	Missouri,	3
Pennsylvania,	12	Minnesota,	3
Connecticut,	11	Rhode Island,	2
Ohio,	11	Nebraska,	2
Illinois,	9	Michigan,	2
Maine,	6	Kansas,	2
New Hampshire,	6	India,	1
Iowa,	6	Kentucky,	1
Vermont,	5	Cape Breton,	1
Texas,	5	Canada,	1
Colorado,	4	Utah,	1
Montana,	3	Wisconsin,	1
New Jersey,	3	W. Virginia,	1
California,	3	Washington,	1

The exchange column in a school paper should be an important one, for through this column we are able to keep in touch with the students of other institutions. The exchanges are placed in the library, and after they have been read, they may be had by any of the students.

This month we have received the following papers: The Mount Holyoke, The Mirror, The Shamrock, The Polymnian, The Wesleyan Literary Monthly, The Argosy, The Harvard Lampoon, The Pennsylvanian, The Crescent, The Pennant, The Yale Review, and The Bowdoin Quill.

LASELL LEAVES

"DUX FEMINA FACTI."

VOL. XXVI   LASELL SEMINARY, AUBURNDALE, MASS., DECEMBER, 1900.   NUMBER 3

Published monthly during the School year by the Lasell Publishing Association.

EDITOR-IN-CHIEF.
GEORGIE M. DUNCAN, '02.

ASSOCIATE EDITORS.
ANNA M. PINKHAM, '02.   BESSIE Y. FULLER, '02.   IDA M. MALLORY, '03

LOCAL EDITOR.   SUBSCRIPTION AGENT.   EXCHANGE EDITOR.
RUTH M. TALCOTT.   ETHEL M. GALLAGHER, '01.   MABEL MARTIN, '01.

BUSINESS MANAGER.   ASST. BUSINESS MANAGER.
ETHLYN F. BARBER, '01.   JOANNA F. DEERING, '02.

TERMS, in Advance: One copy, one year (including Postage), $1.00.   Single copies, 15 cents.

ADVERTISING RATES.

SPACE.	3 months	6 months	9 months	SPACE.	3 months	6 months	9 months
1-8 Column, ...	$2.00	$3.75	$5.00	1-2 Column, ...	$6.50	$11.00	$15.00
1-6 "	3.00	5.00	6.50	3-4 "	9.00	15.00	20.00
1-4 "	4.00	6.50	9.00	1 "	12.00	19.00	25.00

The Editors will be glad to receive from the students and Alumnæ any communications and items of interest to the school.

Editorials.

WE are now entering upon a course of lectures in Business Law for Women, which we feel will be of great benefit. Last year certain of the girls did not take so kindly to these lectures as might have been expected, seeing that they are very evidently intended to be of the utmost practical advantage to us, and consequently these misguided ones did not get so much help from them as they might have gotten, as was clearly shown in the results of the examinations, which, we must say, with shamefacedness, were not in every case a great success. The girls who did pass last year have been excused from taking the course this year, but have been kindly invited to attend when they can. This some of them intend to do, as this year we have a different lecturer, and may, therefore, expect to have the subject presented from a somewhat different point of view, perhaps, or to have additional matter of an interesting kind brought in. Some will say, "What is the advantage of law to women?" We answer, "Law is relatively as important to women as to men." No girl can tell what she is to be in the future; she cannot look ahead and plan for herself; but she must take things as they come. I do not mean by this that she must give up trying, for that is the worst thing a girl can do. She must strive to do her best, and if reverses come, try to overcome them and start afresh. No matter what her station in life, a good understanding of the principles of law is likely at some time to be of great service to any woman. One who has charge of a home would indeed find herself lacking without it; one who is interested in public affairs must have it, in order intelligently to understand them. Any woman is likely, at one time or another, to have charge of her own business affairs, and to manage them well is difficult to do successfully without knowing, at least, the foundations of law. Every wise girl, then, will do her best to get all the information possible from these lectures. If she does not want it now, she will, perhaps, be very glad to have it in the future.

JUST at this time our thoughts turn to Thanksgiving, which, perhaps, we might say is a forerunner of Christmas. We think of the pleasures it brings us in being reunited with our dear ones once more, but do we really think of its true significance? We might consider the Thanksgiving of the past and that of the present, and notice the difference between them. A little over two centuries ago the Pilgrims, after suffering severest trials and sorrows, after enduring the discomforts of a scarcity of food that at times almost amounted to actual want, were at last rejoiced by bountiful harvests, and in sincere gratitude, therefore, set apart one day in the fall of the year, in which to give thanks to God for his gracious answer to their prayers; and on this day they not only worshiped the Great Giver, but spread a bountiful feast by way of celebrating his goodness to them. For some time this day was observed strictly in accordance with the ideas of its founders.

Gradually, however, custom has departed from these ideas, and the chief purpose of the day, that of earnest and heartfelt thanks for God's fostering care, has become obscured by the delight of the people in mere feasting and making merry on this holiday. At the present time it would seem that most of us do not consider very seriously how many things we have to be thankful for, but think only of the social and convivial pleasures the day brings us, regarding it purely and simply as a holiday, a day of fun and feasting. I fear our forefathers, if they should come among us at the present time, would be greatly shocked to see how far we have departed from their old established customs.

A MISSPELLED TAIL.

A little buoy said: "Mother, deer,
  May Eye go out to play?
The son is bright, the heir is clear,
  Owe! mother, don't say neigh!

"Go fourth, my sun," the mother said;
  His ant said: "Take ewer slay,
Your gniess new sled, awl painted read,
  Butt dew not lose ewer weigh."

"Ah, know!" he cried, and sought the street
  With hart sew full of glee—
The weather changed and snow and sleet
  And reign fell fierce and free.

Threw snow-drifts grate, threw watry pool,
  He flue with mite and mane—
Said he: "Though I wood walk by rule,
  Eye am knot write, 'tis plane.

"Ide like to meat some kindly sole,
  For hear gnu dangers weight,
And yonder stairs a treacherous whole;
  To sloe has bin my gate.

"A peace of bred, a gniess hot stake,
  Eyed chews if Eye were home;
This cruel fate my hart will brake,
  I love not thus too Rome.

"I'm weak and pail; I've mist my rode!"
  Butt hear a carte came passed—
He and his sled were safely toad
  Back to his home at last.
                              —*Exchange.*

The Servant Girl Problem.

IN this discussion of the servant girl problem, which is one of vital importance to the housewife, I shall confine myself to the consideration of a modest, rather than an elaborate establishment. In homes where there is a large retinue of servants, the mistress of the house does not, as a general rule, find time to trouble herself much with affairs of the kitchen, and as the mistress is to play no unimportant part in this paper, let us think in our application of the various points made, of the usual house in which are employed but two maids, the house where the mistress personally superintends affairs.

The difficulty of finding good servants, and of keeping them when found, has caused a great deal of discussion to be brought to bear upon the subject within the last few years, and finally there seems to have been found a solution, probably the only one possible.

Of course the great trouble with the average servant girl is incompetency; but does this arise from unwillingness to perform the necessary duties of her position aright, or rather from utter ignorance of how they should be done? In most instances it will be found that the latter is the case, in part, certainly, if not wholly; and when we consider the homes from which the majority of our servants come, it is not surprising. To begin with, a great many of the servant girls employed in our large cities and towns are foreigners, and come from countries where not only are the customs of housekeeping different from ours, but the very food substances themselves differ often from those which we expect them to cook and serve for us, and in such ways as shall accord with our tastes, fixed by long habits, and totally unlike theirs. Is it any wonder that they fail? Who of us, placed in similar circumstances,

could do better? Besides these, there are also to be considered those native-born girls who have come from homes where they have been used to only the bare necessities of life and have had no chance to learn how things may best and most advantageously be done, having had no other training than that afforded by their own homes. Surely it is foolish of us to expect such to prove themselves capable servants during their first experience in household service under such widely differing circumstances.

The mistress in many cases cannot hold herself blameless if she find difficulty in keeping servants. There are certain things she may properly demand of them, but they likewise have a right to expect certain things of her. Honesty, neatness, and good common sense are indispensable requisites in every servant girl, and with these as a foundation, there is no reason why, with time, any girl of average ability should not develop into a capable and trustworthy maid. On the other hand, the mistress should not complain if the maid asks certain privileges, such as a weekly "afternoon out," and her Sunday evenings free. A little leniency in unimportant matters, while making small difference to the mistress, serves to keep the servant much more contented and happy.

In many other ways, often lamentably ignored by the employers, could a servant's life be made pleasanter, nay, even positively attractive. For example, if she has had sufficient education to make reading a pleasure to her, why should not her mistress allow her to read the books in the home library? Certainly, unless the maid should neglect her work for this, it would prove of very great benefit to her, and if the mistress took a little pains personally to find out her tastes, and to help her in selection, it would lead to the establishing of a very desirable mutual understanding and basis of friendship between the two, by which state of things the mistress would profit no less surely than the recipient of these small favors. Of course this is possible only in the case of a girl who has proved herself worthy of such privileges and advantages. It is another matter with the insolent and careless servant we sometimes meet. It is hard to take any interest in these, except to get rid of them; and, indeed, there seems little else to be done with them.

The solution of this weighty problem, to which I had reference in the beginning, is the establishment of schools for working girls, where every department of housework is thoroughly taught, and at a price within the reach of all. Such a school, with a competent woman at the head, cannot fail to be a blessing to housekeepers the world over. There girls may be taught, in a careful, systematic way, the various branches of housework, from that of the laundry up to that of lady's maid. It is one of the most noteworthy events of the past few years that such schools have begun to be established in our large cities, and are meeting with such success. Attention has been called more and more of late years in colleges and boarding schools to the study of what is called Domestic Science, and surely if that is becoming a feature in such schools, of how much more value it must be, if placed within the grasp of those who make such work a means of livelihood.

I have read that there is one other plan which is finding favor, especially in Chicago, where it originated. Housekeepers there are threatening to discharge all regular servants, or rather to give up the search for them, and employ so-called "household assistants" who will come at seven o'clock in the morning and remain until six in the evening. This would leave the servant enough free time to suit even that somewhat exacting individual; and also, it is thought, do

away with the prejudice of native American women against household employment. While in some ways the plan seems practicable, it would necessitate too many radical changes in the household to make it especially popular, at least, at first. All evening entertainments would necessarily be put into the hands of caterers, which would be undesirable, for the housekeeper of average means, in point of expense, if in nothing else. What is more, the evening dinner hour would have to be changed to the middle of the day, to the great inconvenience of the business man, who, lunching down town, naturally desires a warm dinner with some social family cheer on his return home at night.

It would seem, then, as if the first suggestion, that of servant education, were the best way out of the difficulty. Since it is evident that something must be done, let us not choose that the "something" be of benefit to ourselves alone, but to the servant class as well. Education has ever proved one of the greatest blessings to mankind, and we who have known its advantages, should be the first to give our less fortunate sisters the benefit of it; and those who are not unselfish enough to be moved by this consideration alone, will hardly be indifferent to the fact that thus doing they will best subserve their own interests, and minister to their own home comfort.

Experiment Hall.

THE first attempt ever made in a school of high literary grade to combine actual housekeeping with daily studies was last year put in practice at Lasell and was a gratifying success. The entire lower floor of Experiment Hall (the old Annex) was devoted to it, the kitchen and dining-room being refurnished with the latest and most approved apparatus, and sleeping-rooms assigned to the temporary use of those of the class who chose to stay in the Hall over night; all under the care of a resident assistant in the Domestic Science Department.

In this first attempt to teach Practical Housekeeping, it was clearly demonstrated that Domestic Science may go hand in hand with other branches of education. This practice work was supplemented by two courses of lectures on "Science Applied to Housekeeping." The course of lessons on Invalid Cookery was very popular. The work took the place of the daily prescribed physical exercise, and seemed a perfect antidote for nervous prostration. The regular line of studies was in no way interfered with. These classes are divided into three sorts. The first consists of our regular third year classes, the second consists of our graduates or former pupils by the month, and the third consists of graduates of other schools who may come by the month for this special training. We want our former pupils to know that this opportunity is open to them and their friends by the month. We want our readers to take pains to tell it abroad, and to tell other friends that they may come, too. The terms are $50 per month, including everything. Ten per cent. discount to Lasell graduates or former pupils.

BATTALION OFFICERS.

Adj. Lieut.—Edith A. Harris.
Sar. Maj.—Marion Cole.
Company A.
Capt.—Ethel L. Gallagher.
Lieut.—Georgie M. Duncan.
1st Sar.—Ida M. Mallory.
2nd Sar.—Annie Mae Pinkham.
3rd Sar.—Emily A. Clemens.
Company B.
Capt.—Florence G. Plum.
Lieut.—Harriet S. Ward.
1st Sar.—Ellen Chase.
2nd Sar.—Florence Brewer.
3rd Sar.—Leila A. Walker.
Company C.
Capt.—Mabel Martin.
Lieut.—Ina Scott.
1st Sar.—Bessie S. Krag.
2nd Sar.—Ethlyn F. Barber.
3rd Sar.—Ruth M. Talcott.

LORD'S PRAYER BY BOOTH.

"I think," said James O'Neill, in his talk about the Booths, "the most thrilling experience I ever passed through was in New York city one time, when quite by accident a number of foreign diplomats from Washington, a few American statesmen, some prominent New Yorkers, and one or two of us professionals were gathered together in a smoking room of the Fifth Avenue Hotel, when somebody asked Booth, who by the merest chance happened to be there, if he would not repeat the Lord's Prayer for the assemblage. I was sitting not far from the tragedian when he fixed his eyes upon the man who made the request. I think that it was Lord Sackville West, at that time British minister to the United States, and I shall never forget the peculiarly searching expression that Booth shot out of his dark eyes. They seemed to penetrate the very soul of the man at whom they were directed, and then, as if satisfied, resumed their wonted vacuous density.

"We were all breathless with anxiety, at least I was, for seldom would he ever recite off the stage, but at length he arose, walked to a little cleared space at one end of the room, and began a recital that even after all these years makes me thrill through and through. He said 'Our Father', and never before had those two words been clothed with the majesty and reverence with which his look and tone enveloped them. And then he carried us into celestial regions, our spirits seeming to leave our bodies and to follow his behest; he lowered us into depths too dark for Dante's genius to conceive or Doré's pen to portray; the power exerted over us was simply unnatural. His musically resonant tones sounded slowly through the room, and as he swayed his lithe body we unconsciously followed his motion. It was something horrible, beautiful, terrible, fascinating—I cannot find words in the language to express it. There are none.

"I would not go through the scene again for a thousand worlds, and yet if I had the opportunity I would brave any danger to hear it once more. Do you understand? Those few score words as delivered by Edwin Booth were the most powerful argument for Christianity that I ever heard, and could every being on the face of the globe have heard them there would no longer be atheism. Booth strode out of the room when he finished, and a simultaneous sigh of relief arose, while without a word we stole away singly and on tiptoe, and I do not believe that any of us think of that thrilling evening without a shudder. He was a great man, a great man."—*Kansas City Times.*

THE BRAVEST BATTLE THAT EVER WAS FOUGHT.

BY JOAQUIN MILLER.

The bravest battle that ever was fought;
  Shall I tell you where and when?
On the maps of the world you will find it not;
  'Twas fought by the mothers of men.

Nay, not with cannon or battle shot,
  With sword or nobler pen;
Nay not with eloquent word or thought,
  From mouths of wonderful men.

But deep in a walled-up woman's heart—
  Of woman that would not yield,
But bravely, silently bore her part—
  Lo! there is that battlefield.

No marshaling troop, no bivouac song;
  No banner to gleam and wave;
But oh! these battles they last so long—
  From babyhood to the grave!

Yet, faithful still as a bridge of stars,
  She fights in her walled-up town—
Fights on and on in the endless wars,
  Then silent, unseen—goes down.

O, ye with banners and battle shot,
  And soldiers to shout and praise,
I tell you the kingliest victories fought
  Were fought in these silent ways.

O, spotless woman in world of shame!
  With splendid and silent scorn,
Go back to God as white as you came,
  The kingliest warrior born.

PERSONALS.

—The engagement is announced of Miss May Louise Gurley, to Mr. Edgar Hayes Betts, of Lansingburgh, New York.

—The engagement is announced of Miss Alice Rix Taylor, to Mr. E. Clifford Potter, of Newton Centre, Mass.

—Mrs. Nellie Alling Thayer of Newton Center, with Mrs. Bennett, called upon Miss Bennett on the 19th. She says her Margaret (eight years old) is anxiously wondering when she shall pick out her room at Lasell, and thinks she would like the same one her mother had. Mrs. Nellie is President of the Ladies' Aid Society, and in general a woman much in demand, as all Lasell girls are, practical, capable and useful. Mr. Thayer is much engaged with his singing. His rare tenor voice and musical ability are in much demand.

—Bessie Risser, mention of whose recent bereavement will be found in another column, will not be able to return to us, as we had hoped she might.

—Edith Gale ('89) is teaching in the Allen Normal School, Thomasville, Ga.—music and some regular branches. The school is under the auspices of the American Miss. Association. The climate she finds delightful, and the work interesting. The place is something of a resort for northern people, many of whom have winter homes there, Mark Hanna being one. Edith is to spend the holidays in St. Augustine.

—Daisy Seasongood writes that she is

"attending the university, for the purpose of studying logic, French literature of the 19th century, and English literature of the 17th, 18th and 19th centuries." She finds a very great amount of reading necessary, and this she is finding helpful and suggestive in many ways. She speaks of the recent death of a very dear cousin, a young man.

—Edith Bailey (1900) writes of enjoying the LEAVES.

—Esther Bridgman Lane writes that Mary Strickland Whitney has been abroad for nearly three years with her sister, Fanny. She thinks of returning in the spring, but Esther thinks it unlikely, since, having lost her father, mother, husband, and child, she has nothing to call her back to America. Esther has three fine boys, of whom she writes with all a mother's pride; with these and her good husband, her life, she says, is full of peace and happiness. Her years at Lasell she counts among the brightest and most treasured of her life, and says, "The little lessons learned there outside books have been always helpful."

—Nellie Carnahan is attending the Indiana State Normal School, expecting to teach after finishing her course there. Her address is 441 N. Fifth St., Terre Haute, Ind.

—Mabel Marston has been in New York almost ever since her graduation, though in May she visited Anna Wells in Le Roy. She is at present at home busy with housekeeping duties, and with music, to which she gives some four hours daily. Expects soon to begin vocal, too, she says, despite "the fact that I haven't any voice." She attended on Good Friday last the services at the Marble Collegiate, on 5th Ave., and found the music very beautiful. Among other things they sang Mr. Bragdon's favorite hymn, "We may not climb the heavenly steps." She may look in upon us at Lasell some time this winter.

—During her recent business trip West, Mabel Lutes ('95) had the pleasure of a charming visit with Clara Souther, whom she almost missed, however, since Clara was out of the city—Indianapolis—when Mabel arrived there. Coming back in time, though, she packed Mabel off home with her, and they had a fine time together. She—Clara—is well, and "just as nice as ever," and that's *very* nice, as we all know who knew her here. Mabel also saw Mrs. Carnahan, who said that Nellie was well and enjoying her studies.

—Mabel Martin and Bess Krag can make good bread—Mr. Bragdon says so. He tried it—and so can Florence Brewer. Splendid!

—Grace Houghton is studying art at the Cincinnati Art Academy, her father having moved this fall from Columbus to Cincinnati. Grace hopes to become a portrait painter. She has had a recent visit from Edith Moulton ('99). The address Grace gives is Elberson Avenue, Cincinnati.

—Alice Magoun planned to attend the October meeting of the New England History Teachers' Association, in Boston, and was expected at that time to come out to Lasell to see us, but was disappointed, and did not get to Boston at all. She speaks of certain history work, which she did last year under the direction of Dr. Hart, of Cambridge, and which she found very congenial and inspiring work. She saw Alice Hall in August, and had a delightful afternoon with her. Hattie Clark Van Doren wrote her in August of a projected trip to Europe with her husband and the two boys, bright, interesting little fellows of seven and five. Of her school work, English and history, Alice speaks with evident pleasure, and with no less evident appreciation of the College lecture courses at Amherst which she is enabled to enjoy through her residence in that town, mentioning especially in this line Professor Genung's readings in Browning.

—Edith Grant ('98) tells us that they have moved again, this time to Hotel Beresford, 81st St., and Central Park West, where they have a very comfortable place, with delightful views on both sides of them. Her health, she says, has put a veto upon her carrying out her plan of entering Barnard College. The election this fall put her in mind of that held at Lasell when she was here, four years ago, and the attendant excitement. Ada Cadmus ('98) and Edith spent some time together at St. Hubert's Inn, in the Adirondacks, last summer presumably, though she doesn't say when.

—We learn through a clipping that Hattie Pendexter was one of a party of girls who enjoyed last summer a White Mountain trip together. Certain others of the party were Lasell-girls-to-be, so it seems. Who were they?

—We saw Clara Lewis recently for a too brief chat on the street car, coming out from the city one day. She looks the picture of health and contentment. Is with her sister in Brookline now. She mentioned having been housekeeper for awhile during her sister's absence on a trip away, and spoke also of being regularly engaged to sing at one of the Brookline churches.

We have had a splendid time this month with old girls. Carol Case and Helen Campbell came and stayed at Mrs. Walker's from Wednesday to Friday, and kindly gave us some of their time. I have no idea what they did with the rest of it. Carol said she had to get back so as to be at that barbarous Harvard-Yale football game on Saturday. She keeps her interest in the battalion. She may come next year to have charge of the whole drill. Helen doesn't know what she is doing for a living. At the same time May Rice, of Evanston, and Alice Maloon, of

Beverly, came for a bit. May Rice's folks have started on a two years' tour of the known world. Alice Maloon is having fine success at massage. All our girls look well. Then Alice Taylor called. She was visiting her future husband's family in Newton Centre (to see if they approved?) Then Frances Wood and Emily Bissell smiled upon us. They had a great time in Europe.

But the bright, particular visit of the month was that of Mrs. Gilman (Adelaide L. Sears, 1857), Mrs. May, (Emma E. Sears, 1857), and Mrs. T. D. Chamberlain (Delia Jarvis, almost of 1857). This is Mrs. Chamberlain's first visit since 1856. Her late husband's brother was the gallant Gen'l Joshua L. Chamberlain of Maine.

It was delightful to see their interest in everything new and old. They went to the rooms where they used to live. They told about pranks they used to play. They talked about the old girls in the pictures of the classes of 1855, 1856, and 1857; made fun of themselves in old time costume, and admired all the improvements, and wished they were girls to begin again.

Then the next day came Alice Ashley and Agnes Flaherty of 1900. Agnes didn't stay long. She is living in Cambridge, and taking singing lessons of Miss White. Alice Ashley took Thanksgiving dinner with Alice Jenckes, who has just spent seven weeks with her. Then Alice J. came up here with Alice A. Then Beulah Smith came with the daughter of an old friend of Mr. B.'s. Then Mabel Gamwell and Bertha Metcalf looked ed just a bit. She was spending Sunday with Miss Dresser.

The following have been favored with calls from members of their family: Misses Kneeland, Nelson, Bennett, Rogers, McLean, Martin, Bowers, Pendexter, Noyes, Woodbury, North, M. Whitney, Brewer, Barker, Clokey, Kimball, Bullock, McKinnie,

Matthews, Lapouski, Walter, L. Whitney, Krag.

Former pupils: Clara Robbins, Ella Cotton, Agnes Flaherty, Ethel Walton, Alice Taylor, Frances Wood, Emily Bissell, Lucy Curtis, Helen Campbell, Maude Case, May Rice, Alice Maloon, Beulah Smith, Bertha Metcalf, Mabel Gamwell, Bertha Warren, Alice Kimball, Ada Marsh.

MARRIAGES.

—Lillian Mason Baker to Joseph Foss Humphrey, on Wednesday, Nov. 7, at Denver, Colo. Home address: 1537 Vine St., Denver.

—Louese Chase Horton to Edward Wright McKinstry, on Wednesday, Nov. 7, at Cleveland, Ohio.

—Lily Flagg to the Rev. Charles Henry Duncan, on Monday, Nov. 12, in New York City. Home address, Millbrook, New York.

—Helen Holman ('96) to Livingston Pearne Moore, on Wednesday, Nov. 21, in Chicago. Home address, after Feb. 1, 938 Flournoy St.

—Mary Walker to Robert Milton Leach, on Wednesday, Nov. 28, at Taunton, Mass. Home address: 57 Berkely St., Taunton.

—Ruth Alice Cleaveland to Benjamin Franklin Bates, on Wednesday, Nov. 28, at Denver, Colo. Home address: 1225 Twelfth Ave., Denver.

—Myrna Lamson to Pierre Kissam Tyng, on Monday, Dec. 17, at Chicago. Home address, after Feb. 1: 57 Johnson Park, Buffalo, N. Y.

A WORD TO LASELL SHOPPERS.

The importance of trading with the firms who advertise in the LASELL LEAVES cannot be overestimated. We should not expect their patronage if we do not give them our support in return. Another way for Lasell girls to be loyal!

November 10.—A Waltham orchestra played during the dinner hour, and afterwards in the gymnasium, much to the delight of the girls, many of whom spent the evening in dancing.

November 15.—About thirty girls, under the care of Mr. Bragdon, attended the Strauss concert at Symphony Hall. The house, although not crowded, was well filled to hear the court musical director of Germany, with his orchestra, and all enjoyed the evening very much.

November 16.—On this evening a party chaperoned by Mrs. Martin, attended the impersonation of "The Merchant of Venice" by Mrs. Southwick. Between the acts were two harp solos. The evening was one to be remembered.

On the evening of November 19, several of the girls went into Boston with Mr. Bragdon to hear Elbert Hubbard lecture on the "Roycrofters," at Tremont Temple. Mr. Hubbard looks rather peculiar with his hair falling to his shoulders, and his odd-looking, rolling collar, but these little things are forgotten when one hears him speak. He told very entertainingly of his shop at East Aurora, where "books and things" are made, and of the workers, who have increased from the one or two assistants employed at first to two hundred and fifty, and are most of them people who would usually be refused employment elsewhere, one of the most trusted persons in the shop, for instance, being a released convict. Mr. Hubbard goes by the nickname of "John" among his employes, who do not stand on ceremony. A clue to his popularity with his men was in one of several things that he said by way of conclusion. This was that, in his opinion, it is a very poor way of doing business to strike from the payroll sick persons, or those who have grown old in their employer's service, and this opinion was heartily applauded by the audience.

Mr. Hills has given to the pupils of the piano department this term three lectures, which have been very interesting and instructive. In these lectures upon Technical Analysis, he has particularly emphasized the importance to the player of a correct position, and of those conditions which produce it. Two ensemble classes have already been formed. This department is flourishing, as under Mr. Hills it must always be.

November 22.—The Rev. S. M. Crothers lectured upon "The Spiritual Message of Browning." Among other good things he said, "We are often told that Browning is obscure, but after all no poet was ever clearer than he in the purpose he had in view. He leads us to something higher and better in religion, and shows us divine love in man and nature." Mr. Crothers, who is a prominent minister in Cambridge, is also a well-known writer of very interesting magazine articles on sundry literary subjects.

November 24.—Surely the gymnasium never looked prettier than on this evening, when arranged to represent a large drawing-room, in which the Juniors received and entertained the Seniors. "A Salamagundi Party" was the entertainment of the evening, and after play was over, and while the refreshments were being served, the prizes were announced and presented to the winners. The first prize, a handsome belt buckle, was won by Miss Gamwell; the second, a picture of the Countess Potocka, by Miss Lum, while to Miss Isabella Clemens was awarded the booby prize, a small drum with the words "Here's something you can beat" upon it. All had a good time, and the guests of the evening heartily expressed their pleasure to the Juniors.

November 25.—As the weather was quite unpleasant, and all were excused from going to church, more time than would otherwise have been possible was allowed to listen to the very interesting talk in the chapel about the work at the North End Mission in Boston, by Miss Cooke, founder of this mission, and one of its most faithful and enthusiastic workers. She spoke particularly of the medical work there, and of the many to whom it has brought, and is still bringing, help and relief from physical ills. Its efficiency and usefulness is greatly hindered through lack of room, but there is prospect now of having presently a new and more spacious building for this purpose, which we hope will greatly advance this good work.

In the evening Mr. Bragdon took a party to the People's Temple in Boston to hear Mr. Warren W. Adams, with a chorus of fifty trained singers, assisted by several well known soloists, present Rossini's "Stabat Mater." The music, being finely rendered, was greatly enjoyed.

November 29.—Thanksgiving was thoroughly enjoyed by all who remained here. A very creditable number went to the morning service with Mr. Bragdon, while others went for a brisk walk in the keen air; and both church-goers and pedestrians seemed to have gained appetites sharp enough to enable them to do full justice to the generous dinner that came later. At 1.30 a throng of merry faces gathered round the prettily arrayed tables. The place of each was designated by a card bearing the name of the guest, accompanied by a menu card and an orchestra program. Dr. Watkins gave thanks, and the guests were seated. During the feasting the orchestra rendered many familiar and attractive selections, while all enjoyed talking together and listening to amusing stories, jokes, and the like. After dinner the party adjourned to the gymnasium, where social fun and frolic continued. In the evening a large number of the girls went to see Willard, in "The Professor's Love Story." Everyone reported a happy Thanksgiving.

December 1.—Dr. Winslow having finished his course of lectures upon "Household Economy," Dr. Mary Greene gave the first of her lectures upon "Business Law for Women," on Saturday afternoon. Although those who passed in this course last year are not required to attend, yet several of them do, wisely realizing that this is a subject about which one cannot know too much.

JEFFERSON'S TEN RULES.
Rules that governed Thomas Jefferson's daily life:
1. Never put off till tomorrow what you can do today.
2. Never trouble another for what you can do yourself.
3. Never spend your money before you have it.
4. Never buy what you do not want because it is cheap; it will be dear to you.
5. Pride costs us more than hunger, thirst and cold.
6. We never repent of having eaten too little.
7. Nothing is troublesome that we do willingly.
8. How much pain have cost us the evils which never happened.
9. Take things always by the smooth handle.
10. When angry, count ten before you speak; when very angry, a hundred.

PASSED AWAY.
—The earth is resting, yet she is not idle, though she seem so; she is gathering strength for days yet to come; preparing robes of beauty to wear under blue skies in brighter sunshine; quietly, and in manifold unnoticed and unknown ways, getting herself ready for a richness and fulness of renewed life that shall wave myriads of green banners in the air, and fill it with the fragrance and beauty of countless delicate blossoms. And we say of her, "She is dead! Rigid she lies, shrouded in snow, her poor old face wrinkled and drawn—no beauty left, no life—dead." But because we choose thus to dwell upon the picture of death, is she, then, "dead"? Wait till May, till June, then answer, when apple boughs are abloom from tip to tip, the air instinct with the very essence of life, the grass greenly springing, and the tidal-wave of beauty overflowing the world. Is it not thus with our beloved dead? Only resting awhile, to rejoice our longing eyes later with a finer, an immortal loveliness; with a fresher, an undying love to repay our long and lonely days of waiting. Ah, the resurrection spring! what shall it show to us in those whom with tear-blinded eyes we call "dead," and think of as lost? Wait till the Master shall say to us, as Philip to Nathaniel, "Come and see."

—Again to Bessie Risser's home has come the sorrow of parting, in the loss of her loved sister, Mary Lois, a young girl of nineteen, with whom Bessie was last year at Asheville, N. C. Readers of the LEAVES will remember the sad blow sustained last April by the family in the death of Albert, a 15-year-old brother of Bessie's, and but a short time ago a young cousin was taken away, after a lingering illness. In all these troubles, and especially in this last bitter grief, she and her suffering family have our heartfelt sympathy.

—Daisy Seasongood and her family mourn the loss of a dear cousin of hers, a young man of twenty-seven. With these, too, we sympathize in their sorrow.

The Lion ramps around the cage,
The Lady smiles to see him rage.
The little Mouse outside the bars
Looks on and laughs. "Well bless my stars!"
Quoth he, "to think they call that thing
The King of Beasts! If he's a King,
Who cannot make the Lady wince,
What must I be? When, not long since,
Inside the cage I chanced to slip,
You should have seen that Lady skip
Upon the Lion's back. 'Help! Murder!
A Mouse!' she screamed; you should have heard her!
And then with brooms the keepers came
And drove me out (but, all the same,
I got the crumb that I was after).
A King, indeed! Excuse my laughter!"
—*Oliver Herford.*

If you have built castles in the air, your work need not be lost; that is where they should be built; now put the foundations under them.—*Thoreau.*

Foot Anatomy.

Is a branch of science that the skilled shoe maker has to thoroughly master. The makers of

 Sorosis

have, after years of experience, acquired a knowledge enabling them to produce shoes that have a snug, glove-like fit at the heel, ankle and instep, seldom found even in the finest custom-made shoes, and they reveal a style and individuality of their own which all good dressers appreciate.

(Forty styles in all Leathers.)

Always **$3.50** Pair.

Shepard, Norwell & Co.,

Winter Street, Boston.

Business Established 1817.

JOHN H. PRAY & SONS CO.

Wholesale and retail dealers in

CARPETS AND RUGS

of both Foreign and Domestic Manufacture; also

Curtains, Draperies, Portieres and all descriptions of choice Upholstery Fabrics,

PRICES ALWAYS MODERATE

JOHN H. PRAY & SONS CO.,

Oldest and Largest Carpet House in New England.

PRAY BUILDING, Opposite Boylston St.

658 WASHINGTON STREET, BOSTON, 658

EXCHANGES

—At the University of Pennsylvania a war memorial tower has recently been erected in memory of those who fell in the late war with Spain.—*Ex.*

—There are four Filipinos registered at the University of Minnesota, and six at California.—*Ex.*

—Exchanges received this month are: Classic, The Tiltonian, The Kalends, Chauncy Hall, The Pennsylvanian, College Rambler, Ryan Classic, The Olympian, The Argosy, The Harvard Lampoon, The Porcupine, The Radiator, and The Question Mark.

SUBSCRIBE NOW.

Now is the time to send in your subscription to the LEAVES, girls. You all enjoy the items about the girls you knew here, and should not deprive yourself of this bond of union with your old friends and your school home. If you have any news of yourself, or of any of the girls, let us have it for our "Personals." We thank those who have already done this.

LASELL LEAVES

"DUX FEMINA FACTI."

VOL. XXVI   LASELL SEMINARY, AUBURNDALE, MASS., JANUARY, 1901.   NUMBER 4

Published monthly during the School year by the Lasell Publishing Association.

EDITOR-IN-CHIEF.
KATHERINE E. McCOY, '01.

ASSOCIATE EDITORS.
FLORENCE BREWER.   BESSIE M. DRAPER, '02.   IDA M. MALLORY, '03

LOCAL EDITOR.   SUBSCRIPTION AGENT.   EXCHANGE EDITOR.
JOANNA F. DEERING, '02.   RUE McKINNIE.   LELIA A. WALKER, '01.

BUSINESS MANAGER.   ASST. BUSINESS MANAGER.
ETHLYN F. BARBER, '01.   JOANNA F. DEERING, '02.

TERMS, in Advance: One copy, one year (including Postage), $1.00.   Single copies, 15 cents.

Editorials.

WHEN it was announced last fall that the Faculty had decided to make a change in the programme, having only one chapel service a day and that at noon, most of the old girls felt that it would be very hard to accustom themselves to the change, and only a few were in favor of the new plan. The girls adapted themselves very readily to the change, however, and now but few, if any, would care to return to the old plan. One of the greatest advantages is that it gives a definite amount of time for Mrs. Martin's exercises in the morning. These exercises, and Mrs. Martin's work in general, cannot be too highly praised and are certainly one of Lasell's best advantages. The longer one remains at Lasell the more one realizes how much this work does for the girls. It is often hard and trying, and we sometimes think that we disapprove of the methods employed, but we cannot deny that the results are good. Another advantage of the new order is that, having chapel at noon, a break is thus made in our work, which is a rest and enables us to perform better the remainder of our duties. We have now more time in the evening than formerly for both study and recreation. Making our walking period ten minutes shorter, is a disadvantage, for it was not long enough before, although some of us on these cold, winter days cannot help wishing it only twenty minutes long instead of forty. It is not at all necessary, however, that we should confine ourselves to the one walking period; but American girls have not yet learned to appreciate walking, and very few walk more than they are obliged to. Considered on all sides, the new plan seems to have more advantages than disadvantages, and we hope that its adoption is permanent.

Some Curious Facts.

There are some curious facts about our calendar. It is said that no century can begin on Wednesday, Friday, or Sunday. The same calendars can be used every twenty years. September always begins on the same day of the week as December. The months of February, March, and November always begin on the same days. May, June, and August always begin on different days from each other, and from every other month in the year. The first and last days of the year are always the same. These rules do not apply to leap year, when comparison is made between days before and after Feb. 29. *Christian Work.*

Wise or Otherwise.

It was not a Lasell girl who sent the following order by her young husband, when he went to the office in the morning: Five pounds of paralyzed sugar; two cans condemned milk; one box of fresh salt; three pounds of desecrated cod-fish; one-half pound consecrated yeast. And when the store-keeper asked her if she wouldn't like some horse radish, said, "horse radish, no! we haven't any horse."

Again, it *was* a Lasell girl who in history recitation spoke guilelessly of the *excavation* of Henry IV, meaning, it was generously supposed, *excommunication,* instead.

Where the New Century Begun.

THERE is a good deal of sentimental interest attaching to the opening of a new century. Which land will see it first? Whose eye will be the first to note its advent? Whose hail will usher in its earliest moment? Like so many of the phenomena, such as the eclipse and the transit of the planets, the incoming of the twentieth century was in a region so sparsely settled as to be almost devoid of human life.

The first moment of the twentieth century, the first second of January 1, 1901, occurred in the midst of the Pacific Ocean, along a line conforming in general to the meridian of one hundred and eighty degrees east and west longitude from Greenwich. There was here no land of consequence to salute the new century; no human eye, save, perchance, that of the watch on board some tiny ship, was there to see its entrance, and its only welcome was, perhaps, the last strokes of the eight bells marking midnight on board some steamship or vessel which, by chance, might cross the meridian at that instant.

The first people to live in the twentieth century were the Friendly Islanders, for the date-line, as it may be called, lies in the Pacific Ocean, just to the east of their group. At that time, although it was already Tuesday to them, all the rest of the world were enjoying some phase of Monday, the last day of the nineteenth century. At Melbourne the people were going to bed, for it was nearly ten o'clock; at Manila it was two hours earlier in the evening; at Calcutta the English residents were sitting at their Monday afternoon dinner, for it was about six o'clock; and in London, "Big Ben," in the tower of the House of Commons, was striking the hour of noon. In Boston, New York and Washington half the people were eating breakfast on Monday morning, while Chicago was barely conscious of the dawn.

At the same moment San Francisco was in the deepest sleep of what is popularly called Sunday night, though really the early, dark hours of Monday morning, and half the Pacific was wrapped in the darkness of the same morning hours, which become earlier to the west until at Midway or Brooks Islands it was but a few minutes past midnight of Sunday night.

Of course, everybody knows that the twentieth century begun on Tuesday, January 1, 1901. It is true that some thoughtless individuals have obscured the matter by hasty expressions of opinion, setting the date for January 1, 1900. But such persons have forgotten that we begin to count with 1, and that the hundred is not completed till the two ciphers have appeared, and then the new hundred begins, as did the old one, with 1. Just as the year 100 with its close marked the completion of the first century, so did the year 1900 with its last moments end our nineteenth century, and 1901 begin the twentieth.

The actual date-line varies from the theoretical one in a number of places. Starting at the North Pole, it follows the meridian of one hundred and eighty degrees to about seventy degrees north latitude, where it curves to the east about ten degrees, so as to pass through Behring Strait and include all of Siberia in the Russian day. Then it takes a reverse curve across to one hundred and seventy degrees east longitude, to include the Aleutian Islands in our American day. Then in the open ocean it regains one hundred and eighty degrees, and passes by Brooks Island and across the Equator. At about five degrees south latitude it curves again to the east nearly ten degrees, so as to give the Friendly Islands the Australian day. It then regains the meridian of one hundred and eighty degrees just to the south of Chatham Islands, and follows this line across the Antartic continent to the South Pole.

All who cross the Pacific Ocean gain a practical knowledge of the change of day at the date-line. Vessels going west, when they reach this line, skip a day, while in going east a day is repeated, so that there are two consecutive days of the same name in a "week" of eight days.

If one could have truly rapid transit, and be able to pass along the meridian of one hundred and eighty degrees from the North Pole to the Equator in a moment, he would have a strange experience, if the time selected for the journey were a few moments after midnight, on the morning of Tuesday, January 1, 1901, the first day of the twentieth century. Near the Pole it would be the twentieth century, Tuesday morning; at sixty degrees north latitude it would be Monday morning that was beginning, the last day of the nineteenth century, for here it is that the western sweep of the date-line includes the Aleutian Islands in the American day. At thirty-five degrees north latitude it would be again Tuesday in the new century.

If a vessel happened to be in the vicinity of the date-line on Sunday night, December 30, 1900, it would be possible, at the moment of crossing the line, for the watch, himself already in the twentieth century, to call back to the helmsman, who would be just at midnight of the next to the last day in the nineteenth century. Or, if the vessel happened to be becalmed just on the meridian, it would be possible to walk aft into the nineteenth century and forward again into the twentieth, a veritable turning back of time in his flight. On the other hand, if an eastbound vessel approached the meridian at night it might see the nineteenth century close at midnight of December 31, 1900, and then have a second closing of the same century the next night at the end of the repeated day.

Such speculations as these may be carried to any desired extent, and serve to show some of the curiosities of the line along which the day, the year and the century all begin.

The meridian of one hundred and eighty degrees east and west of Greenwich traverses the Pacific Ocean from north to south. While it does not cross any important country, still these seas are so well sprinkled with islands that many lie close to the line, some of the larger groups are divided by it, one or two islands are bisected, and at the north and south it encounters parts of continents.

In the extreme north, the line marking one hundred and eighty degrees runs across Wrangel Land in the Arctic Ocean. For one or two hundred miles it stretches across the continent of Asia, passing from Cape North to Cape Tringa, Eastern Siberia, crossing between these places a quite important arm of the ocean, the Gulf of Anadyr. Siberia extends some ten degrees to the east of the meridian, Behring Strait being in longitude one hundred and seventy degrees west. From Asia the meridian crosses Behring Sea to the Aleutian Islands, passing through the narrow channel between Amchitka and two minor islands of the Andreanoffski group. For more than fifteen hundred miles to the south there is open sea uninterrupted by islands important enough to map, till in about twenty-eight degrees north latitude Midway or Brooks Islands, made famous by Stevenson in his story of "The Wreckers," lie quite close to the line on the easterly side. Maurelle Islands, not far distant, lie to the west of the meridian.

For another long distance, nearly thirty degrees, there is open ocean, till at eight degrees south of the Equator the line runs through the Ellice Islands, passing about ninety miles to the east of Funafuti, the largest of the group. Mitchell Island is just east of the meridian and almost touching it. Ten degrees farther south lies the Fiji group. The line barely escapes the eastern point of Vanua Levu, the northern-most of the large islands, and cuts squarely in two the neighboring minor islands, Rambi and Vuna. One hundred miles to the south, Totoya, of the same group, is grazed by the line, which then passes over five hundred miles of ocean to the Kermedec Islands, some three or four hundred miles northeast of New Zealand. The meridian passes about seventy-five miles to the east of New Zealand, but is to the west of the adjacent Chatham Islands. South four or five degrees and just west of the line are the islands of Bounty and Antipodes, the latter of which, in fifty degrees south latitude, are very nearly the antipodes of London. To the south there are no other islands, and the meridian of one hundred and eighty degrees strikes the southern continent in Victoria Land at about eighty degrees south of the Equator.

This is the strict, theoretical position of the date-line, that line along which the day begins, and it would be the actual line itself but for the fact that every rule made by man is subject to exceptions. The exceptions to this rule have gradually crept in through the manner of colonization or settlement or the demands of business. In deference to the latter some of the recent changes have been made.

The Spaniards going west from their possessions in America carried their day to the Philippine Islands. The Dutch sailing east took their day with them to the adjacent islands of Borneo, Sumatra and Java, and to China. The circuit of the earth having thus been completed, there was the difference of a day between Manila and its neighbors,

Manila being behind. As the business interests of the different islands brought them into closer relationships the absurdity of having different day-names in places so close together was the more striking. Accordingly, about the middle of the century the authorities arranged for a unification of the dates, and a day was skipped by the Filipinos, the day being December 31, 1844. They went to bed on the evening of December 30, 1844, and awoke the next morning on January 1, 1845.

The Russians, who possessed Siberia and Alaska, brought eastward the day of St. Petersburg and maintained it on this continent till Alaska became a part of the United States. The Alaskans, in their reckoning of the date, were one day ahead of their neighbors, the Canadians, and of our people. When we acquired Alaska we made a change in the interests of business, deciding that it would be better for all parts of the United States to have the same day. We set the date-line to the west ten degrees past the meridian of one hundred and eighty degrees so as to include in our day our outermost island, Attu. For this reason, Attu, being in east longitude one hundred and seventy degrees, is the latest place on the earth to retain any certain day.

In the same way certain groups of islands in the southern Pacific, whose business relations are mainly with the Austral continent, have been included in the day with Australia and New Zealand, although some of them are to the east of one hundred and eighty degrees. The Friendly Islands and the smaller members of the Fiji group are among these. Near at hand and still to the east lie the Samoa Islands, but authorities differ as to the reckoning of time in them. They probably also have the day of Australia.

Some other time isn't any time at all.

19th Century Summarized.

TRULY this last century of ours has been wonderful in its material advance, which is thus ably summarized by London *Answers.*

This century received from its predecessors the horse; we bequeath the bicycle, the locomotive and the motor car.

We received the goose-quill; we bequeath the typewriter.

We received the scythe; we bequeath the mowing machine.

We received the hand printing press; we bequeath the cylinder press.

We received the painted canvas; we bequeath lithography, photography, and color photography.

We received the hand loom; we bequeath the cotton and woolen factory.

We received gunpowder; we bequeath lyddite.

We received the tallow dip; we bequeath the electric lamp.

We received the galvanic battery; we bequeath the dynamo.

We received the flint-lock; we bequeath Maxims.

We received the sailing-ship; we bequeath the steamship.

We received the beacon signal fire; we bequeath the telephone and wireless telegraphy.

We received ordinary light; we bequeath Roentgen rays.

And all this on the purely material side, to say nothing of the progress in detail that has made this major progress possible—the advances in chemistry and metallurgy; the invention of machinery and its adaptation to manifold processes formerly considered too intricate for aught but patient work by hand. Beyond this is the scientific knowledge acquired and applied to the lives of the race;

the explorations conducted, and the new countries opened up to settlement and progress. In politics is found the growth of liberal institutions; the leaven of inherent rights of manhood has leavened the whole lump. And in art, in literature, in music, the advance throughout the whole social scale is incalculable.

College Athletics for Girls.

Recent statistics show that there is a goodly yearly increase in average chest inflation, total strength, and lung capacity among the students of colleges for women who are compelled to take regular exercise. The increase in capacity in all directions is always more marked in the freshman class, as the students are almost invariably new to regular scientific exercise, but the growth is marked up to the day of graduation. The general health of the student's body is certainly far better than that of the general run of girls of the same age and of the same walk in life.

She Knew the Difference.

They had the words "visit" and "visitation" in the reading lesson in a Washington public school the other day. Nearly every little girl in the class knew quite well what "visit" meant, but they were a little at sea when it came to "visitation."

"Now," said the teacher, "I want you to tell me what you think it means. It is something more serious, more awful, than visit. I don't want to tell you what it means till you have told me what you think it means. What do you think, Anna?"

Anna looked a bit doubtful, but plucking up courage on the teacher's hint, she spoke: "I know what 'visit' means," she said. "That's like when Cousin Jack comes to see us, and visitation—well, when Aunt Jane comes, I guess that's a visitation."

My Christmas Vacation.

It was a six days' trip to Williamsport, Pa., to visit Mrs. Bragdon's relations, and to see Mrs. Bragdon and Belle so far on their way to California. Maybe some of you don't know that Mrs. Bragdon is Miss Ransom's sister, and that each has two other sisters who have been pupils at Lasell, and so are entitled to record on these pages. Sade, Mrs. Hazelet, was the hostess in the fine, old mansion where I wooed and was won by the oldest of these splendid sisters. We numbered fifteen, including Sade and her five children; Minn, Mrs. Wagner, and her two, and we had a royal good time as you girls say. Mrs. Hazelet is a rare mother and manager, never flustered or out of temper, quick to see, and judicious to plan; withal, one who makes everybody instantly at home in her generous hospitality. Of Mrs. Wagner and Miss Ransom, most of you know already.

Of other girls in Williamsport, I enjoyed seeing Jen Hays Stearns, the happy and capable mistress of a cosy home, and the careful mother of six as fine children as one would care to see. She was Miss Ransom's mate here in their school days: Rachel Allen, ('86), whom I met in a store, but missed in calling, and Marie Wilson of New York, (Ella's sister), who was visiting a schoolmate, and with whom I had a very pleasant chat about Lasell friends and memories.

I called on but missed Alice Williams Huff, (daughter of the present mayor), who boasts a lively group of three children. Florence Slate, who was at Clio Club; Laura Foresman, who lives in Pittsburgh; Florence Ryan Donnellan, who lives in Philadelphia; Nellie Bubb Stevens, who lives in Englewood, N. J. Sorry not to see them all.   C. C. B.

Mr. Bragdon acknowledges, with thanks,

Christmas cards from: Lillian Myer, Columbia, Mo.; Bertha Hax Forman, St. Joseph, Mo.; Mademoiselle LeRoyer, Middletown, Conn.; Josephine B. Chandler, Malden, Mass.; Mrs. Ida F. Burke, Middletown, Conn.; Edith Weeks Burke, Middletown, Conn.; Alice M. Hotchkiss, Middletown, Conn.; Blanche E. Gardner, Wilkes Barre, Penn.; Evelyn Butler, Mexico City, Mexico. Evelyn Butler's card was adorned with a very unique and valuable specimen of Mexican art, which puts one in mind of the priceless feather cloak of the Queens of the Ante Cortes days. It is a beautiful little bird of natural feathers.

By some means this important item has been overlooked in our columns, and our Principal's well-known modesty—or is it his indifference to such things?—has kept us in ignorance of it:

"Principal Charles C. Bragdon, of Lasell Seminary, Auburndale, has received the degree of LL. D. from his Alma Mater, Northwestern University, Evanston, Ill., the only degree of this grade given this year.

Stayed During Christmas Holidays.

Cole, Marion,	Chester, Illinois.
Brooks, Cleora,	Winchester, Kentucky.
Blackstock, Isabella,	Shahjahanpore, India.
Clokey, Mary,	Decatur, Illinois.
Hollenbeck, Madge,	Council Bluffs, Iowa.
Harris, Mollie,	Tyler, Texas.
McConnell, Georgia,	Billings, Montana.
Jones, Nell D.,	Paris, Illinois.
Lapowski, Leonora,	San Angelo, Texas.
Lapowski, Joel,	Abilene, Texas.
Phelps, Adeline,	Springfield, Wisconsin.
Schram, Eo,	Seattle, Washington.
Miller, Mamie,	Dallas, Texas.
Ryder, Ruby,	Kansas City, Mo.
Armstrong, Lena,	Rozeman, Montana.
Bowland, Marie,	New York, N. Y.
Woodbury, Lila,	Burlington, Vermont.

Jobley.—Doing anything now, Hobley?
Hobley.—Yes; writing for the press.
Jobley.—Stories or editorials?
Hobley.—Wrappers.

Christmas Vacation.

CHRISTMAS vacation! How happy were the girls who were going home, leaving us less fortunate ones behind; yet, we, too, were glad, because from all previous accounts we felt confident that we should have a good time, and this, we soon found, was no ill-founded confidence.

The first week every one was busy getting Christmas boxes ready to send home, and much pleasure and thought was taken in packing these.

When Christmas morning at last arrived we were all greeted in the Chapel, at the early hour of seven o'clock, by a big, blazing Christmas fire in the open fireplace, over which hung a row of stockings, one for each of us, filled with all the "goodies" Santa Claus delights to bring. In the dining-room we found, when we went down to breakfast, a very prettily decorated Christmas tree, around which, on floor and table, were heaped the many gifts sent by the friends at home and in school to make our Christmas as happy as possible. After breakfast was over Dr. Gallagher and Miss Genn distributed the presents; and, judging from appearances, each one was made happy by such an armful of gifts as she could hardly carry up-stairs. All through the corridor were to be heard, "What did you get? May I come and see them?" And the answer, "Oh! I got such a lot of pretty things! Do come and look." At two o'clock dinner was announced. It was very much like our Thanksgiving dinner in length, but more interesting, because everybody took part in the sport, contributing to the jokes and conundrums that were bandied about. Mr. Bragdon accompanied six of us into Boston to hear the "Messiah" sung by the Handel and Haydn Society, a treat which we all enjoyed very much.

So much for Christmas Day. Since the principal event of the vacation had now come and gone, our interest was thereafter directed to theatrical pleasures. Nearly every one of the girls that stayed here, have now seen "Ben Hur," "Quo Vadis," "When We Were Twenty-one," and "Oliver Goldsmith." But the theatre was not our only resource. There were concerts. The Symphony concert for December 28 was in memory of Governor Wolcott's death, and was especially interesting to those who went. Moreover, thanks to the kindness of Mr. Bragdon, some of us had the privilege and pleasure of attending a piano recital by Mr. Ossip Gabrilowitsch, a musician of rapidly growing renown, and well worth hearing. There were outdoor frolics, too. Haskell's Pond afforded some good skating, which some of us who had never skated before, were glad to try.

New Year's Eve we all decided to go to the Episcopal church to attend the special service, to watch the Old Year out, and to welcome in the New Year, and New Century, as well, though, I believe, all do not agree on this point. The time between dinner and 10.30 p. m., when we were to start for the church, we spent very enjoyably in the gymnasium, dancing and telling ghost stories.

Those of us who hail from India or Texas, were expecting a sleigh ride by New Year's Day, but we were sadly disappointed. We hope, though, to have one before very long. Our thanks we feel are due to Mr. Bragdon, Dr. Gallagher and Miss Carpenter for the very pleasant time we have had, and we hope the girls who may stay here next Christmas will get as much pleasure out of their holidays as we have from ours this delightful Christmas and New Year's of 1900.

I. T. B.
L. J. L.

—Irene R. Thomas to John Ashley Cadwell, on Wednesday, December 19, at Proctor, Vermont.

—Myrtle Mae Davis to DuRolle Gage, on Thursday, January 5, at Topeka, Kan. At home Wednesdays in February, Copley Square Hotel, Boston.

—Mary Hannum DeRidder to Waldo Ernest Bullard, on Wednesday, December 19, Saratoga Springs, N. Y.

—Laura Edith Geohegan to Horace Welch, on Wednesday, November 21, Wichita, Kan. Their home address is Tayloa, Texas.

—Alice Rix Taylor to Edgar Clifford Potter, on Tuesday, January 15, Buffalo, N. Y. Their address (after February), will be 65 Oxford Road, Newton Centre, Mass.

—Elsa Katherine Doepke to Dr. Henry Hamilton Wiggers, on Christmas evening, December 25, "Mearstead," Cincinnati. Their address (after Feb 1.) will be 2360 Auburn avenue, Mt. Auburn, Cin.

—Helen Louise White to Herbert Augustus Fogg, on Tuesday, January 15, Bangor, Maine.

His Quotation.

"Algernon is very interesting," said the stockbroker's daughter.

"What does he talk about?" inquired her father.

"Why, he's ever so well posted in Shakespearian quotations."

"Young woman," said the financier, sternly, "don't you let him deceive you. Don't you let him make sport of your ignorance. There ain't no such stock on the market."—*Tid Bits.*

When all treasures are tried, truth is the best.—*William Langland.*

Conformity to the world will never convert it.—*Theodore L. Cuyler, D. D.*

PERSONALS.

—Carita Curtis, ('99), is in Omaha, and is soon to make her début.

—Nellie Richards, ('93), sends a pretty Christmas card, by way of greeting for the holidays, and Mr. Henry Turner, a unique check, calling for three hundred and sixty-five and a fourth days, to be paid to the principal. Father Time's Banking House is responsible for the payment. One wonders whether Mr. Turner may not have overdrawn his *deposit* at Time's bank.

—Jane Myrick Gibbs, ('98), sends subscription to the LEAVES, best wishes for the New Year, and an interesting scrap of news about Gertrude Watson Linscott, ('99), now mother of a diminutive Miss Linscott, whose other name we as yet do not know.

—Dorothy Manning, ('95) sends us greetings and good wishes. Elsa Doepke was married, she says, on Christmas evening to Dr. Wiggers—a quiet wedding. Margie Schuberth, ('96), was at Dayton when Dorothy wrote, and Ella Ampt Haman, ('96), and her husband spent Christmas in Wyoming. Dorothy is housekeeper at home now, and likes it. Besides this she is giving her attention to music, and is a member of a literary club. She puts her name on the LEAVES' subscription list.

—Florence Roby is to continue her violin lessons this winter under Mr. Goldstein.

—Avila Grubbs, ('99), tells of her pleasant visit with Katherine White, ('00), and of having seen one day during her stay in Paris, Grace Washburn, ('97), but with no chance to speak to her. Nellie Feagles, ('97), and her mother she met, and had several chats with. They are enjoying very much their days in Europe, and are disposed to stay on for awhile. Avila and her mother and brother met Elizabeth Cossar at Munich—Elizabeth and her sister, Mrs. Smith, with whom she was traveling. They all went together to see the Passion Play. Avila's brother is at Paris for perhaps two years, so that Mrs. Grubbs and Avila may go over next year, also, for awhile. This trip they spent a month in Paris, and the rest of their time in Switzerland, Germany, Holland, and Austria, staying awhile in Carlsbad for Mrs. Grubb's health. On her way home, after returning to America, Avila spent a day or so with Clara Davis, ('98), who is in better health than she was, and saw there Anna Ampt, ('98), "as jolly as ever, and eager for Lasell news." A New Year's card sent by the house for which Mr. Grubbs is manager, looks odd with its combination of English and Spanish on the two sides of it. This is how they say it in Spanish, "Feliz Ano Nuevo!"

—The Hartwell girls, we are grieved to learn, lost their mother last year. Abbie expects soon to be married to a gentleman from Orange, N. J.

—Helen Winslow says of herself, "I am a very busy person, both in office hours and outside, and get as much out of life as most people, I think." Thinks she'd like to make us a visit sometime, "to note changes," but doesn't promise one yet awhile.

—Idelle .Phelps sends a pleasant letter She was in Boston last summer, but did not come to Lasell since she learned that Mr. Bragdon was then away. She and the family were south for about six months last year. Of the Denver girls she says she does not see very much, being away so much of her time; but speaks of meeting Mamie McMann Kellogg frequently at luncheons and the like, and of Carrie Brown Carsell's ('89), absorption in her family. Mrs. Kellogg has two fine boys, and her husband's health is much improved. Idelle has in the market a new invention of hers, an eye-glass holder, which she thinks may presently prove profitable.

—Alice Ashley's, ('00), report of herself is, "safe at home again in the land of ice and snow;" she had just been enjoying her first sleigh ride of the year. She is full of appreciation of her visit with us, and of delight in it. She sends an item concerning Laura Geohegan, to be found in another column. Mabel Coffin traveled all over Europe last summer with a friend, with whom she is still—in Paris, Mabel studying French and German; the friend, art.

—Mary Hazlewood Renwick writes of her home and children and husband. Busy days these are to her. Little four-year-old Robert has two baby sisters, twins, Alice and Julia, a little more than a year old now, and very good babies, indeed, Mary says, both being strong and well, that is natural. She sends photo of these tiny, little women, and, if the sun has told the truth on the card, we can assure you that they are as pretty a pair of babies as you'll see in a day's journey. She hears occasionally from Nellie Osgood Card, who lives in Somerville, Mass., and is the happy possessor of three fine boys of her own.

—Julia Aldrich Williams speaks with regret of Annie Young's, ('97), leaving St. Louis for Cincinnati; says all the girls were loth to have her go. Mary Johnson Whitney, ('98), she says, is a good neighbor of hers, with whom she has frequent Lasell chats. Nora Burroughs, ('97), visited Julia in the fall. Of the other girls from

whom she has heard, she says only, "They all seem happy in their several lives."

—For Ada Marsh, in her recent sorrow, we have sincere sympathy. She was in Boston for a few days in December, and came out to see Mr. Bragdon during that time.

—Agnes Flaherty, ('00), is still in Cambridge, studying music with Miss White, and in addition German and French. She sends LEAVES subscription.

—Hattie Freebey, ('95), has taken up the study of law as a profession, and seems quite captivated with it. Is helping herself along nicely at Ann Arbor, and takes a cheery view of things generally; has been chosen vice-president of her class, and when she wrote was expecting to respond at a coming class banquet, to the toast, "Women at the Bar." Hon. George Fred Williams addressed her class a short time since, and was much liked. By the way, Hattie has a sister whose husband is in a law-office. She sends a pretty Michigan banner, and, subscription to the LEAVES.

—Caralyn Ebersole Martin, ('85), sends charming photo of a manly-looking little son of hers. Donald Ebersole Martin, six and a half years old.

—Martina Grubbs Riker also sends a fine picture of herself and her two sweet little daughters, Maria and Martha, nine and two, respectively.

—Mary Smith, who is learning at home the fine arts of housekeeping and sewing, hears, occasionally from Clara Hammond, and has had letters from Emily Eaton Thomas, telling about her early efforts at housekeeping in that new home of hers.

—Our Marion Josselyn, Mrs. Charles N. Young of recent "transformation," is boarding at 7 Belmore Terrace, Jamaica Plain. Take any Jamaica Plain car, and get off at Bolyston street. Some of the neighboring

Lasellians will want to give her welcome, I am sure. Kathryn Bucknum and Lena were with her, and we had a good time. Kathryn is spending a few weeks with Lena, and has just come from being some Lasell girl's bridesmaid—I forget who—she ought to tell you herself!

—The Valkyrie Flats, the three-story brick apartment building in which Emma Goll Dacey, ('98), lives, has recently been purchased by Joseph Jefferson, the famous actor, for $87,500.

—Florence Wilber and Ella Spalding recently made their formal entrance into society.

—Ella Cotton, ('00), saw Alice Kimball, ('98), on the street the other day, well and hearty as ever.

—Sally Ellwood Wirth is to make New York her home henceforth. Carol Case, ('99), was to visit her during the holidays.

—Grace Richardson is at home in Erie, and is enjoying dances and dinners to her heart's content. She expects to visit in Boston this winter.

I had a delightful call the other evening on Annie Mac Keown, Mrs. Geo. M. Chase, 105 Tremont street, Malden, where she "ladies" it over a charming suite of rooms to her heart's content, and apparently to that of Mr. Chase, who seemed on the whole, beautifully resigned to the condition of things.

Then going on to Linden, I had some bread and some cold roast chicken, and some peach preserves, which seemed to me most toothsome, and some cake that I suppose was all right, although being cake I didn't notice it much, all of which, except the chicken, was made by Rosa Best, I mean *the* Rosa Best, the daughter of Rev. E. S. Best, and not the Rosa Best of Portland.

DEATHS.

—Since the last issue of the LEAVES, word has been received of the death of relatives of several of our friends, to whom we would express our sincere sympathy in their distress. Mary Yocum has lost her dear mother; Mary Smith her uncle, Charles Elmer Smith; Grace Garland Etherington, her mother, Mrs. Jas. G. Garland, long prominent in her home city of Biddeford, and highly esteemed for her abilities and high character; and Sophy White her father, Judge J. W. F. White, a notable man in his town and county, admired and loved as a man, trusted and loved as an official. He was nearly eighty years old.

Dec. 6.—A very interesting lecture on Hawthorne given by Mr. Leon Vincent. Among other quotable things Mr. Vincent said that a genius is "anyone who deviates from the normal"; and that to three names especially people are indebted for certain standards of excellence: Irving, the founder of American literature; Poe, and Hawthorne. Mr. Vincent we always hear with great pleasure, as he is a man who has some-

thing to say, and who knows how to say it.

Dec. 13.—Again Mr. Vincent talked to us on American Humorists, dwelling particularly on Artemus Ward and Mark Twain. The dominant note in foreign criticism of things American, he said, is superciliousness and the thing they expect of American literature is a certain coarseness and roughness, failing to find which in any work they straightway pronounce it un-American. American wit they especially fail to appreciate. The lecturer then noted the chief characteristics of our humor, giving courageousness a prominent place among these. The American wit dares to be as funny as it can, which, as in the case of the two humorists mentioned, proves to be very funny indeed. In conclusion he gave a word of advice: "Never praise our own literature. It is not worth speaking of if it does not speak for itself." We hope for the pleasure of hearing Mr. Vincent again. He may be very sure of a hearty welcome from Lasell girls at any time when good luck sends him our way.

Dec. 17.—We were favored with a musical treat in the public rehearsal given by the best talent among our music pupils. The program was as follows:

Pianoforte Quartette, Overture Commedietta, Gurlitt
Misses Schram, J. Lapowski, Bowers and Buffinton.
Chorus. Before the Sun Awakes the Morn, Goate
Orphean Club.
Violin. La Cinquantaine, Gabriel-Marie
Miss Blackstock.
Songs. Wandering.
Whither?
From Die Schöne Müllerin, Schubert
Miss Draper.
Pianoforte. Mazurka, Reinhold
Miss G. Stone.
Song. Norwegian Song, Henri Logé
Miss Gallagher.
Chorus. Ave Maria, Mendelssohn
Orphean Club.
Pianoforte. Valse Lente, Schütt
Miss Lair.

Song. Nightingale's Song, Nevin
Miss Pinkham,
Violin Duo, Wohlfhart
Misses Blackstock and LeSeure.
Songs. When I am dead.
Ask Not. Frederick Barry
Miss Hamilton.
Pianoforte Quartette. Polonaise. Op. 40 Chopin
Misses Noyes, Meissner, Bennett and Lum.
Chorus. Swing Song, Löhr
Orphean Club.

Jan. 9.—Our first night at Lasell, after the Christmas vacation, was enjoyably spent in listening to a lecture on Egyptian Art, by Mr. George Sawyer Kellogg, instructor in the history of art, Teachers' College, Columbia University, N. Y. He took us with him across the seas into Egypt, and there into its mysterious old tombs, making us intensely interested in the beliefs and customs of the ancient Egyptians. Their ideas of the earth and sky seemed strangest of all to us and made us glad that we live in more enlightened times.

A Word to Lasell Shoppers.

The importance of trading with the firms who advertise in the LASELL LEAVES cannot be overestimated. We should not expect their patronage if we do not give them our support in return. Another way for Lasell girls to be loyal!

The lease which conveys the Boston & Albany railroad to the New York Central is still on its travels. It is making a tour of the state from Boston to Berkshire, spending a few days in the registry of deeds of each county. It has already been recorded in Suffolk, in Middlesex, in Norfolk, and in Worcester, and has got as far as Hampden. It is a voluminous document, and it is, apparently travelling by petite vitesse.

Advice is like castor oil—easy enough to give, but dreadful uneasy to take.—*Josh Billings.*

News of the Class of 1900.

Elsie Reynolds is spending a quiet, but busy winter at her home. She says she has been putting into practice her Lasell lessons in cooking, and is now able to make an eatable cream soup. In September she spent a week in New Bedford with Ella Brightman Ricketson, who is housekeeping in a very pleasant home. From there she came to Auburndale and visited Helen Dyer and Lasell for a time. Shortly before Christmas Elsie and Edna Cooke lunched together in Hartford.

Ella Cotton is at Miss Chamberlyn's School in Boston, and has favored Lasell with several calls this winter. She sent us a bright letter full of news of old Lasell girls.

Jessie McCarthy visited Florence Wilber in December, and says that Floss is an ideal hostess. While there she saw Daisy Cook, "who has not changed at all." She met Elizabeth and Katherine Robertson and their mother one day this summer in Chicago, Jeanette Knights and Jess attended Helen Harris' début, which was one of the events of Chicago society. While Joseph Jefferson was filling his engagement in Chicago, Jessie was fortunate enough to have a little chat with him. Mr. Jefferson, who is an old acquaintance of her father's, said that he would be delighted to have an opportunity to visit Lasell. We certainly should all be more than delighted to have him come.

Blanche Gardner is studying music and German this winter. She spent Thanksgiving in Philadelphia with her brother, and then paid Helene Wiedenmayer a visit. She also visited Mary Davis after Christmas.

Anna Ives says she never spent a happier winter, but that she will never fail to appreciate all that Lasell did for her. Between sewing and reading and music, her time is well taken. She has a Sunday-school class, and is a member of a mission study class. She also belongs to a charity club, and goes Friday evenings to a boys' club, which is formed of news-boys.

Helen Ramsdell is spending a quiet winter taking French and German lessons in Boston.

Katharine White is very busy with social and home duties this winter. She is taking music lessons. Her church work is a mission Sunday-chool class, and an Intermediate Christian Endeavor Society. Katharine wrote that she had put her Lasell millinery lessons to good use in making her own hats, and one for her mother this winter. She expects to attend Alice Taylor's wedding this month, and then go home with Amy Kothe for a visit. Alice expects Louise Gurley, Alice Ashley, Mabel Woodward, Alice Jenckes, Mabel Martin and Amy Kothe at her wedding. From a Parkersbury paper we learn of Katharine's formal introduction into society, which was a brilliant event. Mr. and Mrs. White and Katharine, assisted by Mr. and Mrs. William White, received their guests in the drawing-room, which was decorated with southern smilax and red carnations. During the appointed hours about three hundred guests enjoyed Mr. and Mrs. White's hospitality.

We were favored with a visit from Alice Ashley a short time before Christmas. Alice is giving a few music lessons this winter, and when she wrote was busy with a Christmas cantata. She has a position as church organist, and drills a choir class of seventeen little girls.

Edith Bailey is at present visiting Jeanette Knights. While in Chicago she hopes to see Ethel Cornell, Helen Harris, and Jessie McCarthey.

She met Mabel Currie at a reception there. Edith is studying German this winter.

Emilie Kothe is reading German and belongs to a literature class this year. She says that she looks back to the good times she had at Lasell, and almost wishes they could come again, but she feels that she has other duties now. Amy is to be one of Alice Taylor's bridesmaids, and expects to take Katharine White and Alice Jenckes home with her after the wedding. She also hopes to have Blanche Gardner and Edith Bailey pay her a visit soon.

Roe Porter and her mother are spending the winter in Detroit, and are very much delighted with the city. Roe is studying art at the Detroit Art Academy, and taking piano lessons.

A Vassar girl writes: "I haven't seen a man in a month of Sundays. We were out taking a 'constitutional' Saturday and came across a scarecrow in a cornfield. All the girls ran for it at once, and I only managed to secure a part of one of the skirts of its coat. Still, it was something."—*Pittsburg Chronicle-Telegraph.*

January.

Though the long, frosty nights of the winter are here,
This month is the dawn of a happy New Year.
—*Clifford Howard.*

January was named for the old Italian god Janus, the deity with two faces, one looking into the past, and the other into the future. Janus was worshiped as the sun god and was considered the author of the year, with its seasons, months and days. His temples were built with four equal sides, each side containing a door and three windows. The doors were emblematic of the four seasons, and the windows of the three months belonging to each.

The snowdrop, which means consolation, is January's flower, and the garnet, signifying constancy, is its gem. Gabriel is the presiding genius of January.

Little Language Slips.

A teacher in a famous eastern college for women has prepared for the benefit of her students the following list of "word phrases and expressions to be avoided":

Set a watch on your lips, and if you are accustomed to making these "slips" try to substitute the correct expression. But don't be content with that alone.

Learn why the preferred expression is correct, and this of itself will so fix it in your mind that you will soon use it unconsciously:

"Guess" for "suppose" or "think."

"Fix" for "arrange" or "prepare."

"Ride" for "drive" interchangeably.

"Real" as an adverb, in expressions such as "real" good for "really" good.

"Some" or "any" in an adverbial sense; for example; "I have studied some" for "somewhat"; "I have not studied any" for "at all."

"Some" ten days for "about" ten days.

Not "as" I know for "that" I know.

"Try" an experiment for "make" an experiment.

Singular subjects with contracted plural verb; for example: "She don't skate well" for "she doesn't skate well."

"Expect" for "suspect."

"First rate" as an adverb.

"Right away" for "immediately."

"Party" for "person."

"Promise" for "assure."

"Posted" for "informed."

Just "as soon" just "as lief."—*Denver Post.*

The Old and The New.

E'en while he sings, he smiles his last,
And leaves our sphere behind.
The good Old Year is with the past;
Oh, be the New as kind!
—*W. C. Bryant.*

NUTS TO CRACK.

A member of New York's school examining board believes in making children think. Among his test questions in mental arithmetic are the following:

1. "There are four cats. Each sits in the corner of a room. In front of each cat is another cat. Every cat is sitting on a cat's tail. How many cats are in the room?

2. Six birds are sitting on a fence, when along comes a boy with a gun. He shoots one of them. How many birds are left on the fence?"

Many and diverse were the answers. Some children of a larger growth whose school-days are over, had to use their reasoning powers to discover that there were four cats only, each sitting on her own tail, *vis a vis* to Puss in the opposite corner.

In regard to the second question, of course the five unharmed birds would fly away at the first gun-shot, and none would remain on the fence.

After the scholars had been adding and dividing apples and oranges in all their combinations, he gave them another puzzler. Looking up at the time-piece he said: "Children, it is two o'clock. If three clocks hung on the wall, what time would it be?"

"Six o'clock," was the quick and unanimous answer. When, an hour later, the gong struck for dismissal, he said, with a quizzical smile: "It is three o'clock now—time to go home. If three clocks were on the wall, what time would it be?"

Their lesson had been learned.

Kernels.

It is a great thing just to live a fine life. Think: everything noble that you do influences *yourself*. It may not influence another soul (it probably *will*), but your are sure that it will influence *your* soul. And you are to live forever. Forever. Is n't it worth while?

To hear folks talk about an "influential man" you would think that influence meant a big bank account, or at least the control of a squad of voters. But the really influential men of a community are not always those that get into the papers and on the platforms. Often the most "influential man" is—a woman! The person best loved and most imitated is the most influential.

What is your most influential organ? Your tongue. What commandment is most frequently broken? The ninth. (It's against false witness—but you ought to know.) Probably not oftener than once a year will it be necessary or helpful for you to say anything depreciatory of any else. For the rest of the time, if you can't say something good of men, don't talk about them at all. Talk about automobiles.

—"Newtowne, September 3, 1634. At the court held in Newtowne," it was ordered that no person shall take tobacco publicly, under the penalty of eleven shillings, nor privately in his own house, or in the house of another, before strangers; and that two or more persons shall not take it anywhere under aforesaid penalty. Thus the new town was to be kept clean.

ANOTHER ADDRESS.

Some time ago we published in the LEAVES a list of oddities in the line of addresses upon envelopes designed to reach Lasell, usually, of course, penned by strangers. The following is in the same line, though not so amusing altogether as certain of those above mentioned. This was lately received:

To the Regents of
    Laselle College
        for Girls,
            Mass.

Your next duty is just to determine what your next duty is.—*George Macdonald.*

The Centre of Population.

The Census Bureau has issued the following:

The centre of population is in the following position: Latitude, 39.9.36; longitude, 85.48.54.

In ten years the centre of population has moved westward 16 minutes 1 second, about fourteen miles, and southward, 2 minutes, 20 seconds, or about three miles. It now rests in Southern Indiana, at a point about seven miles southeast of the city of Columbus.

SUBSCRIBE NOW.

Now is the time to send in your subscription to the LEAVES, girls. You all enjoy the items about the girls you knew here, and should not deprive yourself of this bond of union with your old friends and your school home. If you have any news of yourself, or of any of the girls, let us have it for our "Personals." We thank those who have already done this.

EX CHANGES

The exchanges received are: The Cresset, The Adelphian, The Mirror, The Pennant, The Mount Holyoke, High School Record, Polytechnian, The Quill, Smith Academy Record, The Wesleyan Literary Monthly, and The College Rambler.

The following have been favored with calls from members of their family: Misses Davis, Kneeland, Clokey, Barker, S. Lawrence, Rogers, A. Smith.

Former pupils:—Katherine Josephine Bucknum, Lena Josselyn, Mrs. Marion Josselyn Young, Marion Safford, Jessie Hayden, Emma Cleaves.

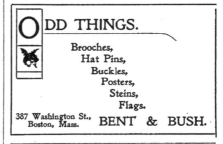

LASELL LEAVES

"DUX FEMINA FACTI."

VOL. XXVI   LASELL SEMINARY, AUBURNDALE, MASS., FEBRUARY, 1901.   NUMBER 5

Published monthly during the School year by the Lasell Publishing Association.

EDITOR-IN-CHIEF.
KATHERINE E. McCOY, 'or.

FLORENCE BREWER.

ASSOCIATE EDITORS.
BESSIE M. DRAPER, '02.

IDA M. MALLORY, '03

LOCAL EDITOR.
JOANNA F. DEERING, '02.

SUBSCRIPTION AGENT.
ANNIE MAE PINKHAM, '02.

EXCHANGE EDITOR.
LELIA A. WALKER, 'or.

BUSINESS MANAGER.
ETHLYN F. BARBER, 'or.

ASST. BUSINESS MANAGER.
JOANNA F. DEERING, '02.

TERMS, in Advance: One copy, one year (including Postage), $1.00.   Single copies, 15 cents.

The Editors will be glad to receive from the students and Alumnæ any communications and items of interest to the school.

Editorials.

THE civilized world is mourning the loss of England's greatest queen, first, because she was a queenly queen, but above all because she was a womanly woman. So much has been written and said about Queen Victoria that the record of her spotless life is familiar to all. She has shown more than any other sovereign of the world that royalty is not inconsistent with goodness. Kings and Queens have not always been examples of purity, but the Queen of Great Britian led a pure, simple life, and wished such qualities to characterize her court. Her moral influence upon England and upon the world was of the greatest value. The Victorian Age has been one of great prosperity and advancement, but the name of Victoria will go down in the annals of history, not as the Great Queen, but as the Good Queen. She inspired the deepest respect and affection of her subjects, for she always had their interests at heart. She disliked war, and doubtless if her power had been supreme, her reign would have contained less bloodshed. To her personally, in a great degree, has been due the growth of the pleasant relations between England and the United States, for which we cannot be too thankful. While performing her royal duties so well the Queen never neglected her family. She was an affectionate wife, and a devoted mother, and those qualities more than all others make her respected and loved by the American people. Her home life was a model of devotion and love, and should be an example to all people. Her character and her position made her one of the most conspicuous figures of the last century.

We would like to suggest that when our Library is re-catalogued and re-arranged, (which we hope will be in the near future) the History of Art reference books be placed in one of the lower shelves, instead of at the top where they are now. These books are used as much as any others in the Library, if not more, and there seems to be no reason why they should not be in a convenient place.

We all extend our thanks to the Seminary for the large mail box which has been placed in the hall, near the post office, to take the place of the two small ones formerly used.

—Where we cannot cure, it is our duty to alleviate; and how much the presence of a loved object tends to take from the imagination destructive power; how it changes an impetuous longing to a peaceful looking.— *Goethe.*

—The French schools are already in advance of us. Girls who attend grammar schools in France begin at fifteen a course of study in manners and morals which extends over three years. No less distinguished a person than Mme. Blanc-Bentzon prepared the textbook for the first year's lessons upon duties to the family, to society, to the state, to self, and to God. Beginning with these practical talks on conduct, the study passes on to moral philosophy and even psychology as applied to ethics and education.

The Royal Mews.

DURING our short stay in London we wished to see all that was possible, and one day my friend asked me if I would like to go to the Royal Mews. Naturally I answered "Yes," for I thought that anything she might suggest would well be worth seeing. And so it was that one day while we were out for a long walk, we presently came to an imposing building.

"Where are we?" I asked. "What is this?" Great was my surprise when I was told that we were at Buckingham Palace. "And where are we going?" I asked again. "We are going," said she, "to the Royal Mews. Don't you want to see them?"

Then for the first time I thought, "What is the Royal Mews?" and my surprise was great when I was told that it was simply the royal stables. You may be very certain I was anxious to see them, and great was my disappointment to learn that we could not gain admittance that day. The coachman, however, very kindly told us that by writing to the Master of Horses for permission, a ticket would be sent us which would admit a party of six. This we did, and receiving the ticket our party of three again made its way to the Royal Mews. After we had registered, a young footman, who attends the queen, acted as our guide.

Perhaps I had better tell you first of all that the stables are built around a square court. Once within, you would hardly believe yourself to be in a stable, for it is better kept than many good houses. The place is heated, of course, and kept at a temperature of 60 degrees. In the different divisions of the stable there are from ten to thirty horses. And, oh, how beautifully they are groomed! Such magnificent horses, and all so gentle! I went in the stall beside two or three of them, and they were evidently quite accustomed to being petted. One of the carriage horses, chestnut in color, was eighteen hands high, and was certainly a splendid animal. After this we saw the saddle horses. Among these I petted one that was the favorite of all the princes and princesses. As one goes on through the several parts of the stables, one comes now and then across a very comfortable looking cat, which enjoys being caressed. One black cat, snugly curled up in the clean straw, fast asleep, the groom awoke for us, and made him jump over his foot.

Presently, we are conducted to the rooms where the harness is kept. We saw that which was made for the Queen's Jubilee. It was of beautiful red leather trimmed heavily with gold plated mountings. The groom said that it was used on eight cream horses, whose heavy manes were matted with blue ribbon, so that they presented very vividly the three colors, red, white and blue. What a gorgeous sight it must have been! Those same cream horses we saw. How beautiful they were, and what magnificent manes and tails they had! Their tails almost touched the ground. The groom said they were not allowed to comb the tails of the horses, but could only brush the snarls out, and that what could not be disentangled in that way, must be picked out with the fingers. Since the Jubilee these horses have had nothing to do. When I was told that, I immediately wondered how these hundred and twenty horses, which surely were not all used every day, were exercised, for of course they must have daily exercise of some sort. I asked about this and was told that before breakfast the horses are taken in pairs and exercised in the stable yard.

In another place we saw the harness used on the queen's horses on ordinary occasions. She always used plain bits as was her fancy, instead of those adorned with the coat of arms, though the rest of the harness is thus decorated. On ordinary occasions the sovereign drives four horses, but on state occasions, the state carriage with postillions is used.

There is yet more to be seen! Can you think what? The carriages. I saw the one that was used at the Jubilee, the one that the queen used ordinarily, and the one used by the ladies in waiting, and last but not least, the coronation carriage of Queen Victoria. It had been used nearly a hundred years previously, and the last occasion of its use was the coronation of Victoria. I sat in this carriage for a few moments. I wish I could describe the beauty of it! Carved oak, heavily gilded, and the panels hand painted by Cipriani.

But before we leave, I wonder if the same question occurs to you that occurred to me. If all these horses are not used often, how do they know how to act when suddenly they come out in the street amid the pomp and excitement of state occasions? But just then we came to the riding school where the Royal family used to take lessons, and where the horses are trained. Here they stand in a row, with flags hung above them so that they touch their heads, and before them are crowds of children waving flags, shouting, blowing horns, etc., and with all that, you see, they are pretty well prepared for "the duties of public life," and take the shout and noise without fright.

After thanking our guide for his kind attentions, we departed, feeling pleased to think that we had had the pleasure and honor of seeing the Royal Mews.   V. I. W.

———

—His real meaning—"When a man asserts that he is just as good as anybody else, do you think he really believes it?" "Certainly not. He believes he is better."—

The Legend of the Holy Grail.

SIR Percival, a knight of the Round Table, so runs the tale, a short time before his death, was sitting under an old yew-tree with his friend Ambrosius, who was curious to know the reason for Percival's leaving the merry company of the Round Table to share in the dull and solitary life of the monks, for this he had done.   Percival told him that it was the sweet vision of the Holy Grail which had so changed his life and made him meditative and fond of solitude.   Then Ambrosius asked him what the Holy Grail was for; he said he had often wondered, but could never find out; and now Percival told him all he knew about it.   "It was the very cup," said he, "that our Lord drank from at the last supper."   This cup the good Saint Joseph of Arimathea brought with him to Glastonbury, where it remained for a long time.   If anyone was fortunate enough to see or touch it, he was immediately healed of any hurt or disease he might have. But after a time the people became very wicked, and the Holy Grail disappeared, caught up to heaven, and was with men no more.

The first woman of Percival's time to see the cup was a nun, and his own sister. She was a holy maid, and gave herself up to prayer and almsgiving, but being accused of sinning against King Arthur she was put in prison.   Here she prayed more than ever before, and the old man to whom she confessed, who was nearly a hundred years old, often sat and talked to her of this Holy Grail. There it was that she came to know about it, and to desire a sight of it.   She was very anxious, indeed, to see it, and asked the priest whether he thought that, by much prayer and fasting, she would be able to do so; but that he could not tell her.   One night she sent for her brother to come to her,

and as he entered he thought her eyes looked more beautiful than usual; they seemed to have a holy light in them.   He was right; those eyes had looked upon a wonderful and a holy vision, and they shone still with the light of it.   She told him that she had seen the Holy Grail.   It was in the dead of night, when she was awakened by beautiful, soft music, and as she watched, a silver beam shone through her cell, and down the beam slid the Holy Grail, rosy red and brightening all the walls, throwing marvelous rosy colors on them.   She told Percival that she wanted him and his brother knights to fast and pray, so that they, too, could see it.   Soon after Sir Percival left her, and returned to the knights.   He told them what he had heard, and as he spoke, he noticed that when the tale was done the eyes of Galahad shone with the same holy light that he had seen in the eyes of the nun, and when the pure, sweet maid knew of Galahad's devoted and stainless character, she cut off all her beautiful hair and making a girdle of it, bound it around Galahad, telling him to go search for the Holy Grail.

Now in the great hall of Arthur there stood a vacant chair, which was carved by Merlin.   In and out among the figures on it ran a scroll which looked like a serpent, and which formed letters that no one could read, but that meant, Merlin said, "Perilous for good and ill," for no man could sit down in this chair without losing himself.   One night Merlin, by mistake, sat down in his own chair and was lost, after which every one was careful to avoid it.   But Galahad said, "If I lose myself, I save myself," and sat down in this chair, whereupon all the knights gathered around him heard a sound like thunder, and beheld a beam of light stream along the hall, and the Holy Grail pass down the beam.   Every man stood as if struck dumb, until Percival cried out, "I make a vow that I will ride a year and a day, trying to find this Holy Grail which my sister has seen." Many other knights made the same vow, among them Launcelot and Sir Bors. Next day the monk Ambrosius, who did not hear King Arthur's name mentioned among those of the knights who had taken the oath, asked what Arthur had said to this. Percival told him that the king was away on business, and was just returning when it happened. When he entered the hall, finding his knights in confusion, he asked Percival, who was nearest to him, what was the matter, and when he learned the truth, his face darkened and he was very angry, and said that if he had been there they would not have done it. But Percival said, "My King, if you had been there, you would have done the same thing." Then Arthur asked why they searched for an empty cloud. And Galahad answered, "I saw it, and I heard a voice say, 'Follow me!'" Then the king told them to go and leave him. "But," said he, "you go in vain; you will never find it."

The next morning at sunrise the knights started out on their journey, going together to the gates of the city where they separated, each one taking his own way. When Percival started out, he was sure that he would soon see the Holy Grail; but as he rode on, he thought to himself that he could never see this cup, the sight was not for him. As he journeyed, he became very hungry and thirsty, but could find nothing to eat or drink, for everything that he saw turned to dust at his approach. Finally he came to a hermitage, where he told the hermit all his troubles, and was taken into the chapel and given food and water. There suddenly Galahad appeared and told Percival that he had not once lost sight of the cup since he had seen it, but that it had followed him day and night. He told Percival to follow him and

he would see the vision when he was crowned king of the Spiritual city. Accordingly they started off together the next morning, but Percival was not able to follow Galahad very far, but he saw him move far out on the sea, the Holy Grail hanging over his head. Suddenly the heavens opened and in a flash he saw the Spiritual city and the Holy Grail, and then all the vision vanished and he rode back alone towards Arthur's gate. On his way back, however, he proved faithless to the holy vision, for meeting a lady that he had loved many years ago, he abode with her, forgetting his quest. But one night he was tormented with the thought of his faithlessness, and fled from the enchantress, and when he returned to Arthur's court, he told his story to the king, saying that he should like to live henceforth a quiet life with the monks, which was granted him. Among the other knights Sir Bors and Launcelot were the only ones who had been fortunate enough to see the Holy Grail. Sir Bors had seen it face to face, but Launcelot could scarcely tell whether it had been a dream or whether he had really seen this holy cup.

This is the story as told by Sir Percival to the monk Ambrosius only a short time before the good knight's death.

DON'T WORRY.

When things go contrary, as often they do,
  And fortune seems burdened with spite,
Don't give way to grieving all dismal and blue—
  That never set anything right!
But cheerfully face what the day may reveal,
  Make the best of whatever befall;
Since the more that you worry the worse you must feel,
  Why waste time in worry at all?

We all have our troubles, some more and some less,
  And this is the knowledge we gain—
It's work and a brave heart that lighten the stress
  Of a life's share of sorrow and pain.
Then face with this knowledge fate's cruelest deal,
  Too plucky to faint or to fall;
Since the more that you worry the worse you must feel,
  Is it wisdom to worry at all?
    Ripley D. Saunders in St. Louis Republic.

How a Rich Woman Regards a Business Training.

WHEN I say that all women should have a business training, I mean women of all classes—poor, middling rich and well-to-do. The assertion does not apply merely to those whose circumstances seem to indicate that they may one day be compelled to make their own way in the world. Every class of girl will make a better and happier woman if she has a business education, whether her womanhood sees her a maid, wife, mother or widow. I have heard it stated that for a woman to get a business training is to crush all the poetry out of her life. This is sheer nonsense. A woman with a knowledge of business appreciates music, painting and the other finer things of life just as much as the woman who is ignorant of all business matters; and the former has the decided advantage in that she is able to turn her knowledge of business into securing more opportunities of seeing and appreciating these fine things. She can get more tickets to concerts and art galleries, she will have more money to become the possessor of more beautiful things than a woman without business training, and a woman with a sure income before her feels a great deal more like studying poetry than a woman who is compelled to worry about her future bread and butter. I have been a business woman for fifty years, and am just as fond of pictures and music as anyone of my age. A business training is but one more accomplishment added to the list which the young woman of today is expected to acquire, and it is absurd to say that its possession will interfere with the proper enjoyment of any of the other accomplishments. Then, every housekeeper is a business woman, the degree of her excellence as a housekeeper being the degree of the business training she was provided with before she entered upon her domestic duties. The successful and economical management of the house calls for the same kind of ability and judgment that is necessary to the successful management of a commercial enterprise.— *Hetty Green, in Woman's Home Companion.*

About Women.

—Mlle. Chauvin, the first woman barrister in France, will shortly make her *debut* before the fourth chamber of the civil court of the Seine.

—Miss Adeline M. Jenney, of Huron, S. D., has won the *Century Magazine* prize of $250 for the best original story not exceeding 10,000 words. She is the daughter of Rev. E. W. Jenney, a Congregational minister, and late missionary to Turkey. She graduated from Oberlin in 1899. Her story is entitled, "An Old-World Wooing."

—Miss Ionia Ivan Roe, aged twenty-four years, daughter of C. C. Roe, a rich Buffalo man, recently took the government examination for a steamboat pilot's license and passed most creditably, says the Baltimore *Sun.* She is the first woman ever granted a pilot's license in Virginia. Miss Roe was born in Belding, Mich., in 1876, and for the last sixteen years has been accompanying her father in various yachting tours. Her papers show that she has seen sixteen years' service at the wheel, and has served on three vessels.

—Madame Berosthorn, wife of the Austrian *charge d' affaires* at Pekin, has been given the cross of the Legion of Honor for her heroic conduct and her assistance to the French during the siege of the legation. Only one other foreign woman has been thus decorated—Marie Schellenck, a Belgian woman who disguised herself as a man and joined Napoleon's army as a private soldier. She became a corporal, a sergeant, and then a lieutenant. She served seventeen years, went through twelve campaigns, and was eight times wounded. Napoleon decorated her personally in 1808.

—Mrs. Mary Hatch Willard, of New York city, has built herself up a business that commends itself to dainty cooks in large towns. When thrown on her own resources and looking for something to do, a friend, the wife of a physician, fell seriously ill, and could keep no food on her stomach. This assumed a serious condition, when Mrs. Willard sent her some delicacies, which worked like a charm and kept Mrs. Willard busy, while the illness lasted, in devising dishes to tempt a capricious appetite. The success was so pronounced that Mrs. Willard asked the physician if he would recommend her dishes to invalids. She soon built up a reputation, and now has all that she can do.

—Mrs. Rosalie Mauff is one of the oldest and most prominent business women in Denver, Col., says the *Daily Times* of that city. Seventeen years ago Mrs. Mauff had one small hothouse heated by a stove. Today she is the sole owner of the largest greenhouses in the West. Her six greenhouses on Logan avenue are mostly devoted to ferns and palms. The cut flowers are raised in Harman, where there are twelve large houses and the only asparagus farmhouses in the West. Mrs. Mauff is a native of Germany, and a woman of rare business ability. She manages every detail of the business herself, from planting the seeds to decorating the churches.

He. "They can photograph the voice now."
She. "Goodness! I hope I'll never live to see a picture of the things you say when your collar-button drops down your back."

Said Little Johnny Green,
This is the funniest world I ever seen;
A fellow is sent off to bed
When he hain't got a bit of sleep in his head,
And he's hustled out of it, don't you see,
When he's just as sleepy as he can be!
—*Boston Transcript.*

What Girls Can Do.

I KNOW a large family of sisters—eight of them—who used to live in the country, years ago, when they were girls. It was so much in the country that servants were hard to get; and, as the mother was an invalid, the eight girls all learned to help with household work. It ended in each one taking a specialty, and learning to do it very well. One could iron the daintiest laces and ruffles; another cooked as well as an expert; another was an excellent laundress, and so on. It was delightful to see what thorough work they made of it, and what real "accomplishments" these household arts became in their eyes. They were proud of doing these things well; and when they had servants they trained them so successfully that to have been in their kitchen for a year or two was like having a diploma. "Miss Eleanor H—— taught me how to iron," or "Miss Mary H—— showed me how to wash flannels," was often heard from such servants when seeking another place, and it was always a recommendation in their favor.

All of the eight sisters now, except one, have gone to homes of their own, and the old house in the country is vacant. But I always remember it as the place where I first realized, as a girl myself, what a beautiful thing it was to be able to do household work exquisitely well. I have wished a great many times since that I was able, as Eleanor H—— was able then, to iron some especially dainty bit of lace and insertion for myself, instead of putting it into the hands of a careless ironer. But I cannot, and so I have to see it poorly done, and perhaps torn in the process. And I often have to see good food spoiled in the cooking because I cannot direct the cook myself, as Emily H—— would have done.—*Priscilla Leonard.*

Envelopes were first used in 1839.

A Greek Service.

IT is seldom that one, who has not been abroad, has an opportunity. to attend the service of a Greek church, for even in our largest cities, there are few representatives of this denomination. But the last Sunday in January Mr. Bragdon took a small party into Boston to such a service.

The place where the worship is conducted is a good sized room at the top of one of the buildings on Kneeland street. Before entering we were aware of the odor of incense, and heard the intoning of the prayers, but were not prepared to find all the congregation standing, and only five or six women among them. The reason for this is that few of the women who are adherents of this faith come to our country. Near the door stood a colored picture representing the Baptism of Christ, which every one kissed upon entering, afterwards putting some small coin upon a tray close at hand. This, we learned, was for the purchase of a candle to be burned as an offering before the altar. To those who have no knowledge of modern Greek, the words of the service are, of course unintelligible; but it was very interesting, nevertheless, to watch the priest, who, gorgeously clothed, was performing his part of the ceremony. About the beginning of the service he presented to the people the Bible to kiss, in which salute the hand that held it was also included; and several times the censer was brought out and waved over the congregation. The service throughout was almost wholly intoned, the sentence, "Christ is risen" being particularly noticeable. Even the children are communicants in this church, and on the occasion of our visit two very small babies were given wine. At the end of the service, each person as he went out took a piece of bread from the hand of the priest.

After having witnessed this strange mode of worship, we all felt desirous of visiting the native land of these people, so that we might see them in their every day life.

The New York Lasell Club Luncheon.

THE luncheon given this winter by the New York Lasell Club was an exceptionally enjoyable and interesting affair. About thirty were present, and on this occasion Mrs. Etherington and Ella Wilson, who have so admirably performed their official duties for the club, retired to private life, being succeeded in office by Mrs. Geyer (Jennie Raymond) and Ada Cadmus, as president and vice president. Katherine Pierce Martin is secretary and treasurer. The special entertainment provided for this occasion consisted mainly of readings, by Miss Foster, of Boston, Mr. Victor Baillard (Maude Littlefield's husband) sang several songs. Two brides were among those present—Edith Howe Kip, and Laura Chapman Anderson.

Following is the list of those who attended: Anna Ampt ('98), Laura Chapman Anderson, Maude Littlefield Baillard, Lida Curtis Bass, Annie Brown, Ada Cadmus ('98), Cornelia Cushing Carpenter, Kittiebel Chapman ('98), Caroline Church, Elizabeth Day, Grace Garland Etherington, Daisy Fischer, Jennie Raymond Geyer, Laura Place Gadsden, May Blair Goodell, Annie Gwinnell ('88), Grace Myton Ireland, Edith Howe Kip ('97), Lee Lufkin, Katherine Pierce Martin, Sara Harvey McChesney ('91), Virginia Johnson Milbank, Lena Foster Nichols, Virginia Phoebus, Florence Rankin, Gertrude Vreeland, Susan Griggs Wilson, Ella Wilson, Marie Wilson ('96).

From a false point of view the truth itself always looks false.—*James Lane Allen.*

PERSONALS.

—Florence Thompson, who is studying at the Emerson School of Oratory, made us a call in January, and looks well, and is improving, it seems to us, in every way.

—Myrtle Davis Gage did right in coming directly to the seminary and bringing Mr. Gage and taking us in as partners in her new joys and hopes. We are very glad to be allowed in sympathy to enter these new lives. Myrtle (Mrs. DuRelle Gage) is at the Copley Square. Lasellians in Boston ought to take notice.

—The chorus teaching is taking new importance, dignity and effectiveness under Mr. A. E. French, a conductor and composer of some note in Boston. It is upon a scientific and scholarly basis that impresses itself upon the pupils, and they are taking hold with new courage after the interim of last year.

—Mr. Bragdon met Abbie Congdon and a friend of hers, Miss Trowbridge (not our Ida) on the train the other day. She says Elizabeth Merriam is spending the winter in college settlement work in Boston.

—Mrs. Leavitt, Frances' mother, is trying her hand at housekeeping.

—Ada Cadmus' engagement to Edwin McCoy is announced. They are to be married in June, and go to housekeeping in East Orange. She was expecting a visit from Sophie Hall when she wrote. Sophie is going to Europe soon, she says, to be gone six months. One of Ada's prospective sisters-in-law is to go with her, and another was expected to accompany Ada and her mother on a trip to Jamaica, which they were to take this month. Mr. McCoy and his brother were also to be of the party. Ada is still busy studying violin and singing.

—Ella Ampt Hamann ('96) writes from her new home in Cleveland, to express her pleasure in receiving the LEAVES, to which she is a loyal subscriber, and to tell us sundry bits of interesting news. She is housekeeping, and says that she regrets not having been more attentive in cooking class while here. Her mother has been visiting her, and she was expecting Anna shortly, together with a cousin, the two of them having made various plans for a fine time while at Ella's. Anna has been visiting Ada Cadmus ('98) who, by the way, has announced her engagement to an East Orange gentleman, and expects to be at the Cornell Junior Prom. Bessie Smith Dechant has a small boy—new—in her home, says Ella.

—Carita Curtis ('99) was present at Louise Thatcher's wedding, as was also Elizabeth Snow. Helene Little was married on the same day. Kittiebel was too much occupied with Laura's wedding to attend Louise's. Carita is now at home helping keep the household wheels well oiled.

—Elizabeth Eddy Holden ('88) writes that her husband has quite recovered from his recent illness. "We are finding," she says, "a pleasant home here in Dorchester, and are very happy in our work."

—Grace Garland Etherington says that she has thoroughly enjoyed the work for the Lasell Club of New York, during the three years of her presidency. Her successor is Jennie Raymond Geyer.

—Through the courtesy of Lieut. Ranlett, the officers of the Lasell Battalion enjoyed the pleasure of an exhibition of bouts with duelling sword, bayonet, sabre and foils, given at the Posse Gymnasium, Boston, on the 7th of February.

—Jessie Gaskill ('93) is well once more, and at home. Mollie Lathrop, she tells us, is engaged to a young gentleman, who is a friend of Jessie's. We quote from her letter: "I met last summer at Naples, Me., a Mrs. Garland, from Saco, at Lasell in 1883, and at Bethlehem Effie Prickett was stopping at the same hotel. Grace Johnson was there also. She visited me in the early winter, and was quite enthusiastic over Sunday school kindergarten work. She's a real worker, always busy."

—Julia Aldrich Williams sends LEAVES subscription. She is housekeeping, and thinks her Lasell training stands her in good stead in this line, and has conceived a real affection for Mrs. Lincoln's book. "We have lost Mr. and Mrs. Whitney (Mary Johnson, '98) as neighbors," she writes; "they have given up their flat and are boarding. Mrs. Whitney expects to make a home visit in the spring." Nora Burroughs ('97) visited Julia recently. She is quite well again. Alice Kendall ('99) lives so near St. Louis that Julia sees her every now and then, and she "counts in" with the Lasell girls of the city.

—Grace Allen's letter tells of an October visit to Chicago and another in December to Denver. In the former city she saw Emma Goll Dacy ('98) and Jess Hutchinson, and visited Julia Hammond in the latter, whither she went, she and Elizabeth, to act as bridesmaids at Ruth Cleaveland's wedding; she saw Gertrude Bucknum and Clara Heath. Eva Kennard Wallace is housekeeping in northern England. She has a baby boy a few weeks old. Lil Tukey Morrison spent the holidays with her parents in Omaha. Marie McDonald lately met with an accident, while coming home from a visit to Ella Eddy. She was thrown from a carriage

and her ankle broken. Mae Burr and Martha Stone Adams are both well and enjoying life. Grace gives us a list of engagements unusually long for one letter; her own, to begin with, to Henry Tefft Clarke, of Omaha; Mabel Taylor ('95) to Herbert Gannett; Julia Hammond to George Joseph McBride, of Chicago; Elizabeth Stephenson ('95) to J. Earl Morgan, of Oshkosh, Wisconsin, and Helen Medsker ('94) to Dr. Humphreysville, of St. Joseph. Grace's engagement was announced, she says, at a buffet luncheon given by her mother in honor of Ruth Cleaveland Bates and her husband, on their return wedding trip, during which they visited at Grace's for a few days.

—Gertrude Taggart ('97) thinks a Middle West Lasell Club would be a good thing, the club to include girls of Illinois, Ohio, and Indiana. She tells us of the death of Bess Bailey's brother—a sad blow to the family.

—Annie Clark Butterworth and her family are living now at Marion, Indiana. They have three bright, happy children, two little girls, who have just entered school, and a little four-year-old mannie, "every inch a boy."

—Jessie McCarthy ('00) gave a Lasell luncheon, January 18th, for Florence Wilbur, then her guest. There were present eight Lasell girls: Gertrude Moore, Helen Harris, Jeanette Knights, Ethel Cornell, Elizabeth Hitchcock, Jennie Maxwell, Flos, and Jessie. Needless to say that that luncheon was not eaten in silence.

—Blanche Goll has been visiting Marietta Sisson ('99), and Kittiebel Chapman ('98). Blanche lives in New York now—134 West 93d St. She intends going abroad in the spring.

—From Martha Baker ('98), now at home in Bowden, Ja., we hear that her mother is improving so much that the family feel greatly encouraged about her. Martha speaks of coming to Boston again next summer.

—Edith Allen ('99) says that Emily Bissell ('99) visited Frances Wood in December, at which time Edith attended a whist party given by Frances, who, by the way, expected to start off on a round of visits this month, Emily and Elsie Burdick ('99) being among the favored ones. Edith's new address is 79 Williams street, Worcester, Mass. Helen Campbell, she informs us, is at St. Andrew's Bay, Florida, for the winter; and Mabel Currie's engagement to Mr. E. Hill, Jr., is announced. The '99 class letter has been the rounds, and Edith started it on its second trip early in December.

—Ella Wilson ('96) to whom we are indebted for news of the New York Lasell club luncheon, tells us that Winifred Conlin Cooke has lost her husband. They were south when he died, after only a four day's illness.

—Some one has kindly sent us a clipping concerning the recent wedding of Florence Harding and Mr. Harry Emmons. According to this she had a very pretty wedding.

—From Eva Couch ('93) we learn the sad news of the death of Florence Williams Nason and her husband. They had been living in New York for some time, about a year, which sums up the duration of their married life. Florence's baby lived but a few hours, and Florence herself almost followed the little one, but through skilful treatment was slowly recovering, when on Wednesday, the 30th, the hotel in which they were living burned, the guests barely escaping with their lives. Mr. Nason was ill with grippe, and the part of the building where they were was cut off by the fire from ordinary means of escape. Florence was swung by a rope from the hotel window, after several vain attempts, till those in an opposite house were able to reach and rescue her, and afterwards Mr. Nason was also saved. The shock, however, was too much for him in his weakened condition, and he died on Saturday morning. Florence, who had begun to rally, seemed now to have had her every tie to life severed, and lived only a day longer, dying on Monday. Her brother Harry was with them at the time, and brought the remains on to Newton. Florence's mother was seriously ill at the time, and it was feared that the news might prove disastrous to her, so that it was kept from her for a time. The one thought that sweetens and brightens all this sad story is that Florence and her husband were both such sunny and helpful people that their spirit of kindliness and of loving interest in others made itself felt wherever they went, and they came as a blessing into all the lives that they touched. Could one wish to leave a more shining record?

—Of herself and family Eva says that they are well. She is assisting her father in the bookkeeping and correspondence, like the good daughter that she is.

—Louise Hubbard ('96) has been receiving high praise for her talents as a reader. She took part recently in a benefit entertainment at Jamestown, N. Y., and here showed the fine results of that training to which she has devoted her energies so assiduously for the last few years—two, we think—and, as a consequence, the papers are sounding her praises.

—Clifford Dasher Stevens ('98) is the proud possessor of a small boy, not long a resident of this country, and known by the family as Hugh. She is authority for the statement that Alvena Chase is in Sandusky, doing club work, which she much enjoys, and that Alice West is in Altadena, trying her hand at housekeeping. Clifford adds her name to our subscription list. Has her address been given in the LEAVES?   It is 110 Thirty-Fifth St., E., Savannah.

—Mrs. Stuckenberg, the much esteemed wife of the former much esteemed pastor of the American Church in Berlin, to whom more than to any other one is due the large collection in this country of money for the building of the fine church there for the American Colony, in connection with a letter about that enterprise (which, by the way, is reviving, a lot has been purchased, and the successor of Dr. Stuckenberg is in this country soliciting funds) writes:

"What wise attractive plans you make for Lasell!   I was delighted with the outline of your scientific housekeeping.   It lies at the basis of good home-making.   Will not the time soon come when school attention will be shown to preparation for home government and direction in all of the relations women may or must occupy?   *In Germany there is more instruction along these lines than is manifest here.*   The mothers are prepared for giving it in the best families."

—Alice M. Ashley ('99) leaves Chicago February 25 for San Francisco, expecting there to take a steamer for Honolulu.   She is going with her father and mother, and expects to be away about six weeks.

—Alice Taylor Potter is now living in Newton Centre, 65 Oxford Road.   She has a pleasant little home there.   On Monday, February 4, Edith Dustin, Ruth Talcott and Mabel Martin spent the day with her.

—Myrtle Davis hasn't had a very pleasant time for her honeymoon, her husband having suffered with a sore throat until now. We saw them at the Senior entertainment on Saturday evening, and he was better.   .

Mr. Bragdon very much regrets missing, on Jan. 26, the call of Joseph G. Ebersole, manager of the Smith & Nixon Piano Manufacturing Co., at Cincinnati and Chicago, the brother of our Caralyn Ebersole Martin

and Mary Ebersole Crawford.   By no means would Mr. Bragdon have allowed anything to interfere if he had known of the call, of which he was not aware until after Mr. Ebersole had gone.

—I met Mary Marshall Call and her husband, brother of Miss Call, on the train the other day.   They had been attending the funeral of the mother, Mrs. Whiston.   Mary doesn't seem to have changed a particle in the last five years.   Both looked and acted like happy and prosperous people, and Mary says her eldest is almost up to her shoulder.

Who is for Washington?

If any former Lasell pupils and members of their families want to join the Easter Washington party, leaving Boston Wednesday, April 3, and returning Wednesday, April 10, at an inclusive cost of $40, Mr. Bragdon would be pleased to have the names.   Those who understand anything about Lasell parties, know that when we say "$40 inclusive," that means there are no extras at all, and that we go to good hotels and do things in first class shape, and take excellent care of our parties.   Owing to Mr. Shepherd's western trip, he ought to know about this a little earlier than usual.

C. C. B.

—No man of conscience can do easily and instinctively that which he knows he cannot do well.   The worker must have therefore the serenity that comes from confidence in the adequacy of his preparation.   A man can even fail with a clear conscience if he has taken every precaution against the possibility of failure.—*Outlook.*

A life spent with a purpose grand
Has simply not been "spent";
It's really an investment, and
Will yield a large per cent.
If you are bald, don't get the blues,
You're not beyond repair;
Just ask your doctor for advice,
His bill will raise your hair.

On the evening of January 24, the members of Charles Ward Post 62, G. A. R., were entertained by the Lasell battalion. After watching the amusing drill given by the veterans, each soldier led two girls down to the dining-room, where a delicious supper was served. The toasts were bright and interesting, and the old war songs filled us with the spirit of '62. Later, the men left with three rousing cheers for Lasell, and a very cordial invitation to the girls to visit the Post at some future time, which we hope will not be far distant.

January 31, was observed here as Day of Prayer, the program being as follows:

10.30 Morning Service.
     Sermon: Rev. George H. Spencer,
          Newton Centre, Mass.
4.30. Afternoon Service.
     Under the direction of the Christian
          Endeavor Society.
7.30. Evening Service.
     Sermon: Rev. Ozora S. Davis,
          Newtonville, Mass.

It was a beautiful day, and it is certain that there were few of the girls who did not feel the earnest spirit that characterized it. It would be well, if, instead of having only one such day in the year, there were more of them to help us in our trying to lead Christian lives.

February 4. Those of us who were lucky enough to have tickets, enjoyed a great treat at the Sembrick afternoon concert. With no apparent effort, she filled the entire hall with the sweet tones of her powerful voice. Each selection seemed more beautiful than the last, and when the program was finished, the audience refused to be satisfied until she responded with an encore, the accompaniment of which she herself played.

On the evening of February 7th, the officers of the drill, and members of Company C., attended a fencing exhibition and tournament at the Posse Gymnasium, given by the pupils of Charles A. Ranlett, Master of Sword, Posse Gymnasium, and those of Captain A. William Seaholm, instructor in the Roxbury Latin School. Being very much interested in exhibitions of this sort, we were glad of the opportunity of seeing the work of both professionals, and amateurs. The score was five to four in favor of the Posse Gymnasium. Lieut. Ranlett, while at West Point, was champion fencer, and was named with another cadet to fence, in exhibitions given before the Congressional Board of Visitors and the General commanding the United States Army in 1895. For quickness in movement and in sight, he can scarcely be equalled. We shall take an added interest in our drill after this, and try to attain more skill in this very graceful exercise.

Mr. Amos R. Wells gave a very interesting talk to the Christian Endeavor Society on the evening of January 20th. He spoke of the way in which many people perform their religious duties, often just to get them off their hands, and he gave by way of illustration an anecdote of a child, who, hearing his mother exclaim in the midst of her house-work that there was "so much to do," later in the day was discovered by her on his knees in a corner. "Why, my dear," said she, "what are you doing?" The little fellow replied, "I des fought I would say my prayers and det dat out of de way." The lesson to be derived is obvious. Mr. Wells emphasized the privilege and the duty of liv-ing Christian lives, glad and hopeful in char-acter, rather than dull or gloomy.

Saturday evening, February 2, a small party of our students attended a reading given at Newtonville by the Rev. Henry Van-Dyke, Professor of English in Princeton University. His first selection was from "Fisherman's Luck," and was followed by portions of other stories, and a number of short poems of his own composition. All who heard him felt fully repaid for going, by the excellence of the performance. Dr. Van-Dyke possesses a fine voice, a pleasing man-ner, and a rare sense of humor. Some were so well pleased with this reading that they went to hear the reader preach in the Chapel at Wellesley on the following Sunday morn-ing. Here they heard a most excellent ser-mon, the theme of which was, "The Uniting of the Real and the Ideal in Life." "We must provide for both the spiritual and the physical man in life," said he, "but must not carry the thought of, or the provision of either to extremes. We should all realize the ideal, and idealize the real, in our lives, more than we do." Certainly these thoughts are worth remembering and living up to every day.

—On Monday evening, February 11, a woman suffrage meeting was held at the Seminary by the Newton Woman Suffrage League, on which occasion Miss Sara Cone Bryant, of Melrose, and Mrs. Maud Wood Park, president of the College League, ad-dressed the girls on the subject of woman

suffrage. There was music by Mrs. Nelson Freeman. The addresses were bright, in-teresting, and logical.

RECITAL OF SACRED SONG
by
Mrs. May Sleeper Ruggles.

There is an Hour of Hallowed Peace,	*Cheney*
Rock of Ages. Hark, My Soul! It is the Lord,	
	Gounod
Angels Bright and Angels Fair,	*Boex*
One Sweetly Solemn Thought,	*Ambroise*
There is a Blessed Home,	*Rotoli*
Ave Maria,	*Mascagni*
Virgin's Cradle Song,	*Bartlett*

Lasell Seminary, Feb. 10, 1901.

New Girls.

Falk, Bella, Boise, Idaho.
French, Mabel, New York, N. Y.
Hayden, Bertha, East Hartford, Conn.
Hawley, Edith, Albany, N. Y.
Robinson, Belle, Newport, Vt. (Day pupil.)

Anecdotes About Children.

—A little four-year-old occupied an upper berth in the sleeping-car. Awakening once in the middle of the night, his mother asked him if he knew where he was. "Tourse I do," he replied, "I'm in the top drawer."

—A prominent scientist was telling the story of Pandora's box to his little son. He was telling it with all possible dramatic ef-fect. "And she slowly lifted that lid and peeped within; and then what do you think came out?" "Germs!" cried his little son, promptly.

—Little four-year-old Harry was not feel-ing well, and his father suggested that he might be taking the chicken pox, then preva-lent. Harry went to bed laughing at the idea, but early next morning he came down stairs looking very serious, and said, "You're right, papa, it is the chicken pox. I found a feather in the bed."

—Little Tommy and his younger sister were going to bed without a light. They had just reached the bottom of the stairs, when Tommy, after vainly endeavoring to pierce the darkness, turned round and said:

"Ma, is it polite for a gentleman to precede a lady when they have to walk in single file?"

"No, my son," replied the mother, "the lady should always take the lead."

"I thought so," said Tommy delightedly; "go ahead, Sue!"—*Primary Education*.

—I wonder if the majority of people realize the full necessity of meeting obligations to friends. Those of us who gladly break our costly boxes, giving our all in some supreme moment of adoration, may be great sinners when we meet the small demands of friendship. Do we comprehend the need of the steady purpose to show the one for whom we have a real regard that she is not forgotten?—*Anon*.

SUBSCRIBE NOW.

Now is the time to send in your subscription to the LEAVES, girls. You all enjoy the items about the girls you knew here; and should not deprive yourself of this bond of union with your old friends and your school home. If you have any news of yourself, or of any of the girls, let us have it for our "Personals." We thank those who have already done this.

—We can be thankful to a friend for a few acres or a little money; and yet for the freedom and command of the whole earth, and for the great benefits of our being, our life, health, and reason, we look upon ourselves as under no obligation.—*Seneca*.

—Not every cloud that appears on the horizon developes into a storm.—*The Rev. Allan Krichbaum*.

—Knavery is supple, and can bend; but honesty is firm and upright, and yields not.—*Colton*.

THE RINGER OF THE CHIMES.

He had never heard the music,
 Though every day it swept
Out over the sea and the city,
 And in lingering echoes crept.
He knew not how many sorrows
 Were cheered by that evening strain,
And how often men paused to listen,
 When they heard that sweet refrain.

He only knew his duty,
 And he did it with patient care,
But he could not hear the music
 That flooded the quiet air;
Only the jar and the clamor
 Fell harshly on his ear,
And he missed the mellow chiming
 That every one else could hear.

So we, from our quiet watch-tower,
 May be sending a sweet refrain,
And gladdening the lives of the lowly,
 Though we hear not a single strain.
Our work may seem but a discord,
 Though we do the best we can,
But others will hear the music
 If we carry out God's plan.

M. E. Paull.

Any Other Questions?

The lecturer on health had finished his discourse and invited his auditors to ask any question they chose concerning points that might seem to need clearing up, when a lean, skinny man asked:

"Professor, what do you do when you can't sleep at night?"

"I usually stay awake, although of course everybody should feel at liberty to do otherwise. Are there any other questions?"—*The King*.

A Word to Lasell Shoppers.

The importance of trading with the firms who advertise in the LASELL LEAVES cannot be overestimated. We should not expect their patronage if we do not give them our support in return. Another way for Lasell girls to be loyal!

PASSED AWAY.

Rarely, indeed, has it happened that death invades the circle of those who year by year are gathered together within Lasell's walls, but this year it has done so, and we miss from hall and classroom one of the sweetest tempered and best loved among our girls, Alice Bingham, who died at her home in Waltham a short time after the re-opening of school. A number of her schoolmates attended with Mr. Bragdon her funeral services. We feel deeply her untimely death, and sympathize with her afflicted family.

Early in February occurred the death of Florence Williams Nason and her husband, within a day of each other, and under especially distressing circumstances, detailed elsewhere in this issue. We crave for the bereaved families the comfort of the Great Healer of all life's ills.

Just as we go to press we hear with sorrow of the death of Josephine Chandler's mother. She died of pneumonia, on the 10th of February.

Home-Makers.

One of the greatest social dangers today is the indiscriminate employment of married women and minors.

In ten years the number of employed minors increased two hundred and thirty-eight per cent., and the number of employed married women five-fold, or three-fold more than single women. By earning pin money from choice, too many become bread winners from necessity.

Every principal and every woman's club should denounce the pernicious doctrine that girls must become self-supporting before they have finished the ward school. The hands, the heads, and the hearts of our girls should be trained for home making. It requires more mental, moral, and spiritual acumen to conduct a good home than it does to steer the Ship of State through a Presidential campaign or a Chinese complication.

The January number of the *Academia* contains an article worth reading: "What Is a Great Man?"

The last number of the *Adelphian* was an interesting number, taking on the form of a review of the latest books.

Dartmouth College was the first to issue a college paper, and has the honor of having had Daniel Webster as editor-in-chief.—*Ex.*

Exchanges received last month are: *The Bowdoin Quill, The Mount Holyoke, High School Gleaner, Nesinus College Bulletin, The Newton High School Review, The Rac-* quet, *The College Rambler, The Polymnian, The Pennant, The Classic, The University Beacon, The Cresset, The Polytechnic, The Kalends* and *Acta Victoriana.*

The following have been favored with calls from members of their family: Misses George DeGroff Clokey, White, Walker, Curtis, J. Lapowski, Rogers, Armstrong, A. Smith, Brewer, Crosby, Shields, Whitney, M. Harris, Dwinell.

Former pupils: Florence Thompson, Emma Ferris, Grace E. Graffarn, Nettie Woodbury, Roxie Green, Marion Safford, Carol Maude Case ('99), Grace Washburn ('97).

—I have thought how careful one ought to be, to be kind and thoughtful to one's old friends. It is so soon too late to be good to them, and then one is always so sorry.—*Sarah Orne Jewett.*

LASELL LEAVES

"DUX FEMINA FACTI."

VOL. XXVI　　　LASELL SEMINARY, AUBURNDALE, MASS., MARCH, 1901.　　　NUMBER 6

Published monthly during the School year by the Lasell Publishing Association.

EDITOR-IN-CHIEF.
KATHERINE E. McCOY, '01.

FLORENCE BREWER.

ASSOCIATE EDITORS.
BESSIE M. DRAPER, '02.

IDA M. MALLORY, '03

LOCAL EDITOR,
JOANNA F. DEERING, '02.

SUBSCRIPTION AGENT.
ANNIE MAE PINKHAM, '02.

EXCHANGE EDITOR.
LELIA A. WALKER, '01.

BUSINESS MANAGER.
ETHLYN F. BARBER, '01.

ASST. BUSINESS MANAGER.
JOANNA F. DEERING, '02.

TERMS, in Advance: One copy, one year (including Postage), $1.00.　Single copies, 15 cents.

ADVERTISING RATES.

SPACE.	3 months	6 months	9 months	SPACE.	3 months	6 months	9 months
1-8 Column, ...	$2.00	$3.75	$5.00	1-2 Column, ...	$6.50	$11.00	$15.00
1-6 "	3.00	5.00	6.50	3-4 "	9.00	15.00	20.00
1-4 "	4.00	6.50	9.00	1 "	12.00	19.00	25.00

The Editors will be glad to receive from the students and Alumnæ any communications and items of interest to the school.

Editorials.

"The principals and teachers of the Chicago High schools have declared themselves in favor of abolishing formal exercises on graduation days. At their meeting Feb. 1 they passed a resolution of sympathy and support to Assistant Supt. Nightingale in his efforts to have the present graduation exercises done away with. Mr. Nightingale's objection to these exercises is that they are attended with needless expense, often causing suffering and sacrifice among the parents of children; that the exercises tend to make the graduates conceited, and that the addresses delivered to them on these occasions, though well-meant, do more harm than good.

Dr. Nightingale's suggestions were adopted Feb. 2 by the school management committee of the board of education

It would be interesting to know what the scholars of the Chicago schools think of this new plan. Graduation is always looked forward to by young people as one of the most important events in their lives, and if the graduation exercises should be abolished much of the pleasure and interest now attending the close of their school course would be lost. That this custom has some evils is apparent, and we acknowledge that they are evils not easy to correct, but we find it difficult to say that we approve of entirely doing away with these exercises. It is true that the expense connected with graduation is often needless and often demands of parents no little sacrifice, in the case of those of slender means. This is especially true in the case of public schools, where there are all classes of scholars, from the rich to the very poor, than in private schools, where the pupils are more nearly of the same social standing. In public schools, when graduation time comes, the poor pupils naturally wish to look as well and to contribute as much to the class expenses as the rich children. This desire is usually shared by the parents; consequently the scholars often spend far beyond their means. We cannot so easily see why the exercises should tend to make the graduates conceited. Surely, if those who receive honors and praise are worthy, they will not be so weak as to be puffed up by this. The addresses given on these occasions are very often inappropriate and uninteresting, and may sometimes, perhaps, do harm, but we venture to say, although it is not to the credit of the student, that nine times out of ten he does not remember ten days thereafter any of the opinions, sentiments, or advice given in his graduation address. This is only from the student's pont of view, and we do not wish anyone to suppose that we think we know the facts of the case better than do the instructors and superintendents of schools. Young people very often dislike most the things that are best for them, and *vice versa;* and this may not impossibly be a case in point.

A DAILY THOUGHT.—There is no mortification, however keen, no misery, however desperate, which the spirit of woman cannot in some degree lighten or alleviate.—*Lord Beaconsfield.*

—It comes naturally for some women to put on their clothes straight. Others will use innumerable hooks and buttons and fourteen extra safety pins, and yet look like the trail of a cyclone.

Queen Wilhelmina.

THE recent marriage of this young sovereign, who has always been sincerely beloved and reverenced by her people, has again brought her prominently into public notice; hence it is especially interesting at this time to study her life and her personality.

Her mother, the Queen Regent, brought up her little daughter as simply as possible, and, as a girl, Wilhelmina spent most of her time quietly at The Hague with only the occasional excitement of a visit to relatives in Germany, her mother's native land. Of course her girlhood was necessarily different from that of most children. She was obliged to spend much time upon various difficult branches of learning which ordinary girls are not obliged to study, under the direction of an English lady, who was her teacher until she was nearly eighteen. Nevertheless this little queen found time to indulge in many of the innocent pastimes of childhood, although her rank deprived her of the intimates which make such amusements doubly enjoyable. The following story illustrates the loneliness of her early childhood. "Wilhelmina, when a small child was one day overheard by her governess while thus scolding a favorite doll: 'Now be good and quiet; because if you don't, I will turn you into a queen, and then you'll not have anyone to play with at all!'" Despite this fact we are told that as a child she was "a merry, sunshiny little girl, usually seen in white, a large, broad-brimmed hat with a white ostrich feather, half hiding the pretty face, and the long, fair hair rippling down her shoulders. Now she has changed into a tall, slender maiden, full of grace and royal majesty," but is still so young that it might seem as if the duties and responsibilities, which every sovereign must face, would prove too difficult for her—indeed they would had she not the love of the whole nation to strengthen her, and no little good mother-wit to aid her.

Both the Queen and her mother have won their way deep into the hearts of the Dutch by their cheerful dispositions, their sincere kindness of heart, and their consideration and courtesy for their people. "Fortunately for them," says one writer, the heir apparent, an unpromising youth, died in Paris some years ago, and his little sister, with her native sweetness of disposition and her wise bringing up, has become ruler by inheritance over their beloved Holland."

When Wilhelmina was about seventeen years old, she and her mother took a journey to England to visit the latter's sister. Here she first met Queen Victoria, who heartily welcomed her. The early lives and love affairs of these two queens seems strangely similar. Both came to the throne at an early age, one to rule one of the most powerful nations, the other a country comparatively small, yet owning some of the richest colonies of the world; both married about two years after receiving the crown; and the motive of both marriages was love, and not politics as is so often the case among sovereigns.

In the *Outlook* we find the following interesting statement concerning the proposed change in the wording of the marriage ceremony by which the Queen of Holland was united to Duke Henry of Mecklenburg-Schwerin: "It is stated that the marriage contract provides that the Queen shall yield obedience to her husband as a wife, but not as a Queen, but that, by the Queen's own desire no modification was made in the usual vows of obedience in the marriage ceremony." The people participated for two days in the festivities of the occasion, and seemingly they entertain only kindly feelings towards Prince Henry, as his Royal Highness is now called, in spite of the fact that he is a German, a people of whose influence the Dutch have for years been jealous.

Of her three palaces, the one which Wilhelmina likes best is called the "Queen's Palace in the Wood." Situated on the border of a beautiful park, just outside of Amsterdam and completely hidden from view among the trees which surround it, this is described as a "veritable fairy palace, which calls to mind the fabled abode of the Sleeping Beauty." It is here, amid these beautiful surroundings, that she and her husband will doubtless spend many happy hours together, when from time to time their duties permit them a few leisure days.

Probably no queen, except Victoria, has ever been so well beloved by her people as is this youthful sovereign, and although her future cannot be so magnificent, or her influence as far-reaching, yet we all hope that her reign may be as noble and elevating as was that of her who has so recently passed away from her earthly kingdom; and we, as Americans, echo with great good will the prayer of the people of Holland: "God save good Queen Wilhelmina."

M. H. G., '02·

—The wise man who always knows just which way the wind is going to blow is apt to be a little vane.

—Bear your own burdens first; after that try to help carry those of other people.— *George Washington.*

—In this world it is not what we take up, but what we give up, that makes us rich.— *Henry Ward Beecher.*

—It is the *root* of bitterness which must be struck at, else we labor in vain. "Crucify the flesh." In vain do we go about to purge the streams if we are at no pains about the muddy fountain.—*John Wesley.*

From London to Paris via Newhaven and Dieppe.

Having been in London two weeks and a half, it was time that we should go on to Paris. We had decided that we would go via Newhaven and Dieppe. The question now came up whether we should travel second or third class. Of course one most desires to go first class; but in traveling abroad unless one has almost unlimited means, one has to be on the constant lookout for the farthings, sous or pfenninge, as the case may be. It may at first seem mean to calculate so closely as that, but there are always so many uses for money that unless tourists are constantly on the watch, they suddenly find their means greatly reduced, and are yet far from having done what they intended to do. In America one does not think about the cost of one's ticket, but in England and on the continent, this question has to be considered, and it is surprising how comfortably one can travel second class; in fact, most people travel that way from choice. Even third class traveling is very comfortable; that is, on some lines.

For our own part, we concluded to travel second class, since thus we should journey in the day time, so that we could see the country, which was new to me; and we anticipated a very pleasant time. The night before we started, however, the wind blew hard in London, and I made the remark to my friend that I thought we should have a rather rough crossing, and then thought no more about it. In the morning the other people in the house seemed to be rather surprised that we were going, but we said, "Why, yes," in answer to their inquiries, and wondered what they meant by speaking in that depreciating way.

We drove to the Victoria station, all the way rejoicing that we had such a pleasant day for our trip. After purchasing our tickets we entered our compartment in the train. Unless you have seen these compartments, I think they would seem very queer to you. The mode of travel here is so entirely unlike our way of traveling in America.

Our ride to Newhaven was but an hour and a half, yet in that short space of time the wind increased to a gale. In fact, it seemed as if the howling wind was so strong that it impeded the progress of the train; besides this, a driving rain came on. By this time we had come to the conclusion that we should not have a very pleasant crossing, but little did we suspect all that we should have to endure before reaching our rooms in Paris.

The train was a little late in arriving at the dock, but we were soon all aboard, although in going along the platform to the boat we seemed in great danger of being blown off our feet, particularly just as we reached the deck. *"Personne n'est permis de rester sur le pont!"* We were ordered below immediately. This was a great disappointment, as we had looked forward to being up on deck; but it was inevitable, and down some narrow, steep, dark stairs we had to go. There were in the cabin about twelve ladies of various nationalities.

You know by this time that we were on a French boat. The stewardess, naturally, was French, also, and talking like lightning all the time. I could understand but little of what she said. All made themselves as comfortable as possible. The stewardess asked me when I was going to lie down, and seemed very indignant when I said that I did not wish to lie down yet, receiving this reply with the remark that soon I'd be glad enough to do so, a remark I did not understand till my friend translated it for me. As for the stewardess herself, she came and comfortably lay down on the sofa, and the one little surging several feet high, and the spray gleam of the kerosene lamp was turned out, & blowing many feet above that. "Crossing and there we were in the close, dark cabin, the bar!" So often I had heard those thinking how glad we should be when the words, but never seemed to have thought of rough trip was over. their true meaning; but now it was evident. The boat presently made a start, or seemed to me. And later I realized it all the more to do so, and we thought we were off; but fully. If we could only have crossed the in looking out of the tiny portholes, I could bar, we could then have made the passage discern all the time the same posts of the easily. dock, and the only motion of the boat was Some of us now settled ourselves to take that made by the waves. In a few minutes a nap, but soon after several men came in the stewardess went to see what the trouble and began to hammer and pound in putting was, and brought us back word that it was up side-boards to the berths. My friend, so rough that the boat could not get out. who went out to the station to send a tele- This, she said, was the first time any of the gram, saw, while walking on the platform, boats on that line had been unable to leave a lady lifted off her feet, and blown to the port. Upon receiving this unwelcome news middle of the track. This perhaps will every lady arose, all beginning to speculate give you some idea of the force of the gale. as to when we should be able to start, while At last the rain ceased, and the blue sky be- the stewardess began to tell us about her ter- gan to appear They told us now that we rible passage of the night before,—how ill should start in the evening. We had dinner she was and how little able to be on the boat on the boat. We had become so tired and she now felt. We thought that was a rather hungry that the meal was refreshing, even dismal outlook for us, if the boat should though the room was not of the cleanest and start, and we should be ill. We seemed the men had been smoking there shortly be- hardly likely to receive much care or atten- fore it was served. Again we were in- tion. formed that it was doubtful whether we

Then came a period of conflicting reports. One minute we would hear that probably the boat would not go till the next day, and then we would hear that it might start in a few minutes. I have heard it said that the fascination of life is its uncertainty. If uncertainty, then, had been all that was needed, we should surely have been greatly fascinated. Many of us had brought a lunch along, and this we found very convenient. At last we heard that if the boat did not go between three and half past, it would not go at all; and now all anxiously awaited that time. It came at last, but the boat did not start. Some of us went up on deck and looked out to sea. Not far from us, just at the bar, we could see the waves rising and

should get out that night, and were ordered to transfer to another boat. So, with our grips, we made our way thither. By this time the stars were twinkling in the sky like diamonds, and the wind was not quite so boisterous. We made our way on to the other boat and through sundry dark passages, but when we came to some very dark stairs, where it seemed as if we were going into an unknown abyss, we remonstrated, only to be told that no lights were to be turned on till later, and had to make our way as well as we could down the dark stairs. I expected most certainly to land on my head, rather than on my feet. It was a pleasant disappointment to find when once I had safely reached the cabin, that it was a great improvement on that we had just left. This was an English boat. But here, too, the stewardess told us how ill she was, and how little she felt like making another crossing. It seemed as though we were fated. Everybody was tired, and we immediately settled ourselves for the night, caring little whether we crossed or not. After waiting till eleven for the arrival of another train with more passengers, we at last left port, after *only twelve hours' delay.*

For five hours we knew what it is to be rocked "in the cradle of the deep." The boat rocked, rolled, plunged, pitched, creaked and groaned in an awful way, but most of us were too ill to care for that. My friend was never so seasick in her life, and I, who never had a qualm in my nine days' crossing the ocean, though we had what is called "a whole gale, and very rough sea,"—I was sick after having been out only two hours!

At last, at 4 a. m., we reached Dieppe. When we came up on deck the stars and moon were shining as brightly as though there had been no commotion so short a time previously. The fresh air was so reviving that the minute it struck my face I laughed and wondered whether it were possible that I had been ill, or whether I had dreamed it all. Unfortunately my friend was not thus quickly revived.

We had to stop at the station to have part of our luggage examined, after which we established ourselves in our compartment in the train for Paris,—a four hours' ride. After all that we had been through we had to resort to our little bottle of champagne and our oranges for refreshment. Had it not been for these, I doubt if we should be here to tell the tale. After over an hour's waiting, we finally started. We tried to get what sleep we could, but this consisted only of cat-naps. After awhile my friend said that we were near Rouen. I was too tired

to know or care where we were, yet I dimly recollected that the name of Rouen sounded rather familiar. "What about Rouen? I have heard of it before."

"Yes, it is where Joan of Arc was burned."

"Oh, yes," I said. "I remember."

At the station we thought we ought to get something to eat, though I assure you that neither of us felt like eating anything. However, we ordered two cups of coffee to be brought to the carriage door. Coffee! The word *"mud"* hardly describes what appeared before us. We could not drink it, but had the pleasure of paying a fabulous price for it.

Finally, by nine o'clock, we found ourselves in Paris. Here we had to have the rest of our baggage examined, and after that was done we looked about for a carriage. An Austrian girl who could not speak a word of French had come with us, and my friend saw that she had a carriage, and was about to leave her, when the driver said, "Are n't you coming, too?"

"Why, I have a trunk, too."

"That doesn't make any difference."

"But I have a friend with me who has two trunks."

"But that doesn't make any difference!"

"But the three of us are not going to the same place."

"Oh, that doesn't make a bit of difference!"

The capacity of the cab and the power of the horse seemed to be unlimited. So, with four heavy trunks on top of the hack, and three persons with hand luggage inside, we started, and it seemed as if the whole thing must tip over and spill all of us out into the street. But no such thing happened, and we reached our several destinations safely, and were safely deposited, both luggage and persons.

You see, then, that even across the water,

one is not free from all vexations and annoyances. After hearing all this, would you dare to cross the ocean? I assure you it pays, though travelling, like some other things, is a matter of "better or worse"; yet, if one is determined to make the best of it, there is more "better" than at first appears.

V. I. W.

College Christianity.

It is not a novel fact to college men, but it needs to be restated now and then for the benefit of others that the proportion of Christian students in our colleges and universities never was larger than at present. Moreover, they include more than ever before of the leaders. At the annual Yale dinner in this city last week it was emphasized by more than one of the visitors from New Haven that a large number of the foremost Yale athletes, members of the football team, university crew, etc., not only are scholars of good, or even high, rank but also are active in Christian Association and other philanthropic and religious work. Presumably the same thing is true in other institutions. The student world has learned that to be a Christian renders one more of a man instead of narrowing his range of interests and abridging his opportunities. When such men take the lead in study or sport, the whole tone and temper of the college life is elevated. We have believed for years, and often have insisted, that the moral perils of college life are apt to be exaggerated by those who do not know it intimately, and that its influence is distinctly and increasingly elevating and Christian. Such facts as those just mentioned confirm this belief.

The first air pump was made in 1650.

—If a man love the labor of any trade, apart from any question of success or fame, the gods have called him.—*Robert Louis Stevenson.*

PERSONALS.

—Bess Bailey ('96), writes from Orlando, Florida, where she and Margaret have been spending the winter. Her sister Lillian, who went thither with them, married a Dr. Mayo, of Indianapolis, "and," says Bess, "they both went away at once, leaving us here in a boarding house, to miss them dreadfully." She saw May and Lucy Muth in Cincinnati, called on them, indeed, at their lovely Avondale home. Ella Ampt ('96)—she was then—was in the city at the time, with her mother, and Bess saw them also.

—Eva Cole still remembers old friends. She has had a delightful western trip, she writes, she and one of her friends accompanying as guests Ex-governor Fifer, of the Interstate Commerce Commission, and his wife in their trip by special train and private car to California and back, going by the southern route and returning by way of Portland, Seattle, Salt Lake City and Denver. She was east also during the fall, and regrets not having been able to come to Boston before returning home. At Helene Little Peck's wedding she was a guest, and at Laura Chapman Anderson's, as was also Helen Morris—Helen Thresher Hartzell lives at Bloomington now. She and Eva meet often.

—Lee Lufkin, (here in '83,) has recently had several noticeably good portraits on exhibition at the Boston Art Club. She has spent much of the time since leaving Lasell in the study of art, and for the past two years has made it profitable as well as pleasant. She was one of those who attended the Lasell luncheon in New York this winter. She expects to be at Ogunquit this summer; and will take pupils in drawing and painting, from the figure and head. /

—Margie Schuberth has had a visit from Dorothy Manning.

—Edith Moulton ('99), visited Nellie Edmonds in October, Nellie is living at Meadville now, where the family moved over a year ago. She has a brother in Allegheny college. Minta Henne, who lives only a few miles from Meadville, Edith did not see, since she was then at Minneapolis. In November she visited Grace Houghton, who is doing fine work there. While with Grace she saw in some of their trips about the country, the tomb of William Henry Harrison at North Bend, and the famous Rookwood Pottery. As guests of Mr. George Stone, one of the stock-holders of the electric railway in Cincinnati, she and Grace had a delightful trip through the city and suburbs in a director's car. Lucy Muth, she says, is teaching in a kindergarten. From Cincinnati Edith went to Washington, via West Virginia and Virginia, and had a fine time at the capital. Then on to New Brunswick, New Jersey, to see Lucy Carter Lee, whose husband is principal of the high school there. Lucy was here in '96. "She is a good housekeeper," says Edith. Mary Vance she sees occasionally.

—Anna Bartlett Shepard attended the D. A. R. Congress held recently in Washington. She speaks of having met during this trip a Mrs. Davis of Portland, one of our old girls, and a friend of Grace Fribley Pennell's. Anna has three little boys, eleven, nine, and seven, respectively, and seems quite happy.

—Miss Lucy Tappan, who in the early eighties was here as head of the mathematic's department, is, after a long absence, again at home, in Gloucester, Mass. In French, German and Spanish, as in English language and literature, she is a teacher of exceptional qualification. She taught for awhile in Denver University—French and German. The text-book, "Topical Notes on American Authors," is her work.

—Alma Widstrand Rogers and her husband are planning a spring trip to Seattle to see Mr. Rogers' parents, stopping on the way to see Alma's, also. Mr. and Mrs. Rogers are living now in Roxbury, 73 Ruthven street.

—A copy of the *Brooklyn Eagle*, recently sent us, contains an article descriptive of the attractive home of Dr. and Mrs. Victor Baillard—our Maud Littlefield of former days. This home is the old Coe mansion on Washington avenue, Brooklyn, which is described as most delightfully arranged and furnished. It is styled "Bohemia" by the appreciative guests there entertained, because of the unusual degree to which they are accorded the freedom of the house, "from drawing-room to roof," says the paper. The drawing-room, by the way, is styled the music room, and among its other furnishings, has in it an Alexander organ of noticeably fine tone. The Baillard's are musical. A December glee club concert and dance, given at the Pouch Gallery by Dr. Baillard's glee club, was enthusiastically praised by many who had the pleasure of being present.

—Mr. J. D. Smith, whose wife—our Amy Hall—died January 6, leaving her two dear little girls motherless, sends a photograph of these little ones for the Lasell album. Bright, attractive-looking children they are. Sad that they should so early have lost the priceless gift of a mother's love and care. Amy's illness (a long one) and death were peculiarly sad.

—Julia Hogg Powell's father tells us that she and the children are "pictures of health," and that Julia is doing her own housework. Evidently enough she is no longer an invalid. Lulie sends LEAVES subscriptions, and Nan, he says, has gone to the farm to live.

—Nettie Woodbury has developed into a full-fledged school-ma'am—with a school all her own, beautifully located near Beverly, Mass., and "preparatory to Lasell," her pretty catalogue announces. This little pamphlet contains views round about the school, and one the house, exterior, and one of a very attractive-looking study. The school receives but a small number of pupils, and only under fifteen, but these will be well taken care of, and must find school-life here very pleasant.

—One day in the Christmas vacation, Miss Ransom was very much surprised to see Dr. George Shinn, of Newton, enter the church in Williamsport and preach. Williamsport seems such an out of the way place from Newton; but it appears that his daughter married and moved to Williamsport. Hence his visit there.

—Born to Mr. and Mrs. Guy Shepard of Glen avenue, Omaha, Neb., a daughter. Mrs. Shepard was formerly Gertrude I. Gleason, (here from '91 to '92) of Council Bluffs, Iowa.

—Rosie Best wants it understood that she is no more Rosie, but Rosamond. All correspondents please take notice.

—We are sorry to hear that Caraline Ebersole Martin ('85), has been very ill—invalided for six long months! Too bad. But we rejoice that she is now better and steadily improving. She writes a sweet letter breathing so beautiful a spirit that we are shamed of our impatience at little ills!

—Mr. Bragdon had a delightful luncheon with Mrs. William and Miss Clementina Butler. Mr. Clancy, who will be our next Missionary Bishop for India, was the guest of honor. These friends are always such genial hosts that it is one of the most delightful places to visit on the whole continent. Mrs. Butler is in fine health, and just her same self. Clementina can make the best curry out of India. So Mr. Clancy said, and he knows.

—Henry P. Moulton, who has lately been appointed United States District Attorney, is the father of our Edith Moulton, of Salem, of the class of '99.

—Mabel Lutes ('95), although she lives at Newton, keeps her membership in the Church of the Messiah, which she attended when a pupil here, and has a Sunday-school class of sixteen girls.

—Cora Shackford Tilton writes: "I have always the happiest memories of Lasell, and trust I may be able to influence others to go there." She has in Salem a pleasant home, and enjoys, too, her church life in that city. Her two bright children are boys,—no girls for Lasell.

—Blanche Gardner ('00), Katherine White ('00), and Alice Jenckes ('99) had a pleasant visit at Emilie Kothe's ('00), shortly after Alice Taylor's wedding. While there they were entertained by Gertrude and Lilian Taggart, who gave a luncheon in their honor. Here they met Flora Ketcham, and Mrs. Thompson, Floss Plum's sister. Jessie Eckhouse, too, gave a party for them. Alice Jenckes, after the termination of this visit, went to see Alice Kendall ('99), and thence to Rhode Island, where she saw Marion Stafford and Jo Milliken ('99). Alice Ashley ('00) is enjoying herself in Honolulu, and Carita Curtis ('99) is to "come out" soon. Katherine Mason ('99) is making a trip east which is to include Boston.

—The misfortunes hardest to bear are those which never come.—*Lowell.*

On the evening of February 9 the seniors gave an entertainment consisting of a scarf drill, living pictures, a burlesque drama, and music.   Owing to the good management of the stage directors, the curtain rose promptly at eight, on a well-filled gymnasium. The opening number on the program, music by the Lasell Mandolin and Guitar Club, was followed by the scarf drill by twelve girls dressed in pink.   The grace and ease with which they moved was really beautiful, and the final tableau, one to be remembered. The living pictures were unusually well presented, and much credit is due the girls who selected such fine subjects.   The play entitled "Hamlet's Brides," was bright and well acted.   We are all proud of our seniors, and think that another class of equal originality and talent would be hard to find.

February 10.—The S. D.'s gave the Lasellia Club their long talked of sleigh ride. It was a beautiful night, and cold, but thanks to Miss Nutt, we were well wrapped up and did not mind it in the least.   There were about fifty in all, and the only thing we regretted was that we could not sing louder, although possibly we were heard as it was. Returning at about ten o'clock, we went down to the dining-room where a delicious supper was served, after which we went to our rooms, thanking the S. D. girls for one of the most enjoyable evenings of the year.

February 14—Mr. Wharton James gave a lecture upon the novel "Ramona."   The speaker having lived in the very places spoken of by H. H. in this book, was eminently fitted to take it as his theme, and aided by a series of good stereopticon views, he made it easy for us to imagine ourselves in California, living over the sad life of Ramona, and aflame with indignation at her causeless injuries and wrongs.   Mr. James said that although the novel itself was wholly fictitious, there nevertheless had been a real Ramona, whose husband was actually killed for horse stealing.   As we were all familiar with Mrs. Jackson's novel, we were delighted to hear about it from so able a speaker as Mr. James, and when, afterwards by means of a gramophone we were given the unusual pleasure of hearing the story of the horse stealing from the lips of the very man who killed the real Ramona's husband, we felt almost as if we had been witnesses of the murder.

On the morning of February 15 Mr. James again talke dto us about one, whom he called one of our greatest American poets, Joaquin Miller.   Mr. Miller received his name Joaquin from one of his own poems, which, at the time of publication met much unfavorable criticism.   The subject of this poem was a well-known Indian bandit and robber, by the name of Joaquin Murietta, who had been cruelly wronged by whites, and was unable to obtain any redress, and who for this reason had turned his hand against men in general.   Because the poet tried to show that there might still be something good in the heart of this man, and pointed out that he had been hounded to this course by injustice and cruelty, Miller himself was derisively called Joaquin, a name which he proudly adopted, signing it to his published work, so that few people know now, that the real name of this sweet singer of California, is Cincinnatus. The speaker also told a story of Mr. Miller which he said is characteristic of his simple, beautiful soul and his dislike for conventionalities. He had long been desirous to meet Mrs. Langtry, which pleasure was his upon the occasion of a reception given by Lady Constance Flower. Mr. Miller had been told to come as a Californian, and accordingly, on the appointed evening presented himself, dressed in an old red cotton shirt, blue overalls tucked inside large boots, and wearing an immense sombrero which he did not for awhile take off. Lady Constance knowing him, was hardly shocked at his attire, though she must have been a little surprised. When he was introduced to Mrs. Langtry, instead of responding in the usual conventional way, he took off his sombrero with a sweeping movement, showering down upon her from its capacious crown a myriad of pink rose leaves, saying at the same time, "California's tribute to the Jersey Lily." We were very grateful to Mr. James for giving us this little insight into the life of such a poet. After hearing the beautiful poem, we were all eager to look up more about a man of whom America may well be proud.

It is seldom that our schoolmates favor us with entertainments of their own devising, but on February 28 we spent a delightful evening listening to an organ recital given by Misses Ward and Walker. The program was as follows:

Aria,	Bach
Andante in Ab,	Dunham
Offertory,	Batiste
MISS WALKER.	
Agnus Dei della Requiem,	Verdi
Pastorale,	Guilmant
MISS WALKER AND MISS WARD.	
Præludium,	Bach
Offertory in D,	Salome
Processional March,	Whitney
MISS WARD.	

We are proud to have two such fine organists as Miss Ward and Miss Walker, and are looking forward to the time when we may hear them again.

On the evening of the 16th of February the Christian Endeavor Society listened with interest to Mrs. Frances E. Clarke, who spoke of the recent Portland Convention held on February 2, the twentieth anniversary of the founding of the society by Dr. Clarke. Mrs. Clarke told of the pleasant trip from Auburndale to Portland; of the meeting with old friends and new; of the pleasure in listening to the speakers at the Convention; leading workers in the Christian Endeavor field, and gave us bits of several of the speeches.

February 18—This evening a number of the girls were given the opportunity of seeing Ben Hur, which is being played at the Colonial Theatre in Boston. The staging was very good, and the scenic effects very realistic. Our interest did not flag from first to last, indeed we were sorry it was not longer. We shall not often have the advantage of seeing a more finely staged play.

Through the kindness of Melle LeRoyer the Senior French class were given the opportunity of attending the course of lectures given by Monsieur Gaston Deschamps at Harvard during the last month. Monsieur Deschamps spoke on the French Drama, a subject especially interesting to the class, since they have just been reading several of the best French plays, and were very glad to hear so distinguished a scholar talk on that subject.

Of course patriotic Lasell girls could not

allow February 22 to go by unnoticed, and this year we celebrated it with due ceremony. The dining-room was prettily decorated in red, white and blue, and the girls dressed in light gowns, with powdered hair, made it a prettier picture than ever. When the orchestra played the tune, "The Red, White and Blue," we could stand it no longer, and rising sang heartily the dear old song. The menu printed on cardboard hatchets was as follows:

Mock Bisque
Radishes
Roast Turkey,   Cranberry Jelly
Boiled Ham,   Currant Jelly Sauce
Mashed Potatoes   Corn
Lemon Sherbet
Cherry Pie   Bombe Glacée
Candy   Cake   Fruit
Coffee
Brigden's Orchestra

On the reverse side was the program of toasts, which was to follow the dinner. Miss Zoe Hill acted as toast mistress, and introduced the speakers with her usual charming manner, the first being Miss Ruth Skinner with a toast, "To the Mother of our Country."

Should you ask to whom these verses,
Should you ask to whom this toast is,
I would answer, I would tell you,—
Martha Washington the mother,
Mother of our glorious country;
To the helpful wife and tender,
To the well beloved Martha.

She was neither proud nor haughty,
Neither was she false and fickle;
But a woman pure and loving,
Worthy of our great devotion,

Can you picture her, our mother,
With her snowy powdered tresses—
Part in curls, which fell behind her,
Part a crown of silver making—
Clad in silk with dainty bodice,
Clad in flowing robe and stately?

She had courtliest of manners,
Perfect and yet unaffected;
Talked so low with voice so gentle
That none save those near could hear her;
Sat with both feet on the floor;
Quiet, she, yet sweetly, gracious;
Smiled, but never laughed out loudly.

If we think of our great parents,
Parents of our mighty country,

Can we say as evolutionists,
Man is ever growing better,
Growing to a higher level,
Higher minded, nearer perfect?

Rather, must we as their children,
Think ourselves far, far below them,
Yet we'll follow in their footsteps;
Draw from them our needed lessons.
So for you our Lasell mothers,
Mothers until June the eleventh,
And for you, our mother Martha
We are very, very grateful.

Should you ask to whom these verses,
Should you ask to whom this toast is,
I would answer, I would tell you, ·
Martha Washington, the mother,
Mother of our glorious country,
To the helpful wife and tender,
To the well beloved Martha.

The next Miss Bessie Lunn, on, "What Would George Washington Do If He Came to Lasell."

———

THE good Saint Peter heard a knock on the heaven-side of his gate. He looked startled for a moment, because, you know, people usually want to get into heaven and not out, then calmly answered, "Wait." He took his heavy key from its nail beside him there, and as he turned the rusty lock and the gates slowly swung out on their creaking hinges, I beheld a vision fair. Now who was it, do you think? A friar? No; not at all. Guess again! 'Twas the man who never was a liar. George Washington! And, as he stood I heard him say, "Pray, can you tell me, Saint Peter, a way by which I can get into Lasell; for it pleaseth me well to visit that seminary. I have heard that of all boarding-schools that a person may choose, that is the nearest perfection; so, if you've no objection, I should like to go down, for we want soon to start one up here of our own." Saint Peter's face would have melted a stone. He beamed, and chuckled, and rubbed his head. At last, "Fair Sir," he said, "I have a plan. You know it is hard for a man to get into Lasell, and naturally you would not be on any of the calling lists, so

I will give you a pass-port which will make you welcome at that guarded fort of learning. Here it is. Now begone! Take care how you behave when you get there!"

The night was cloudy when Washington arrived at Auburndale. The moon was pale, and the stars were scarcely visible; but after asking the direction in which the school lay, and wishing sincerely that it were day, he climbed the hill leading to the seminary, guided by the many bright lights in the windows. While on the way, the town clock struck half past nine and, I am happy to say, Washington's first impression of our promptness was a good one, for at half past nine the bell is a sign for all lights to be out, and immediately at the peal of this bell, all was dark at Lasell. "Well!" he said, "I hope *everyone* has not gone to bed." He gave up his pass-port in the hall, and announced that he had come to call, to inspect the school. To call at such a late hour was shocking; but he was forgiven, for he had striven to get here earlier, and besides, as soon as our preceptress saw him she recognized him by his portrait, which we all know. Without any show of formality he was taken to his room, and soon, very soon, for he was tired after having traveled such a long distance, was asleep.

He awakened suddenly with a start. Was an old-time army attacking him? What was the din? Where had he been? Then, his presence of mind being strong, he realized that it was the rising gong, and got up the moment he heard it, just as we all do on the first morning after our arrival at Lasell. Not knowing our customs and fearing that he would be late, he was in front of his plate in the dining-room at exactly half past seven. I am sorry to say that eleven girls stared at him when they came in, but not one blushed, for each had had nerve-training and could control her circulation by

relaxation. He did, however, look queer in his old fashioned gear, as we all came in— I felt sorry for him. There he sat, I can see him yet, over at the German table. No one seemed to know what to talk about, except on the subjects of cherry-trees and hatchets, and crossing the Delaware and lying—and *that* in German. But he was polite, in spite of his plight.

That day, to pleasantly pass the time away, he visited a few of the classes. He first went to senior lit., which amused him a bit, when he learned all about ancient history, and the wonderful mystery with which the seniors surround it. He never had known before that Abraham was a descendant of Moses. Even if one is a Washington, one always has something to learn. He went also to French and heard L'Aiglon. Such translations as we had! Not a single one bad, hence no girl made sad. The drill was fine. Each line was as straight as if marked by a tape. Oh—I nearly forgot to state, that no one came to chapel late, because— well—we didn't have steak at lunch. Mr. Washington remarked on the quiet manners of all of the young ladies. He thought that they were just as dignified as the girls of his day, which, really, was to us quite a compliment. He entered into the spirit of the nerve-training class with zeal, and no girl present seemed to feel any desire to giggle, queer as that may seem.

Oh, can't you imagine the rest? . . . I really think it best.

———

After the dinner and the speeches were over, we went into the gymnasium and danced. The evening was throughout a very pleasant one.

March 2.—Prof. Edward S. Morse talked to us upon Japanese Home Decoration. Speaking of the interior furnishing of a Japanese home, he said that the floors are covered with mats which are of the same size all over Japan, and that screens decorated with most artistic designs, serve for partitions. There is in a room only one picture on the wall at a time. After a month or two, this is taken down and another one put in its place, the Japanese custom being thus in strong contrast to our less defensible fashion of having a great number of pictures displayed at once, and all the time, upon our walls. On the floor, or on a stand below and in front of this picture is a vase in front of which is the seat of honor. Among other things Prof. Morse said that although we can teach the Japanese a great deal, they can with equally beneficial results give us lessons in the art of home decoration. The lecture was full of interest.

March 7.—We had the pleasure of hearing on this afternoon Mrs. Alice Gordon Gulick, who gave us an interesting talk on her work in Spain during the last few years. Mrs. Gulick, who, by the way, is an old Lasell girl, has done a great deal toward giving Spanish girls an opportunity of obtaining an education, for until recent years it was in Spain thought unnecessary, nay, even wrong, for girls to have any learning at all. The fact that we were sorry the talk was so short, is enough to show with what great pleasure we listened to it.

Marriages.

—Katharine McDowell to Henry Grant Rowe, on Saturday, February 16, at Medina, Ohio.

—Married on Saturday, February 23, Mabel Cameron Currie, class of ('99), to Mr. Ebenezer Hill, Jr. At home after May 15, Norwalk, Conn.

—Every man's task is his life preserver. The conviction that his work is dear to God, and cannot be spared, defends him.—*Emerson.*

The Midwinter Lasell Reunion.

THE New England Lasell Reunion was held on February 18th, Monday, and was chosen because thus more of the teachers of the seminary would be able to attend. And so it proved. The gathering took place at the Vendome, and the guests numbered about seventy. There was first of all at 2.30 a pleasant program of readings and music, by Mrs. Blanche C. Martin and Miss Evangeline Winn, respectively, followed by a talk from Principal Bragdon, whose presence added the finishing touch to the reunion, his absence from home during the winter having repeatedly kept him from attending these annual gatherings of his old pupils and teachers. His speech, after a few preliminary and characteristic pleasantries, dwelt upon the future of Lasell, and its possible endowment. It was, he said, his dearest wish for the school that it should be in the hands of its own alumnæ, conducted in accordance with its long avowed principles, and secured from any possibility of embarrassment, by a liberal endowment. This he trusted would eventually come to pass, and then his ambition for Lasell would be satisfied, and the future of the dear old school assured. He emphasized the fine character of the work done there, and the splendid promise for coming days.

Following this came the formal reception of the guests by Miss Carpenter, Miss Blaisdell, Mrs. Martin and Miss Loud.

The refreshments took the shape of an afternoon tea this time, which allowed a freer intermingling of those present, with much more satisfactory renewal of old acquaintance and forming of new than the more formal way of serving dainties to a seated company allows. Miss Packard, Miss Kendrick, Miss Austin and Miss Witherbee filled the cups with steaming chocolate, tea or coffee, as desired, and quick hands passed sandwiches, wafers and cakes around, while to those who preferred ices to hot beverages, Miss Ransom ministered.

The unavoidable absence of Mrs. Parker, President of the Association of Alumnæ, was regretted by all. The matters pertaining to arrangements were in the capable hands of Miss Jennie Macmillan, '82, and Miss Elise Scott, '99, and were admirably managed. The following were present:

Dr. C. C. Bragdon, '74-1901, Auburndale, Mass.
Miss Caroline Carpenter, '73-1901, Auburndale. Mass.
Miss Angeline C. Blaisdell, '67, Auburndale, Mass.
Miss Jessie J. Macmillan, '82, 305 Central Street, Auburndale, Mass.
Miss Helen Rishell, '99, 20 Turner Street, Newtonville, Mass.
Mrs. Emma Fernald Brock, West End, Malden, Mass.
Mrs. Blanche C. Martin, Waltham, Mass.
Miss Nellie S. Wilson, Nahant, Mass.
Miss Martha E. Avery, '96, Plymouth, Mass.
Miss Sara Hayden, '95, East Hartford, Conn.
Mrs. Jennie Arnold Felt, '93, 71 Main Street, Peabody, Mass.
Miss Grace E. Loud, '95, 201 Linden Street, Everett, Mass.
Miss Annie F. Cushing, '96, Foxcroft, Maine.
Mrs. Blanche Busell Hofmann, Somerville, Mass.
Miss Emma F. Cleaves, '99, Rockport, Mass.
Miss Edith F. Moulton, '99, 10 Mall Street, Salem, Mass.
Miss Ida F. Trowbridge, South Framingham, Mass.
Miss Marion A. Safford, Sharon, Mass.
Mrs. Gertrude Watson Linscott, '99, Woburn, Mass.
Mrs. Jennie Myrick Gibbs, '98, Jamaica Plain, Mass.
Mrs. Abbie Hills Holbrook, '57, 77 Arlington Street, Newton, Mass.
Mrs. Addie Rich Treadwell, 50 York Terrace, Brookline, Mass.
Miss Florence E. Tower, Auburndale, Mass.
Miss Lillie R. Potter, 12 Union Park, Boston, Mass.
Mrs. Mira Sweet Hall, Auburndale, Mass.
Mrs. Augusta Damon Nickerson, Newton Highlands, Mass.
Mrs. Carrie Kendig Kellogg, '79, 86 Vernon Street, Brookline, Mass.
Miss Jessie M. Gaskill, '93, Woonsocket, R. I.
Mrs. Annie Kendig Peirce, '80, 34 Centre Street, Brookline, Mass.
Miss Irene G. Sanford, '79, United States Hotel, Boston, Mass.
Mrs. Rosa Best Pike, 8 Gaylord Street, Dorchester, Mass.
Mrs. Lizzie Burnham Low, '87, Essex, Mass.
Miss Edith T. Grant, '98, Beresford Hotel, New York, N. Y.
Miss Louise W. Richards, '97, Weymouth, Mass.
Mrs. Alma Widstrand Rogers, '73, Ruthven Street, Roxbury; Mass.
Mrs. Inez Bragg Johnson, 28 Wigglesworth Street, East Somerville, Mass.
Mrs. Carrie Wallace Hussey, '82, Rochester, N. H.

Mrs. Grace Fribley Pennell, Portland, Me.
Miss Martha B. Lucas; '60, 32 St. Stephen Street, Boston, Mass.
Mrs. Ella Richardson Cushing, '73, 158 West Newton Street, Boston, Mass.
Mrs. Marietta Rose Green, '86, 22 Lincoln Street, Newton Highlands, Mass.
Mrs. Adelaide Sears Gilman, '57, 9 Baldwin Street, Newton, Mass.
Mrs. Sadie Perkins Johnson, 62 Harvard avenue, Hyde Park, Mass.
Miss A. Elizabeth Mann, Randolph, Mass.
Mrs. Mary Hathaway Farnham, '88, 11 Kearsage avenue, Roxbury, Mass.
Mrs. Mary Cole Seaver, 16 Homestead Street, Roxbury, Mass.
Mrs. Bessie Sayford Bacon, 52 Hyde avenue, Newton, Mass.
Mrs. Mary Colby Walworth, Newton Centre, Mass.
Miss Rosamond Ridgaway Best, Malden, Mass.
Mrs. Myrtle Davis Gage, '97, Copley Square Hotel, Boston, Mass.
Miss Mary C. Penniman, '58, 5 Alverton Street, Jamaica Plain, Mass.
Miss C. A. K. Bancroft, '57, Wellesley Hills, Mass.
Miss Gertrude May, 9 Laurel avenue, Auburn, Me.
Miss Mary B. Vance, '99, 1648 Mass. Avenue, Cambridge, Mass.
Miss Elizabeth Starks, 10 Durham Street, Boston, Mass.
Miss Clementina Butler, Newton Centre, Mass.
Miss Evangeline Winn, Northboro, Mass.
Mrs. Lottie Hardy James, 28 Macon Avenue, Haverhill, Mass.
Miss Bertha L. Childs, 469 Haverhill Street, Lawrence, Mass.
Mrs. Margaret Noyes Otis, Andover, Mass.
Mrs. Emma Sears May, '57, 272 Centre Street, Newton, Mass.
Miss Mary P. Witherbee, '92, Auburndale, Mass.
Miss Clara M. Austin, Auburndale, Mass.
Mrs. Louie Best Cummock, 62 Bay State Road, Boston, Mass.
Prof. G. M. Winslow, Auburndale, Mass.
Miss Mary L. Nutt, Auburndale, Mass.
Miss A. Ethel Johnson, '99, Hallowell, Maine.
Miss Ruth Rishell, '99, 20 Turner Street, Newtonville, Mass.
Miss Eliza H. Kendrick, Auburndale, Mass.
Miss Lillian M. Packard, '83, South Boston, Mass.
Miss Martha E. Ransom, Auburndale, Mass.

PASSED AWAY.

—Amy Hall Smith died recently at her home in Ware, Massachusetts. We sympathize with her bereaved husband and little ones.

—Swift, speedy time, feathered with flying hours.—*Daniel.*

—Every evil to which we do not succumb is a benefactor. We gain the strength of the temptation we resist.—*R. W. Emerson.*

Highest Type of Girl.

Julia Ward Howe is convinced that the representative 20th century girl will be the highest type of girl the world has yet seen. In "Success," however, she sounds a warning as to the cultivation of manners, observing that in this respect we have not advanced during the last century. Abroad we are acquiring the reputation of being the best dressed people in the world, but about our manners, which are even more important than dress, there is often a polite but significant silence.

It is Mrs. Howe's belief that our educational system should take more account of deportment, which is in a large measure expressive of what we represent. The social atmosphere is warmed by the enthusiasm of youth. We admire the vitality of the healthy girl, but when youth becomes forgetful of the feelings and opinions of others, the line between good manners and bad manners is crossed. Young women who are fond of outdoor sports, who can do as well as men numerous things that in the past men alone did, and women who are successful in competing with men in the business or professional world, exult in the power and freedom which their mothers did not have.

Mrs. Howe concludes with the statement that the progressive women are in the danger of offending good manners by giving their exultation and their own personality too great emphasis. Some of them feel that their study, work or play is too engrossing to give them time for the delicate amenities and little niceties of social life that in her youth were held in such high esteem.

CONTENTMENT.

It ain't no use to grumble and complain;
It's just as cheap and easy to rejoice;
When God sorts out the weather and sends rain,
W'y, rain's my choice.
—*James Whitcomb Riley.*

—In all the Universities of France, there are no papers, no glee clubs, no fraternities, no athletics, and no commencement exercises.—*Ex.*

—The *Converse Concept* has an article entitled, "True Friendship" that is well worth reading.

—The exchanges received this month are: The Classic, The Adelphian, The K. H. S. Myth, High School Gleaner, The Polytechnic, The College Rambler, Newton High School Review, The Dean Megaphone, The High School Bulletin, The Mount Holyoke, The Cresset, The Bowdoin Quill, and the University Beacon.

The following have been favored with calls from members of their families: Misses Blague, Woodbury, Clokey, Hazleton, McConnell, Upham, Ordway, Bowers, George, Tarbox, DeGroff, Brewer, B. Hayden, Albright; Curtis, Taylor, Rising, Rogers, Bennett, Skinner, Patterson, Talcott.

Former pupils—Ethel Johnson, Emma Cleaves, Evangeline Winn, Florence Roby, Edith Tidd, Sara Hayden, Florence Thompson, Ella Cotton, Josephine Milliken, Edith Grant, Olive Smith, Grace Richardson, Mrs. Jennie Myrick Gibbs, Mrs. Ella Brightman Ricketson, Mrs. Myrtle Davis Gage.

—"Only those who deserve happiness find it."

—Our friends tell us of our virtues, but our enemies, who are even kinder, tell us of our faults.

LASELL LEAVES

"DUX FEMINA FACTI."

VOL. XXVI   LASELL SEMINARY, AUBURNDALE, MASS., APRIL, 1901.   NUMBER 7

Published monthly during the School year by the Lasell Publishing Association.

EDITOR-IN-CHIEF.
NELL DAVIS JONES, '03.

ASSOCIATE EDITORS.

MARINETTE RAMSDELL, '02.   FONNIE E. DAVIS.   EVA L. CHANDLER, '04.

LOCAL EDITOR.   SUBSCRIPTION AGENT.   EXCHANGE EDITOR.
LENA ARMSTRONG.   DORA E. CLARK.   M. BELL CLOKEY, '02.

BUSINESS MANAGER.   ASST. BUSINESS MANAGER.
ETHLYN F. BARBER, '01.   JOANNA F. DEERING, '02.

TERMS, in Advance: One copy, one year (incl uding Postage), $1.00.   Single copies, 15 cents.

Editorials.

WHAT makes the school, the seminary, the college? We can not say the teachers alone; it is largely the students. We sometimes say of a school, "I do not like its spirit," but do we realize in regard to our own school that we students help each in her measure, to make it what it is? Should we not make this a personal matter, and see whether we ourselves are lacking in the proper interest which this question ought to call out? We make each of us our own little circle, of friends, and in this circle, chiefly, we live and enjoy our school year; but is this binding us to our friends alone, or to the school as well? We need not necessarily break up these pleasant little cliques, but we should remember that we have a duty to others as well. Let us, then, be less exclusive in our social spirit. Again in our daily work we do much to create a good spirit in the school simply by doing our best, and not allowing our interest to lag, and our standards to grow less worthy. Outside this matter of class work, too, we have still other responsibilities. Let us not in any way, nor regarding any thing, lower the standard of our school by any thoughtless or reckless conduct, but keep it so high that it may rather stimulate in all the desire to make it yet higher. Now, when there comes to us from this or that source such criticism as denotes dissatisfaction with our paper, it is surely time to awake to the necessities of the case.   All kindly criticisms and friendly suggestions will be very gladly accepted by the editors; but it must be remembered that editors alone can do little, though with the help of all, much can be accomplished.   Come, girls, let us have your ideas, and see your school spirit, in this matter, of what sort it is, the true and loyal, or the indifferent and caviling.

W E are very much indebted to Miss Austin's table for the very pleasant time they gave us a few weeks ago.   May it be the first of a series of such impromptu gatherings.   Let us make the most of our social life here, and take this as a suggestion, to be followed by other pleasant times in the gymnasium.

T HE cream puffs stuffed with cotton, and the coffee sweetened with salt were especially delicious on the first of April. Could the same person who fooled us at dinner have planned it?

Senior Class of History of Art.

Oh, we all love History of Art,
Where we feel so happy and smart;
    For Miss Adams, our teacher, is terribly nice,
    And pictures she brings that really entice.

Ah, we have it but twice in the week,
When Clemens and Scott then do speak;
    Tell what they have seen, and what they like best,
    Until the class all feel quite at rest.

Oh, we really like History of Art,
But the most our beloved chart;
    For there stand the painters all in a row,
    Italian, French, Spanish and Dutch, you know.

Oh, these I expect we will keep,
To remind us of the times twice a week,
    When in room No. 5, we oftener than not,
    Thanked our lucky stars for Clemens and Scott.

Steel pens were first made in 1830.

Where Is Lasell?

A LETTER directed to Auburndale, Mass., will reach it, but—let us go to Boston—there you'll find a hospital owned by the Deaconesses.   Lasell is there represented by a room which bears its name.   In the same city there is the Willard Y. Settlement, the Union Rescue Mission and the Hull Street Medical Mission, all of which have had gifts and Thanksgiving offerings from either the Missionary society or the school as a whole.

Going South we find, at the Allen Normal and Industrial school near Thomasville, Georgia, a much-needed veranda, built by the aid of Lasell.   At Claflin University, Orangeburg, S. C., a scholar, otherwise too poor, is studying there by means of a gift from the Missionary society.

Now let us go to Moradabad, India, and there find the school which the Missionary society supports, and at Bareilly, the orphange which yearly receives money from the same source.

Harpoot, Turkey, is the next place, and from there recently came a package of letters written by some school girls who thanked their kind "care-takers" at Lasell for making an education possible for them. Among them was Caroline Lasell, an orphan, whom the society adopted many years ago.   She will soon lose that name, however, for she is to be married, and come to America to live.

When the American Church is built at Berlin, a Lasell pew will be found there.

The International Institute for Girls in Spain is soon to have a large building, and among the rooms named for the different colleges who have contributed to its erection, a Lasell room will be found.

If Lasell is at Auburndale, then that little village has very wide dimensions. Wherever there is good to be done it is *there* you will find Lasell.

A Typical Lasell Room.

WHAT was my surprise and delight one rainy, gloomy Monday (when, in spite of bad weather, most of the girls had gone to Boston) to find myself at liberty to go where I pleased and into any room I chose. I wandered aimlessly down the hall until a card on one of the doors attracted my attention—the name it bore being Miss Prim, one of the "new girls" who had often invited me to come to her room at any time I chose. It was such a peculiar and old maidish name that I was immediately interested, and wondering what kind of a room she would have, stepped boldly up and rapped several times on the door. Hearing no response, I was fully convinced that Miss Prim, like most of the girls, had gone to Boston for "necessary shopping," so I determined to go in and amuse myself during her absence.

What was my surprise and delight in finding what I termed a typical Lasell room. The room was most artistically arranged, and yet contained many things that one, at first, might think out of place, but were here used in a most unique manner. The first thing that caught my eye was a cozy window seat, luxuriously piled with pillows, many of them tokens of rival colleges; but here they reposed peacefully side by side. I was a little disappointed, though, to notice that Harvard seemed to be most prominent, and my fears were confirmed when I glanced up and saw a rich crimson banner waving over my head. It was useless to protest; this young lady was evidently for Harvard. Not far from the window seat there was a small tea table on which the tiny cups and tea pot were arranged in a most delightful way. Near by was a chafing dish that fairly glittered with brightness, and seemed not to have been recently used—for a reason probably best known to Lasell girls.

I also noticed that our friend seemed to cling to Stanlaus and Gibson, rather than Raphael and Angelo, but we hope that after a short time at Lasell she will learn to appreciate higher art, and may even learn to love Cimabuk's virgin. From the side of the dresser hang numerous candy tongs; but they must be tokens of by gone days—or how would they be there? In one end of the room hangs the inevitable fish net holding many familiar faces, some of which are Lasell "by-gones," and others, perhaps, from home. I notice quite a number of a certain curly-haired youth, and he is also visible on the dresser and desk. Do we need much imagination to guess that he is responsible for the Harvard emblems?

Knowing that this was a bedroom, I began to wonder where my friend enjoyed her dreams, and after a few investigations, found, that with her clever ingenuity, she had deftly transformed her bed into a most inviting lounge. Just beside this, and within easy reach, was her bookcase, well filled with the most choice literature, showing her excellent training and good taste.

Altogether I was very much pleased with the room, thinking it was not only artistically arranged, but showed a great deal of life at Lasell; and I went out with the full determination to make the further acquaintance of Miss Prim.

The LEAVES for May will be a special number published by the Junior Class. It will be full of interest to all Lasell girls, past and present. Orders for extra copies should be sent as soon as possible to Helen Howes.

—We push time from us, and we wish him back.—*Young.*

An Adventure at Lasell.

They were two lovely Seniors,
Their names I dare not tell,,
It is enough if you know
That they are at Lasell.

Both had received permission
To go away and stay
From Saturday after lecture
Until the next Monday.

Light-hearted they did leave us
Not realizing then
What an awful thing would happen
In their own little den.

When they opened the door Monday
Of their room, "Quality Row,"
A sight met their wondering gaze
That made them wish to go.

Seated on each rocking-chair,
And on the other, too,
Were men! The girls knew not where
To run, nor what to do.

Men at Lasell! Awful thought;
But worse is yet to come,
For these men were not disturbed
At the entrance, as would be some.

They neither moved, nor turned 'round,
Nor did they say a word;
In fact, they acted just as if
They really had not heard.

What could those brave Seniors do?
Lasell had not yet taught
What to do when they saw men.
Was education then for nought?

At last the bravest girl spoke; ·
In modesty blushed she,
And vainly sought for fine words,
So as to address the three.

"Prithee, fair sirs, I would ask,
What you are doing here,
You're not on our calling lists,
This is a mistake I fear."

But never a word they spoke,
Those same strange figures three,
But sat there in a silence.
What could the matter be?

And then the girls grew bolder,
And advancing through the door,
Sighed deeply as they discovered,
The terrible suspense was o'er.

The men were simply pillows,
Dressed in an artistic way,
And made to look like gentlemen.
What an awful joke to play!

Now don't ask these Seniors,
At twenty-nine, they stay,
Who played this joke upon them;
They don't know to this day.

Lasell has become interested in the plan to establish at Madrid the International Institute for Girls, now located at San Sebastian, Spain. It is under the direction of Mrs. Alice Gordon Gulick, a former student at Lasell, by whose influence and untiring energy Higher Education for Spanish girls has been made possible. This school is doing a fine work for Spanish girls, and by this change of location will greatly increase its sphere of influence and its power, so that the opportunity seems too good to be lost. To effect the change $100,000 is necessary. Of this sum $70,000 has already been pledged or paid, and various schools in the country are contributing to raise the remainder. In the new building to be erected for the school at Madrid, $300, it is estimated, will provide one room, which will bear the name of the school contributing such sum.

Lasell desires to give $300 for this purpose, and has appointed two committees, one to bring the matter to the notice of present students, the other to present it to the old girls. We feel assured that every loyal Lasell girl will be proud to have the old school thus represented in the land of Columbus and Isabella, and will desire to contribute personally to the sum to be raised. Whatever you wish to give may be sent by check or P. O. order to the undersigned, who will be glad to receive it, and to see that it reaches its proper destination.

Thanking you in advance for whatever aid you may render in this work.

Mr. Bragdon, Miss Packard, Miss Witherbee, Ruby Ryder, Clemens, J., Bessie Fuller, Frances Leavitt, Rose Taylor, Barbara Vail, Committee.

LASELL SONG.

Words.
ZOE HILL.

Dedicated to C. C. Bragdon.

Music by
HARRIETTE SMITH WARD.

1. Dear La - sell, where the happy days slipp'd by, Oft for them in the years to come we'll sigh; They to us will be bless'd for - ev - er - more. Tho' our paths are sev - er'd, for —

rit.

CHORUS.
Tempo.

Tho'ts of thee will ne'er for - got - ten be, No love can e'er be great - er;

f Give three long cheers, 'Mid smiles and tears, For La - sell our dear Al - ma Ma - ter. *rit.*

2 If you've read " Guide to Life " at old Lasell,
Of our trials and restrictions you can tell;
Broken oft, no one ever knew just how,
They seemed dreadful then, but now,— CHO.

3 Time is swiftly bearing us along,
And our school-days shortly will be gone;
But we're true to the dainty white and blue,
Raise it high, long may it fly. CHO.

PERSONALS.

—Rena Goodwin sends remembrances to her old friends. She is at Biddeford, Me.

—Mary Smith has found a "Lasell granddaughter" in a Mrs. Keogh (recently married) of Wheeling. Virginia Brown, she says, is now Mrs. Miller. Mary has been ill with diphtheria.

—Nellie Vaill LaSelle writes of an Easter trip to Denver, with a party of University girls; their object, to establish at Boulder, Colorado, a new chapter of Kappa, Kappa. You may be sure there was to be a gay time—banquets, breakfasts, receptions, and all the rest. Corinne Salisbury is engaged to a Mr. J. E. C. Fisher, and expects to be married June 1, at Corinne's home. Nellie is to be one of six bridesmaids—all cousins. They, Mr. and Mrs. Fisher, are to go, after the wedding, to England, Mr. Fisher's home, to spend several months. They sail June 8, at 11 a. m., from Hoboken, N. J., on Patricia, Hamburg American Line; and Corinne would like to see any of her friends who chance to be in the vicinity at that time. Perhaps this may meet the eye of some of them.

Ida Trowbridge announces her engagement to Dr. Louis D. H. Fuller.

—May Sternbergh, we learn through her sister, is in New York studying music. Another sister, Mrs. Helen Dodds, is in Austin, Texas, 1800 East 20th street.

—Alma Widstrand Rogers and her husband were in Minneapolis, when she last wrote us. They expected soon to leave for Seattle, intending to make during their stay in Washington, a trip through California. Mrs. Knights and Edith are well, she tells us.

—Sara Hitchcock, of Bath, Me., writes us about a Lasell pin. Every Lasell girl, now here, or formerly, should have the school pin. How many have them?

—Sade Hollingsworth Thompson sends a pleasant letter, in which she holds out a hope that we may see her here at Commencement. That will be a treat. She and her husband are planning a little trip to Virginia together in May or June.

—Mrs. May Sleeper Ruggles, who has so delighted us with her charming recitals of sacred song, recently, has an admirer in Mrs. Amy Beach, the most famous lady composer in the land, and one of the most accomplished pianists living. Mrs. Beach says of Mrs. Ruggles, "A voice of such volume, richness, and extent of compass, combined with so much musical feeling, cannot fail to win widespread recognition in the church as well as in the concert room." She thinks Mrs. Ruggles an artist of truly rare power.

—Mrs. F. A. Seiberling—Gertrude Penfield—has scored still another musical success. In the presentation at Easter, by the Akron Tuesday Musical Club, of Mendelssohn's St. Paul, her splendid rendering of this grand music called out especially complimentary notice, though a number of professional vocalists took part in the oratorio.

—As a feature of our Semi-Centennial Celebration, we hoped to have Gertrude Penfield Seiberling's singing. But she writes that she cannot come. She and her splendid family expect to spend the summer, "half on land, half on water," on one of Lake Huron's beautiful islands. She made her first visit to Washington at Inauguration time, and was charmed by our Capital.

—Grace Seiberling's husband, Mr. Chase, will graduate next June at Ann Arbor Medical school. Grace busies herself with literary and historical study, and German.

—Ruth· S. Pflueger is living at Akron, and Kittie at Indianapolis, where Gertrude went last February and received quite a welcome from musical people, meeting Eleanor Young Hord and other Lasell girls. She says Mollie Coe Ninde has· been far from well since her marriage. With all the cares of her growing family, Gertrude keeps at work going always further with her music, taking of German, etc. An example for married women, I say.

—A "beautiful little visit" is what I call a dinner and evening with Carrie Kendig Kellogg and Annie Kendig Peirce and their dear father and husbands. The years do not show on any of these people, perhaps because they have not had enough of them; perhaps because they have been so happy. Dr. Kendig in his leisure time is much occupied with his rare collections. He is an authority, respected on both sides of the Atlantic. I told Mrs. Peirce that she gets more childish every day. I hear that Elizabeth Starks is in Boston training her voice; what a mistake, when she might be with Mrs. Martin! That Carolyn Baldwin is in New York training her voice; what a mistake when she might be with Miss White! And that Laura Birdsey is with her father in Middletown, studying how to make home happy. Mrs. Kellogg is talking about a year in Southern California, and Mr. and Mrs. Peirce and two daughters (who, just think of it, are fifteen and thirteen years!) are planning to start May 22, for a year's absence in Europe.

Lasell Alphabet.

A stands for Armstrong, the Montana girl;
   A typical one, who keeps things in a whirl.
B stands for Bennet, who sits near the door,
   And leaves for her music before lecture's o'er.
C stands for the Chase's, of which there are two,
   And if you live near them you never are blue.
D stands for Dwight, a bright little miss,
   And who, if I knew her, could add much to this.
E stands for Edwards so eager to learn,
   Who answers the questions just after her turn.
F stands for Fonnie who'll have a good time,
   Yet be in her room at a quarter past nine.
G stands for Griffin with hair in a braid,
   Who, in spite of her French, is never afraid.
H stands for Hawley, tall, slender and straight,
   Who managed to get here, altho' she came late.
I stands for Irwin, the sisters so true;
   Whatever one does, the other will do.
J is for Jones, tho' best known as Nell;
   And what she'll do next, we never can tell.
K stands for Krag, who like Sampson of old,
   Exhibits her strength in ways manifold.
L stands for Lapowski, the big and the small;
   One is so short, and the other so tall.
M stands for Miller, you know her, no doubt,
   And that she's from Texas, is quickly found out.
N stands for Nelson, or North if you like;
   They both have good times and are very polite.
O stands for Orcutt, who when she first came,
   Thought she'd add to excitement, by first getting lame.
P stands for F. Plum; if that you don't know,
   Just ask Carrie George, and she'll tell you so.
Q stands for queen, but of those there's so many,
   That I think I will leave that and will not name any.
R stands for Ryder, the girl from the West;
   I need not tell more, for you know the rest.
S stands for G. Stone, such a giddy young girl,
   Who has the idea she sets hearts in a whirl.
T stands for Taylor, that dear little maid,
   Who is everyone's pet as is plainly displayed.
U stands for Uhrich, our little Dutch girl,
   Whom everyone loves for she is such a pearl.
V stands for Vail, little Barbara Vail,
   Who when saying her piece always gets very pale.
W stands for Wheldon, the singer so sweet,
   With great big blue eyes and such dreadful big feet.
X stands for Xmas, which comes once a year,
   And which when it comes brings us all such good cheer. ·
Y stands for young; we can all share in that,
   For here we grow young as well as grow fat.
Z stands for Zeller, the last of the list;
   If you want any more, you may measure your fist.

On Saturday, March 16, we enjoyed an unusual treat in the shape of a lecture by Mrs. Mary A. Livermore. The subject was "Superfluous Women," and the brilliantly satirical and pungent remarks of the speaker showed how deeply she felt and how clearly she saw the facts and the conditions of woman's position, past and present. There was not an uninteresting sentence in the entire talk, and one could not choose but listen and enjoy. Mrs. Livermore's object was to prove that there are no "superfluous" women. Among other things she said that, although she certainly intended to say nothing against marriage, believing it to be one of the happiest and most sacred states, she by no means thought that marriage should be the only aim and ambition of a sensible woman— that, in the advance of civilization, there are now countless fields of work open to any woman with brain and energy enough to hold her place in the sphere of work she chooses. The title of this lecture was suggested to Mrs. Livermore by a lecture she once heard in London. An Englishman, presumably, it seemed, a scholar and gentleman lamented the fact that, owing to war and the loss of men's lives in sundry other ways, there is in human society such a woful surplus of women. "And what," he demanded, "is to be done with these superfluous women— women who can never hope to be married."

And there, in the face of all that audience of women, he dared to suggest that these women for whom no husbands could be provided should—to strip the thought of smooth phrases—be herded together like cattle, driven to the wharf, put on board ship, and sent to remote parts of the world to get along as best they could. What a point of view! Where could be found a woman who would consent to such an outrage! When he had finished the women present promptly undeceived him as to his mistaken notion of the possibility of such a proceeding. "No woman is superfluous who finds work to do in the world and does it well. Neither sex can do without the other. It seems to have been the wish of the Divine Creator that these two should co-operate in the social and industrial, as in the domestic world, in perfect harmony, neither one being the head, nor yet the foot, but that on an equality, they should calmly and strongly work together."

Mrs. Clark led the Christian Endeavor meeting on Sunday, March 17, the subject being, "Christ Our High Priest." She distributed certain printed slips explaining various points about the Jewish High Priests, and showed in her comments that they were typical, how Christ was our High Priest, and how we might apply the truths thus taught to practical life.

On the evening of March 21, Mr. Hill's pupils gave one of their enjoyable musical recitals—"not for exhibition purposes, but for practice in public."

The overture by the first quartette was very well done, the melody being especially pretty. All of the pieces showed faithful and painstaking work. What was particularly noticeable was the ease and confidence with which the girls did their work.

Les Classes Superieures de Francais nous

ont donné, le 23 mars, une reception dans les salons du Seminaire précédee d'une Comedie "Les Reves de Marquerite" interpretée par Mlle. M. A. Ramsdell dans le role de Ferdinand joué avec beaucoup de force masculine et par Mlle. F. Hayden qui nous a montré une Marguerite charmante et gracieuse Mlle. Pinkham a chanté tres gentiment deux chansons francaises. On a servi le chocolat et le café à neuf heures et c'est avec regret que la joyeuse assemblée s'est separée à dix heures.

On Thursday, March 28, instead of our usual Bible lesson, we were surprised and pleased to hear a short talk by Miss Chisholm, a deaconess of the Methodist church. In the few minutes that were hers, she told us much about her work among the poor, and of the good work accomplished by this association of brave and helpful women. In closing she sang for us two of her favorite hymns, which were much appreciated by all present.

"Lasell invites all her children to a rally in the gymnasium at half past six tonight, March 28. Let everybody come and bring Lasell fiags—also bring sofa pillows for reserved seats on the floor." Of course we all went, as our curiosity had been aroused over what *it* could possibly be, and who had gotten it up. After all of us were seated on our pillows the lights were turned out, the curtains parted and a mysterious voice issuing from the side of the stage began to read Joe Chandler Harris' "Tar Baby." Suddenly strange black forms crossed in front of us. What could they be? Surely they were, "Tar Baby," "Bre'er Fox" and "Bre'er Rabbit." We were all more or less frightened until it dawned on us that they were only shadow pictures of the girls from *Miss Austin's table*. This amusing comedy was followed by equally entertaining pictures from Lasell life illustrating the following poem as it was read from behind the scenes:

By the banks of the broad Charles river,
  Not far from Boston town,
There stands a Seminary
  Of old and wide renown.
And fathers wise, and mothers
  Who love their daughters well,
Give them the best of all the land,
  And send them to Lasell.
In September, they come trooping
  From the North, and South and West,
With their mothers, fathers, brothers,
  Old girls, new girls, all the rest.
There is laughing, there is talking,
  Hither, thither, how they run!
But the schedules soon are finished,
  And the year's work has begun.
In the morning from the chapel
  March they all to music gay—
"Girls, girls, throw your heads back,
  Sparkle now with life and play!"
Next they try to march sedately
  To the wedding's solemn note,
To "radiate" they learn completely,—
  Yes, even in the air to float!
A relief from this high tension
  Of slow floating, as they pass,
Comes a form of relaxation,
  Known as the "Nerve-training class."
There, in silence still and solemn
  They to non-existence sink,
Slowly, slowly, fade to nothing,
  Blissful is this Lethe drink.
And the Orphean, do you hear it?
  Through the halls its high notes ring,
One, two three, four, one, two, three, four
  One, two, three, four, sing!
There's another source of pleasure,
  May its memory ne'er grow dim,
In the tank, down in the basement,
  Where they learn to dive and swim.
Think you that is all we're learning?
  Then you are mistaken, quite—
Here is bread of our own making—
  Doughtnuts, too, and pancakes light.
When some pleasant Monday morning
  Boston's balmly breezes blow,
We to White's and Shepard Norwell's
  With a shopping party go.
One a new spring suit must purchase,
  One, some hairpins, one a plate,
Off for pictures flies another,
  While the others calmly wait.

When they all have reassembled
    At Jordan Marsh's entrance door,
Off they haste· for the four fifty,
    Counting bundles by the score.

Sometimes on excursions going,
    Many wondrous sights they. view;
Yet there's one sad thing about it—
    I would tell to none but you.

For, not watching close her leader,
    When a crowded street is crossed,
To·her sorrow and amazement,
    Suddenly she finds she's lost!

Next time that these girls go walking,
    If by night or if by day,
Without doubt they will remember
    To "walk solid" is the way.

Another thing experience teaches—
    Of umbrellas take a score,   ·
Its a way well-known to Boston
    From clear skies dense rain to pour.

Now keep cool and do not wonder—
    True—a man! and at Lasell!
Know you not of Saturday night callers?
    Calm your fears—for all is well.

But there comes a time of terror,
    With a false alarm of fire;
Hasten, children, with your treasures,
    Save your soap and picture wire!

Put your big hat on securely,
    Take your letters in the drawer,
You've escaped the burning building,
    Still—'tis standing, as of yore.

Listen, listen, from the distance
    Comes the tramp of many feet,
Like a mighty army marching,
    Never beating a retreat.

Yes, they come, Lasell's battalion,
    Soldiers true as steel are they;
"Shoulder arms!" the captain orders,
    Then "Right face," they march away.

What, pray, meaneth this deep silence?
    Do not whisper, make no sign;
Lights are out, and all things ended—
    For the time is half-past nine.

March 30.—Mrs. Loomis gave a very interesting lecture on Bacteria.   The first of a course on Home Sanitation.

On Saturday evening, March 30, we all enjoyed seeing "The Merchant of Venice" played by twenty boys from the College Settlement in Boston.   Their rendering of the play showed the result of talent and much study, and that each boy had a clear conception of the character he represented. The Mandolin Club furnished the music for the evening, and this added very much to our pleasure.   The entertainment was under the auspices of the Lasellia Club, and we feel indebted to them for one of .the most pleasant and profitable evenings of the term.

April 1.—A Pupils' Musical Rehearsal was given in the gymnasium.   The girls who took part were unusually self-possessed, and gained great credit both for themselves and their teachers.   The following program was given:

Chorus. Day is at Last Departing,	*Raff*
Orphean Club.	
Pianoforte. Valse,	*Wächs*
Miss Dyer.	
Song. Ecstacy,	*Mrs. Beach*
Miss Day.	
Pianoforte. Melody,	*Von-Wilm*
Miss George.	
Song. Haste Thee, Sweet!	*Hawley*
Miss F. Hayden.	
Violin Quintette.	
Melodie,	*Dancla*
Serenade,	*Hermes*
Misses Winn, Hawley, Blackstock, Biddle and LeSeuer.	
Chorus.	
a. New Century Anthem,	*French*
b. O, Shepherd of Israel!	*Morrison*
Orphean Club.	
Pianoforte. Sonata.	
Op. 10, No. 1, first movement,	*Beethoven*
Miss Hunt.	
Rose Songs.	
If I knew,	
In My Garden,	*Jessie Gaynor*
Because She Kissed It.	
Miss Wheldon.	
Pianoforte. Etude,	*Ravina*
Miss Bowers.	
Violin Quartette.	
Ständchen,	
Pizzicati,	*Pache*
Misses Winn, Blackstock, LeSeure and Biddle	
Song. Irish Love Song,	*Margaret Lang*
Miss Hill.	
Organ and Pianoforte Duet. Pastorale,	*Guilmant*
Misses Ward and Walker,	

Song. My Little Love,   *Hawley*
      Miss Patterson.
Pianoforte. Balancelle,   *Wachs*
      Miss Miller.
Chorus. From Venice,   *Reinecke*
      Orphean Club.

To the Editor of the Lasell Leaves—

Here we are in Washington, and we feel so sorry for the poor girls who could not come with us. Mr. Shepherd is the best kind of a person to travel with, and Mrs. Shepherd looks after us so well.

We left you people at Lasell at 5.11 Wednesday, and at 6 of the same day we left Boston, an irresistable company of twenty-two. Our trip to Fall River was comparatively uneventful, though we felt very much as though we were somebody, for was not our car marked "private." We were given our state-room keys before we left the train, which made it very convenient, for as soon as we arrived at the wharf we went aboard the boat and to our rooms. We had supper at 7.30, and the boat left while we were eating. About 9.30 the wind and sea came up. We were out on deck, and most of us came down to our state-rooms. Of course we were not sea-sick, but several of the girls went to bed without going through the process of disrobing, probably so they would be ready for the early breakfast. The rocking of the boat lulled most of us awake, and we arose at 5.30, feeling as though we preferred the sea on dry land. Breakfast was at 6.30, and we landed in New York at 7, where Mrs. Austin joined our party. The most pleasant part of that trip was the ride into the harbor. We passed seacrafts of every description, and steamed under the Brooklyn suspension bridge. We took the ferry to Jersey City, and the train from there to Philadelphia. We made the most of our two hour stay in the Quaker City visiting the National Museum, Independence Hall, where we saw the Liberty Bell and the

United States Mint. Up stairs in the Mint building were coins of all Nations, among others the shekel and the Widow's Mite. We had a very pleasant walk down Chestnut street, and a nice lunch at the Rittenhouse. We left for Washington at 1.33, arriving here at 4.30. Mrs. Shepherd was waiting to welcome us, and she had already engaged our rooms. One of the girl's brothers was also here. We all left the hotel early Friday morning, and it was such fine weather for sight-seeing. A bystander was heard to remark as we passed, that he felt sorry for the poor man. We first visited the Pension Building, and it was decidedly interesting. In the centre of this is the large hall where the Inauguration ball is held; this room contains eight fine large columns that run from the floor up to the ceiling, and twenty-four smaller columns. It is said that the building contains more brick than any other in the world. In other rooms are cabinets and cabinets, containing lists of the pensions asked for and granted.

The United States Capital, which came next, was well worth coming to Washington to see, even if none of the other buildings were seen. All the senators seats had been taken up, but we found where the different men sat in Congress. The guide showed us the peculiar effects of the echo in Statuary Hall, and they were really quite weird. Some of the reception-rooms, especially the marble room in the Capital, are very beautiful.

It was such a beautiful day that Mr. Shepherd thought that it would be a good plan to go to Mount Vernon in the afternoon, and we quite agreed with him. Two o'clock found us steaming down the broad Potomac. It was a most delightful ride, and passed Alexandria and other points of interest. We reached our destination at 3.15. Here the air was so balmy that we had to take our jackets off and carry them. Mount Vernon certainly is a paradise, the grounds are so beautiful. It seemed just like some old country place with its old-fashioned house, its quaint garden, its deer park, and coach houses. Washington's room is as it was in his time, and the other rooms have been restored so that they are about as they were then. We saw the last resting-place of America's greatest citizen; the vault in which are the graves of our first president and his wife. Our trip back on the boat was equally pleasant as the trip down. Some of the girls took naps, and others took pictures.

In the evening we went to the Library of Congress. Never in all my life have I seen any building that equalled this in magnificence. It is an utter impossibility to do it justice with a description. One has to see it, to realize how beautiful it is.

Saturday morning we went to the White House, and by special arrangements which Mrs. Shepherd had made the day before, we had the pleasure of shaking hands with the President. We afterwards saw the Treasury building, and met Secretary Gage; and we also went through the War and Navy departments.

In the afternoon we went to the Corcoran Gallery, which is indeed a treat to all art lovers. It was raining, but as we went over and came back in buses, we were not at all inconvenienced. There were so many marvelous paintings here that I will not try to tell of them. I must speak of the Veiled Nun though, the marble bust of Nun. It is so cleverly carved that it seems as though you could really see the nun through the Veil. In the evening some of the girls went to the theatre.

This morning we all went to the Metropolitan Church, and enjoyed the services very much. We found it especially interesting, as Mr. McKinley attended.

Sincerely,
M. A. R.

April 7, 1901.

There are few of us who have time to read the newspaper at breakfast, and as a result, many of us do not keep up very well with the news of the day. Last year we enjoyed the bulletin board by the library door very much, because there we found expressed in a few words, every morning, a record of interesting events which had happened throughout the world on the day before. Can't we continue with the good old custom?

Club Notes.

First Term.

Pres.—Helen Howes.
Vice Pres.—Zoe Hill.
Sec.—Frances Leavitt.
Tres.—Florence Hayden.
Ex. Com.—Mann, Lockwood, Hayden.

Second Term.

Pres.—Marion Mann.
Vice Pres.—Florence Toole.
Sec.—Florence Hayden.
Tres.—Marion Cole.
Ex. Com.—Edith Toole, Hill, Talcott.

Third Term.

Pres.—Frances Leavitt.
Vice Pres.—Marion Cole.
Sec.—Lotta Hewson.
Tres.—Grace Lawrence.
Ex. Com.—Goodwin, Hollenbeck, Brooks.

Fourth Term.

Pres.—Marion Cole.

Vice Pres.—Edna Lockwood.
Sec.—Mollie Mower.
Tres.—Mable Shields.
Ex. Com.—Curtis, Lawrence, LeSeure.

—Ella Spalding is visiting Roe Porter in Detroit, her present home, and while there Jeanette Knights took lunch and went to the theatre with them. On the same evening during a party given for Ella, Gertrude Tidd called, unexpectedly, Ella says, "I tell you, we talked and talked."

—Ruth Crouch is studying music at Oberlin Conservatory, Ohio, and enjoys it very much.

—Georgia Lord is studying music at the Metropolian, N. Y. She expects to be with us for commencement. Eleanor Waite spent a few days with her on her visit to N. Y. this winter.

—Mrs. Fred Weston, née Julia Cox, when in Boston on her wedding trip, made us a short call, though long enough to tell us that she was very happy.

—Elsie Burdick ('99) called in March to find very few old girls whom she knew.

—Florence Wilber is at Coronado, Southern California, and is soon going to Pasadena.

—We are all pleased to hear that Zell Rising's operation was successful.

—Clara Eads ('93) is in California spending a pleasant winter.

—Mame Cruikshank ('96) is spending the winter abroad.

—Harriette Lawrence is teaching school at Wayne, Mich.

—Mrs. DuRelle Gage, née Myrtle Davis, ('97) is living in Boston at the Copley Square Hotel this winter. She took lunch with Louise Richards a short while ago.

—Flora Taft expects to come East in the spring, and Lasell hopes to have a visit from her.

—Louise Peycke made her début this winter, and is now enjoying Kansas City society.

—Jeanette Knights expects to visit us in the spring before sailing for Europe.

First Election.
Pres.—Ethlyn Barber.
Vice Pres.—Bessie Lum.
Sec.—Edith Dustin.
Business Mgr.—Joanna Deering.
Critic.—Edith Harris.
Ex. Com.—Ellen Chase, Ward, Martin.
Second Election.
Pres.—Mabel Martin.
Vice Pres.—Isabella Clemens.
Sec.—Bessie Lum.
Business Mgr.—Joanna Deering.
Critic.—Sue T. Lair.
Ex. Com.—Dustin, Jones, Skinner.
Third Election.
Pres.—Florence Plum.
Vice Pres.—Edith Harris.
Sec.—Lelia Walker.
Business Mgr.—Joanna Deering.
Critic.—Katherine McCoy.
Ex. Com.—Clemens I., Lapowski J., Taylor.
Fourth Election.
Pres.—Edith Dustin.
Vice Pres.—Harriette Ward.
Sec.—Elizabeth Kimball.
Business Mgr.—Joanna Deering.
Critic.—Nell Jones.
Ex. Com.—Kendrick, Lair, Deering.

The following notes have come to us of old Lasellias:

—Hortense Watts, just returned from a delightful trip through Florida, and will soon leave for Chicago, where she will be bridesmaid for Elizabeth Hitchcock.

—Alice Kimball ('98) and Ethel Johnson ('99) were among the guests of the French reception, Saturday evening, March 23.

—Helena Hasbrouck is at Wells College this year, and expects to go abroad this summer.

—Alice Conant is to be married in May to Mr. Charles Sisson, Jr.

—Marion Stafford is visiting in South Framingham. She was at the school, Monday, April 1.

—Elizabeth Snow has been visiting Mrs. Elmer Ayers (Louise Thatcher.)

—Louise Gurley is staying in Atlantic City.

—Joe Milliken has been visiting Emily Bissell ('99) in Rockville, Conn.

—Katherine Moses was at school, March 22; she has been visiting in Boston, and is going to New York about the first of April.

—Maud Mayo has been in Boston buying her wedding outfit—she was married, April ninth. On her way home she spent two or three days with Lorena Fellows ('99).

—Mabel Stilson may come North this summer.

—Blanche Gardner and Emily Kothe expect to come for commencement.

A few years ago the Lasellia and S. D. Societies planned a Club House. It was not merely planned, but much money was raised for its erection. Each society was to give $1500, and Mr. Bragdon was to make up the balance. The girls were earnest, and before long over half of the amount had been raised by each society. The house was to be built back of the Crow's Nest, and each society was to have a hall. The old girls gave generously and were anxious for it. For some reason or other the plan was given up and the money returned. Why not talk the matter over? Let us have a Club House.

English, how she was murdered in the German classes.

1. Bertha enters in hunter's *clothes.*
2. They want to take me to the emperor's *yard.*
8. Gessler *to the horse* with an *eagle* on his fist.
4. Gessler steps over the woman *backward.*
5. Bertha steps into the *middle* of the people.
6. This arm can well protect the *bosom* of a man.
7. With a *rapid scream* she fainted away.
8. They made a Gothic *bundle* to conspire against the Romans.
9. His blood *cooked* at the thought that one day he might be a Roman emperor.
10. All the ships were ready for departure and the *linen* was put up.
11. His *accused* wife of the murder.
12. Then I gave up my wife with a *bloody* heart.
13. Everybody goes to see the criminal who is taken to a *peaceful* death.
14. How she was pleased when I let her *make the declaration* how to make dumplings.
15. He was dressed in a loose jacket and a *padded* shirt.
16. I am not the man of *degraded ability.*

Overheard.

First Girl—Did M. B. C. and M. E. F. keep Lent?

Second Girl—Yes; they both gave up chocolate elairs.

Teacher (in Bible class)—Who led the first expedition out from Babylon to Jerusalem? Miss Zerubbabel, you may tell.

M. C. (in explaining the apparent motions of the planets, in astronomy remarked) "Oh! I took Jupiter around the circuit."

(Study hour in "53")—M. M.—Where is that clock, on the folding bed?

J. P.—No; I moved it over on the dresser, but the tick is there.

Miss C. (in History class)—Did Henry VIII. and Catherine ever have any children?

Miss G.—Yes; a son Mary. She was Queen Elizabeth.

It is said that at a certain Frat. House at Yale, they have Sue Tea (Tee) and layer (Lair) cake for every meal, and *one* boy, at least, never tires of them.

The Senior play was so tragic that even the seats were in tears, (tiers).

One of our Freshman girls was puzzled to know why Cæsar always was talking of Sallies.

Pupil—Which is worse, to study on Sunday, or go to class with an unprepared lesson and annoy the teacher?

Miss P-c-rd—To be sure; go to class without the lesson and "be persecuted for righteousness sake."

First girl—Oh, there is a man!
Second Girl—Where?
First Girl—No, it isn't either; it is Mr. Hills.

What is Carrie George's favorite fruit?

—Dr. M. C. Bragdon and family leave on May 18 by the Southern route for four months' absence or more.

The following have been favored with calls from members of their families: Misses Whitney, Brewer, B. Hayden, Upham, Buffinton, Howes, Dwinell, Thorne, Pendexter, Barker, Rogers, C. Stone, Clokey, Bullock, George, Patterson, Tabler.

Former pupils—Marion Stafford, Helen and Ruth Rishell, Catharine Moses, Eleanor Waite, Elsie Burdick, Mabel Lutes, Mary Vance, Emeroy Ginn, Mrs. Annie Burney

Eaton, Mrs. Julia Cox Weston, Mrs. Alice Taylor Potter, Bertha Warren, Ethel Knowlton, Agnes Flaherty, Helen Ramsdell, Bessie Hayward, Alice Kimball, Mrs. Mabel Sawyer Rogers.

The Summer Abroad.

Mr. Wm. T. Shepherd, who has taken so many parties to Europe, has issued a circular describing the proposed *Fourteenth Tour,* which is certainly an attractive one, including, with supplementary tours, the best of Europe from the North Cape, in Norway, to Rome in Italy.

There will be a small party for young ladies, to sail June 29, on the "Lucania," one of the finest of ocean steamers. The tours throughout will be first class. Send for a circular.

Wм. T. SHEPHERD,
372 Boylston St.,
Boston.

Our Seniors.

This is a history, and when it is done,
You will know it's about the class 'oɪ·
  Never was there such a class at Lasell;
  As proof just listen to what I have to tell.

Ethalyn Barber, president, first is named,
For fondness for Gym. she is greatly famed.
  She'll be first married, and they all say,
  She marches best if Frances will play.

Cleora Brooks is the Kentucky Belle,
Very seldom do we get them here at Lasell.
  Though she entered the class late in the day,
  "She is as good as the rest," Mrs. Martin did say.

Marion Cole, though she does appear quiet,
With her room-mate, always has some sort of riot.
  She broke her pitcher, but really she's fine
  At playing the piano, and at drawing divine.

Isabelle Clemins is next, if I could
Ask questions in Shakespeare as she does, I would.
  In arguing she is so good, I will stake
  A wager, a mighty fine lawyer she'd make.

Edith Dustin, indeed, is one of the best,
The source of much fun, but I will stop, lest
  The callers she receives every week now
  Will all come oftener and there'll be a row.

Margaret Fisher many of you have seen.
From her grains of knowledge you all may glean
  Why Auburndale air is best far and near?
  What to do when callers don't really appear?

Ethel Gallagher sings in the Lasell choir.
Her voice is one which all do admire.
  As captain of Co. A she's all right,
  Her eyes are brown and her hair is light.

Zoe Hill whose fondness for Yale we all know;
In singing her musical talent does show.
  In the senior play she did very well
  As a man, but really, I hope you wont tell.

Bessie Lunn is the star, and we do have such fun—
Teasing her about everything under the sun.
  Her pampon is fine, at French she is great,
  And sometimes she gets to her meals rather late.

Mable Martin is nice, but oh, such a tease!
She constantly makes Bess feel ill at ease.
  Miss Carpenter thinks she has too many clothes,
  But Mabel thinks not, and I guess that she knows.

Cathryn McCoy, even though she is small,
Is good in her studies, yes in one and all.
  She is so very independent, and yet
  They say she has always been the class pet.

Florence Plum, the best natured of all,
Is not very short, nor yet very tall.
  She's as fond of fun as she can be;
  What we'll do without her, we don't really see.

Florence Pooler is not known so well,
Because she does not live at Lasell.
  From Wellesley she comes here every day;
  She listens always to what her sup. has to say.

Ina Scott, our artist from Paris does appear,
By far the most dignified girl we have here.
  Her hand is so deft, her voice is so sweet,
  She truly is a girl you all ought to meet.

Leila Walker is the quietest girl in the class,
But though she talks little, she's a mighty fine lass.
  For further information, I'd say \
  Ask Carrie George, who's there night and day.

Harriette Ward from New Haven, is one
Of the Seniors we are all glad that was done.
  The organ and piano she plays with such skill,
  That the hearts of listeners with rapture do thrill.

These are the sixteen girls in the class.
They are very fine girls, but oh, dear! Alas!
  In June from Lasell they'll go away,
  And thus we'll lose them for ever and aye.

Answers to Correspondents.

M. E. F.—Yes; I quite agree with you, that Auburndale is the best place for your trouble.

F. H.—I think you are wise in choosing a front seat in chapel, for as you say, you can hear better, and get to your classes sooner.

G. M.—It is customary to put only the address and stamp on the envelope. I can assure you that it will reach its destination.

I. C.—I really think gym. twice a week would not be too great a tax on your strength.

(Inquiring pupil).—I am unable to give you a clear definition of a cow, but refer you to Joel.

(Industrious girl).—Yes; I quite agree with you, that a new sewing machine would be a very acceptable addition to the school, especially to worthy girls who make stocks.

M. S. (office)—I am unable to tell you where you can find a new book of puns.

(To the public)—All questions not satisfactorily answered may be sent to B. Clokey, who (as the members of the Pol. Econ. class know) we "always fall back upon."

The exchanges received are: The College Rambler, Acta Victoriana, Bowdoin Orient, The Polytechnian, The Havard Lampoon, The R. H. S. Myth, The Bowdoin Quill, The University Beacon, The Mount Holyoke, The Porcupine, The Converse Concept, The Newton High School Review, New England Conservatory Magazine and Radiator.

Marriages.

—Minnie Bachrach to Ben Deutsch, on Tuesday, April 2, in Kansas City, Mo.

—Musette Derby Lovell to Newell Tucker, on Wednesday, April 3, in Newton Upper Falls, Mass.

—Helen Boullt Medsker to Daniel Louis Humfreville, on Tuesday, April 9, in Kansas City, Mo. Home address, after June 1, 604 No. 9th street, St. Joseph, Mo.

—Elizabéth Hitchcock to John Kelly Robinson, on Tuesday, April 9, in Chicago. Home address, after May 1, 2207 Prairie avenue, Chicago.

—Stella Ballou Cady to Robert Torrington Furman, Tuesday, April 16, in North Adams, Mass.

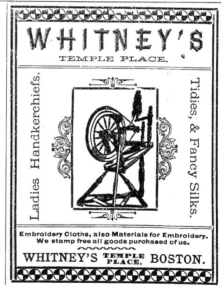

LASELL LEAVES

"DUX FEMINA FACTI."

VOL. XXVI   LASELL SEMINARY, AUBURNDALE, MASS., MAY, 1901.   NUMBER 8

Special number published by the Junior Class.

EDITOR-IN-CHIEF.
EDITH A. HARRIS.

ASSOCIATE EDITORS.
M. BELL CLOKEY.   LOTTA P. HEWSON.   MABEL H. GOODWIN.
SUE T. LAIR.   ANNA MAE PINKHAM.

BUSINESS MANAGER.   ASST. BUSINESS MANAGER.
HELEN L. HOWES.   JOANNA F DEERING.

TERMS, in Advance: One copy, one year (including Postage), $1.00. Single copies, 15 cents.

BOARD OF EDITORS.

This is the State of the Pilgrims.

This is the Town through which runs the rill,
 Which is in the State of the Pilgrims.

This is the School way up on the hill,
Built in the Town through which runs the rill,
 Which is in the State of the Pilgrims.

This is the Class which time cannot kill,
Best in the School way up on the hill,
Built in the Town through which runs the rill,
 Which is in the State of the Pilgrims.

These are the Editors who toil until
The bell rings out so sharp and shrill,
Pride of the Class which time cannot kill,
Best in the School way up on the hill,
Built in the Town through which runs the rill,
 Which is in the State of the Pilgrims.

This is the Book, come now read your fill,
We humbly hope it will fill the bill,
The work of the Editors who toil until
The bell rings out so sharp and shrill;
Pride of the Class which time cannot kill,
Best in the School way up on the hill,
Built in the Town through which runs the rill,
 Which is in the State of the Pilgrims.

HENRY VAN DYKE, D. D., LL. D.

THE Junior Class wishes to introduce to all the school its honorary member, Dr. Henry van Dyke. He is, perhaps, best known to you through his books, especially those charming stories, "The First Christmas Tree," and "Fisherman's Luck." But Dr. van Dyke is also widely known as a preacher and professor. As a minister he has had two charges; he was pastor of the United Congregational Church of Newport, Rhode Island, from 1878 until 1882, when he received a call to the Brick Presbyterian Church of New York City. At present Dr. van Dyke fills the Murray Chair of English Literature at Princeton University. The degree of D. D. has been conferred upon him by Princeton, Harvard and Yale. and that of LL. D. by Union.

The following letter is Dr. van Dyke's own story of his life, as given to the Class of 1902, in reply to a letter asking for a few facts about himself and his work:

"Avalon, Princeton, New Jersey.

My dear classmates—

You say that Lasell does not believe in examinations. Yet just here, at the very beginning, you require the youngest member of your class to pass an entrance examination on the subject about which a man knows least,—himself.

Well, then, I am told (mark you, it is only a matter of hearsay) that this fortunate and inconsiderable person was born on November 10, 1852, in Germantown, Pa. He has always been glad that this event took place, for he has never been able to persuade himself that life is not a blessing. At a very early age, his father taught him to study and to fish. He got his education at the Berkly Polytechnic, the Adirondack Mountains, Princeton College and Seminary, Moosehead Lake, the University of Berlin, the Canadian Camp-fire school, the Woodland Institute of Philosophy, and several other well-known and unknown places of learning. For twenty-one years he tried to preach, in Newport and New York. He kept right on studying life and liking it.\ Then he began to write books about it. Some people cared for them, and some did not. Both of these things seemed strange to him. But he kept right on studying life and liking it more and more. This was chiefly because he had a good wife, and a houseful of real children, and some friends who were fine enough for everyday use. Also because he had to work hard to keep up with his job. Also because the world was full of birds, and books, and places to go a-fishing when he had a day off. Then he got a chance to live with young men and work for them. He took it with prompt joy. He kept right on trying to preach the few things that are worth preaching, faith and hope and love, and at the same time he did not stop studying life, and liking it, and trying to write about it as well as he could. When he told stories he did not preach. When he preached he tried not to tell stories. Some of the things that he did, got into print; and anyone who cares about it can look them up in the Cyclopædias, and Who's Who Books; but they are not of much account.

This picture is said to look like him. I cannot speak from personal knowledge for I never met him face to face. But reflections upon him lead me to think that the photograph presents him in too favorable a light. Really, he is a plain, short fellow, sunburned and growing gray; but he remains,

Faithfully Your Classmate,

March 5, 1901.   HENRY VAN DYKE."

Senior Descriptive Initials.

Ethlyn Barber	Ever Bumming
Cleora Brooks	Considered Beautiful
Isabella C. Clemins	Is Curiously Convincing
Marion Cole	Most Charming
Edith Dustin	Ever Devilish
Madge E. Fisher	Mostly Enjoys Fellows
Ethel L. Gallagher	Ever Loves Gabbing
Zoë D. Hill	Zealous, Dangerous Heart-breaker
Bessie M. Lum	Blesses Many Lives
Mabel Martin	Much Merit
Katherine McCoy	Keeps Marion Cool
Florence Plum	Fascinates People
Florence Pooler	Forever Patient
Ina Scott	Industrious Sketcher
Lelia A. Walker	Likes Ardent Workers
Harriet S. Ward	Has Sensible Ways

JUNIOR PROPHECY.

We all some time must meet our fate,
And 't is for us to now relate;
To tell to you our thoughts and views
Of the future of our Naughty-twos.

Our President, so grand and tall,
Our dear old Nell, beloved by all,
A pastor's helpful wife will be—
And bless the poor with charity.

Our charming Floss, so dear and sweet,
Both fame and glory she will meet;
In acting she will be a star,
And nothing will her triumphs mar.

For our faithful stand-by, Harris, E.,
A literary fame will be;
In books and papers she 'll be known,
And all her wit and brightness shown.

In the dim distance now we see
The stately form of one Sue Tee,
The highest lady of our land—
The President's heart at her command.

To help us with our daily news
And give to us broad-minded views,
Our clever Belle will use her pen,
And interest bring to fellowmen.

A second Sherlock Holmes we see,
Our friend Bess Krag—it cannot be!
All plans and plots are now revealed;
And nothing from her is concealed.

Harris, M., for human ills
Will give her sugar-coated pills.
A few have dared to call her "Quack,"
But better judgment they do lack.

In a little cottage not far away,
Marion Mann now holds full sway;
A cheery housewife she does make,
With never a blunder or mistake.

'Mid roses red and violets blue,
And other flowers of different hue,
Our Bertha roams and sells to all
Her sweet bouquets, both large and small.

Our Cutie, swell in every way,
Will lead the fashions of the day,
In parlor and in social hall,
Her gowns will be admired by all.

At Symphony Hall on the ninth of May,
We will hear the noted Miss Kendrick play,
With fine technique and greatest ease,
She wanders over the ivory keys.

With tasks severe and most strict rule,
Who 's this we see that 's teaching school?

Our Marionette, who 's always wise,
Is teaching children of small size.

Whose book is this that 's made its name,
And shows the writer's wondrous fame?
'T is Mabel Goodwin's, whose keen wit
Has helped her book to make its hit.

Our friend and classmate, Anna Mae,
Soon, very soon, will see the day
When in Grand Opera she will sing,
And loud applause from all will bring.

Our gifted Monk can now be seen
In a French salon, where she is queen.
The nobility flock to share her arts,
Which she with all her grace imparts.

Lida Walters, I do declare!
Is she the wife of a millionaire?
Jewels and gowns she has galore,
And of servants and horses more than a
score.

For both the rich and poor to bless,
Bess Fuller lends her helpfulness.
As deaconess she 's won renown
In the awful slums of Boston town.

Our Georgie Duncan now we see,
Gravely counting, "One, two, three."
The art of swimming she does teach,
Both in the tank and on the beach.

Since for her voice is Jonie noted,
An orator she now is voted;
For Woman's Rights she now stands fast,
And will uphold them to the last.

Filling the church of Trinity,
With all its grand sublimity,
Bess Draper's voice does upward float,
With thrilling, sympathetic note.

As mistress of a home so neat,
Where everything is bright and sweet,
Our Madge presides.   A good helpmate
Of one who 's chosen as her fate.

In the dim future, what do we see?
Our Anna Rouse, an old maid, she!
Birds and tea are her sole pride,
And Pussy 's always at her side.

A most kind nurse with fingers skillful,
And power to soothe her patients willful,
Is Hattie McGregor, who does believe
That all from pain she can relieve.

"McLean—Modiste," is that the sign,
Painted in letters large and fine?
Now for our gowns to her we haste,
Pleased by her skill and wondrous taste.

CLASS OF NINETEEN-ONE.

Motto—*"Non nobis solum."*

Colors, Yellow and white.

Flower, Marguerite.

OFFICERS.

President—Ethlyn F. Barber.

Vice President—Edith Dustin.

Secretary—Isabella C. Clemens.

Treasurer—Bessie M. Lum.

Historian—Zoe Hill.

SENIOR CLASS HISTORY.

C AN it be possible that at last we have reached the goal we have been striving for? Are we the same humble personages who presented themselves four years ago in the spacious halls of learning at Lasell? And now before we leave, let us look back upon the four years, so full of sweet remembrances, and sometimes, painful experiences.

Even in our first year we felt the honor of being Lasell's first Twentieth Century class.   Our first year was rather uneventful, yet as we look back upon it now, we see, what then was not apparent to us, the latent talent, the hidden buds of promise in our class, just waiting for an opportunity to burst upon the world and dazzle it with their greatness.   One thing there was in which our class was not stinted during its first year, and that was advice.   It came from all directions.   It was well for us that we had learned the very first day, the motto in the English room, "A soft answer turneth away wrath," for many's the time we put it in practice during that terrible reign of advice.   We studied hard, made Roman history our own, fought gallantly with Cæsar in the Gallic Wars, and came out at the end of the year with colors flying.

The next fall we were on hand bright and early, and, say it softly, we were called Sophomores.   This year we thoroughly enjoyed ourselves.   We had overcome the greenness of "Freshies," and had not yet taken up the great responsibilities of Juniors. Such good times as our basket-ball team had, and what crowds (?) we had at our class meeting, and what splendid order we kept!   Nevertheless, amid all our fun, we attended well to our lessons, and were fully prepared to enter as Juniors the next fall.   We could then afford to hold our heads high, for are not Juniors next to Seniors?

Now it was our turn to give advice, and as we had been well taught in that art, we imparted our knowledge with wonderful skill.   A class meeting was at once called, officers elected, the colors white and gold decided on, a class flower chosen, and then a stirring yell was composed, after which the class really felt organized, and started in for a good year.   How we enjoyed the Junior reception, and how we worked to give our dear Seniors a good start on their way in life!   Even the "supes" survived, and managed to squeeze in some fun in the midst of their drudgery, and as they toiled for their mighty oppressors cheerfully murmured softly to themselves the class motto, "Non nobis solum."

And now the "naughty ones" (the name belies us) turn to the last page in their four leaved book.   How the girls will miss us!   How can Lasell do without us?   But, better let us say, how can we do without Lasell?   As we take our last look at each familiar spot, a sadness mingles with our triumph.   The dear old chapel, where we set such a good example to the rest of the school, in keeping silence; the gymnasium where we distinguished ourselves in dramatic performances; the room where we held our noted class meetings; in fact, every nook and cranny holds its special recollection.

There are but sixteen of us, yet we are content when we remember the old saying. "The best goods come in the smallest packages."   We cannot be entirely forgotten, for 1901 will be seen on different parts of the building and its furniture for many years to come.   And now as we are about to leave, we give our blessing to all our dear friends, the undergraduates, who have worshipped us from afar; and we do not begrudge them the success they will surely attain if they follow in our illustrious footsteps.   As for us, we will try to be modest, and when great glory crowns our efforts, we will smile quietly and say, "It all came of being one of that extraordinary class of '01's."

Miss K.—What is in Jerusalem nearest the Mount of Olives?
Miss T.—Palestine.

CLASS OF NINETEEN-TWO.

Motto—Lifting Better Up to Best."
Colors, sapphire blue and white.
Flower, white carnation.

OFFICERS.

President—Ellen Chase.

Vice President—Florence Hayden.

Secretary and Treasurer—Edith A. Harris.

Historian—Sue T. Lair.

JUNIOR CLASS HISTORY.

The class of '02 first entered Lasell in the fall of '98.   Having made certain agree-ments with the school not to bring any fancy doo-jons(1) with us, our wardrobe con-sisted of only two strong, sensible dresses(2).   Soon after entering the building we were given the "glad hand" (3) by Mr. Bragdon and the "stony stare" (4) by quite a number of the old girls, who evidently termed us "Pills" (5).   We "sized things up" (6) and concluded that we had "struck it rich" (7), although we were but small Freshmen; but after a few "squelches" (8) and "call-downs" (9), we decided that boarding-school life was not all it was "cracked up to be"(10).   Nevertheless we "hung on"(11) till the next year and found ourselves Sophomores.

By this time we knew that we were the "whole show"(12), and were able to assure the other classes that they were not the "only pebbles on the beach"(13).   We hap-pened sometimes to "gif Mademoiselle a fit"(14), and were promptly "fired"(15) from class.   However, we soon learned how to "work" (16) our teachers and to "bluff" (17) to a "finish"(18), so that life became easier.

NOTES.

1—For the meaning of this word apply to Miss Mann.

2—See page 8, catalogue.

3—Common expression for welcome.   Derivation unknown.

4—Originally applied to the gaze of the Sphinx.   Now used in connection with anyone who looks upon you as their inferior.

5—Pill; a certain form of medicine given by doctors, and very objectionable.   Therefore a person who is objectionable is a pill.

6—To size—to estimate the measure of anything; hence to take its value.

7—Originally used by miners when they found ore; hence to find anything valuable.

8—To squelch; to subdue.   (The meaning of this word was carefully looked up by Miss Nutt.)

9—Probably originated from the fact that children are usually called from up stairs for a scolding. Hence to call down—to scold.

10—To crack up—to powder and make fine.   Hence not what it was cracked up to be—not fine.

11—Applied to one who has great perseverance.   Originally applied to a bull dog whose perseverance is shown in his ability to hang on.

12—To be the entire attraction.

13—This expression originated from the impossibility of there being but one pebble on the beach.

14—The meaning of this can be learned only from experience in the French classes.

15—To fire an engine is to get it ready to go; hence to fire a person from class, which originally meant to get them ready to go, by corruption has come to mean to make them go.

16—To work anyone is to make someone work; hence to get anyone to do something for you.

17—An expression of self confidence, meaning a pretended knowledge.

18—Originally to pursue game in the best way was to pursue it to a finish.   Hence to do anything in the best way is to do it to a finish.

A number of "dandy"(19) girls entered in our Junior year, and everything went on "fine as silk"(20), (our one sad predicament being that we were "busted"(21) most of the time. We got "grouchy"(22) now and then when we thought things were not quite "on the square"(23), but the other girls would "jolly us up"(24) until we were in good spirits again. On the whole we have concluded that no matter how much you "rubber"(25), you won't find a class as "peachy"(26) as ours, and the others "can't touch us with a ten-foot pole"(27).

19—This formerly meant perfection in dress as applied to a dude, but by common usage has come to include perfection both in character and dress.

20—Silk being the finest texture known, anything as fine as silk is very fine.

21—When anything is busted it has no financial value; hence a person who is busted has no financial value.

22—Derivation unknown—meaning out of sorts.

23—When anything is on the square it is fair and just.

24—Make us feel good.

25—When you pull rubber it will stretch. The muscles in your neck stretch when you crane your neck to see anything. Hence to look around—to rubber.

26—Peaches are considered one of the finest fruits on the earth. Hence a peachy class is one of the finest classes on the earth.

27—Anything that can't be touched with a ten-foot pole, must have a very elevated position.

TO THE MAIL BOX.

As I peep in through the window
    At the mail-bag on the floor,
What makes me gaze with longing,
    Waiting by that office door?

What means this hurly-burly,
    These cries from all around?
"Girls! girls! now not so noisy,
    Do not make this deafening sound."

"We are waiting," comes the answer,
    "For the mail to be put out."
But a grave face still looks cloudy,
    And the girls begin to pout.

"You don't seem to have your manners,
    You will shove, and you will scream;
At the table you are boisterous,
    Something must be done, I ween."

From behind, way down the hallway,
    Comes a shrill voice calling out—
"Hey, there, Jen, have you your key here?
    Mine I've looked for all about."

"Yes," comes quickly back the answer,
    "But your mail I cannot get,
For they tell us, none too softly,
    Each her own must not forget."

All at once on comes the head-light.
    Now beware, for danger's near!
Pick your skirts up close around you,
    Then there's not so much to fear.

Some one cries out just behind you:
    "Oh! a note from Mr. Wing!
Says he'll be here for the concert
    If I'll promise him to sing."

Then some muttered words before you,—
    Same old story, by-the-by,—
"If some mail don't come tomorrow,
    Well—I'll just go off and die!"

To your right a dark-haired maiden
    Frowns and looks distracted, quite;
In her hand she holds a paper,
    And she seems most in a fright.

Could we see what there is written,
    We would understand her mood,
For her English—"Not accepted!"
    Teacher says 't is much too crude.

One more weary voice is saying,
    "Oh, dear me! another dun,
Fifteen cents for some old package;
    Fifteen cents' worth less of fun."

Now the crowd begins to scatter,
    And the noise grows almost dim,
To their studies they are starting,
    All the girls, both large and slim.

Left alone, the mail-box ponders,
    And he thinks of years gone by.
Yes, girls, he has been quite faithful,
    And he surely makes time fly.

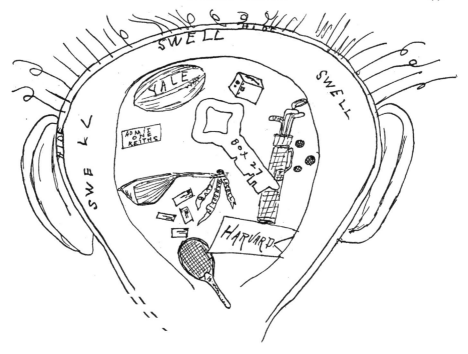

CLASS OF NINETEEN-THREE.

Motto—*"Virtue alone is true nobility."*
Colors, green and gold.
Flower, lily of the valley.
OFFICERS.
President—M. Frances Leavitt.
Vice President—Joel J. Lapowski.
Secretary—Marie Biddle.
Treasurer—Isabella Blackstock.
Historian—Ida M. Mallory.

SOPHOMORE CLASS HISTORY.

IN the ever-memorable year eighteen hundred and ninety-nine, many astronomers in Mars were anxious to see whether the removal of eight from the thousandth's place in earth's calendar, and the substitution of nine would make any change on that queer old star. From January to the middle of September they watched in vain for any sign of unusual occurrences there, but after that came a perceptible difference noticeable in an important place a little way in from that large body of water called the Pedantic. It was then observed with concern that the size and impressiveness of aspect of this place, where but few buildings could be seen, was steadily increasing. They sought everywhere for a solution to the problem, but for a long time none could be found. They fancied it might prove only a temporary change; but during the two following years, from Rebmethes to Eniy (as the Martians reckon time) this alteration and enlargement continued. Then the astronomers, more and more impatient to learn the secret of this odd change, sent down to earth, on a small kite, a message of inquiry, asking for an explanation of the phenomenon. This same kite, as it chanced, alighted on the Lookout, and was there found by a wise young girl who had gone up there one balmy afternoon, lured by the *clemency* of the weather. She carefully took the little æronaut to her chief, the president of the Sophomore class of Lasell Seminary. Instantly a consultation was held by the Sophomores. *"Leave it* to me," said the president, who immediately after sat down and wrote all the particulars of the case, and then sent the news up by return kite.

For fear others may be as much in ignorance about this as the poor Martians (which would be a great pity) it was thought advisable to give an account of the Class of '03, to whom all the disturbance is directly traceable.

Its preparatory year is obscured by time. All we know from ancient manuscripts is that everyone felt a presentiment of the fame which it would in after years attain. It did not, however, in that year gain much distinction. But at the first meeting of the class in its Freshman year, its brillant future was foreshadowed by an unmistakable circumstance—half the number of its members were officers! With due solemnity, color, flower and motto were chosen, and ever since, the first has never faded, the second never wilted, and the motto—ah, the motto—can be recited so fast and with such ease that did you hear us you would think us reciting that coveted Latin motto which, alas! was refused us. As we began, so we have continued. This last year has been full of great promise for the class, and it has done much fine work. Even a Senior, recognizing the high standard of our work has joined one of the classes. If "a nation at peace has no history," certainly a class which keeps the unwritten rules, gets its lessons and goes by the "guide," would scarcely be expected to have one. This must explain why this chronicle is no longer—good class, no scrapes to relate; wise class, no blunders to tell about.

Now all the people in Mars are looking forward to the graduation of the class, who will then have a wider field for their talents. You, dear readers, will have a better opportunity than those remote folk to see how well our class will then employ their talents.

Teacher—Now, Miss M—, give us an illustration of this fact.

Miss M. (edging forward and looking decidedly uncomfortable)—

Teacher (encouragingly)—You don't remember the illustration given of the hammer and the bin of barley? I should think that would be one of the striking things!

CLASS OF NINETEEN-FOUR.

Color, red.   Flower, red rose.

OFFICERS.

President—Rose K. Taylor.
Secretary and Treasurer—Edith E. Sisson.
Historian—Eva L. Chandler.

HISTORY.

WE, the Class of '04, do not claim to be a remarkable class.   Other classes have
lived and worked here in the past and will, no doubt, continue to do so long
after we have said good-bye to dear old Lasell.   They have had the same trials and
gained similar victories, and yet, after all, does that make our triumphs any the less
glorious?

It is far from our intention to boast, but we do fell proud, and not without reason, of the earnest spirit in which the Freshman class have taken up their duties. Nor has this earnestness failed to produce good results, as shown by the high marks earned by some of our number in the various classes. In fact, in certain studies, also pursued by members of other classes, the Freshmen have ranked among the very first, even doing better work, in some cases, than the Seniors themselves. We feel that we have won special distinction in German, since we have contributed quite largely to the book of remarkable sayings, carefully kept by the teacher. In drill, we have learned, among other things, to keep our "hands down in ranks," and our "eyes to the front." We have also been taught the correct way of going up and down stairs, and are trying faithfully to put this knowledge into practice. It does require a good deal of self-control though, especially when, after taking a few steps with the feeling that we are "being drawn up," we are seized with an irresistible desire to rush to the top. It is to be hoped that this impulse will remain with us throughout life, ever stimulating us to "rush to the top."

As for the dignity of the class, we do not feel like boasting much. We could speak with greater confidence if we felt sure that our reader had not happened to be out on Woodland Road one of the first days after a snow fall. If so, he would probably have been somewhat amused at beholding a company of girls, including one of the highest officers of the Freshman class, sliding down the bank, their zeal not being at all checked by the absence of any kind of sled. But then, a Freshman class is not expected to be dignified. That virtue is left to the Seniors, and we trust that by the time we have become learned enough to don caps and gowns, we shall have acquired a suitable stateliness.

But, though we are not very dignified, we certainly are a class united in purpose, in aspiration, and, more than all, in loyalty to dear old Lasell.

Senior (puzzling over letter just received)—Aunt Jennie sent John some—well, it's something and then "chiefs."
Junior (unhesitatingly)—Scottish chiefs!
Special (not to be beaten)—Hawaiian chiefs!
Senior—Oh! I have it now. It's handkerchiefs.

(Seniors waiting nervously before door of Lit. class-room.)
Senior No. 1—What's the difference between a lyrical and an ethical ballad?
Senior No. 2—Why, a lyrical ballad is one that is to be sung, and an ethical ballad is one that sings itself.

Excited Junior (in class meeting)—I nominate Miss Jacket.
President—Who?
Junior (very confused)—Oh! I mean Miss Clokey.

SENIOR PERSONALIA.

ETHLYN FOSTINA BARBER, *Milford, N. H.*   Entered in 1898, Lasellia.   Sophomore year—Guard, Lasellia.   Junior year—Vice President of the class, Business Manager Lasellia, President Lasell Publishing Association.   Senior year—President of
Class, President Lasellia, Business Manager Lasell Publishing Association, 2d Sergeant Company C; exempt from Law.

CLEORA BRIGHT BROOKS, *Winchester, Ky.*   Entered in 1900.   S. D.   Senior
year—Vice president S. D., member of Lasell Missionary Society and Lasell Publishing Association.

ISABELLA CUMMING CLEMENS, *Pottsville, Penn.*   Entered as Freshman.   Lasellia.   Freshman year—Secretary of class, Associate Editor LEAVES.   Junior year—
President of class, Secretary Lasellia, 1st Sergeant Company C, member of Housekeeping Class, winner of First Bread Prize, received Honorable Mention in Bayonet Drill.
Senior year—Secretary of class, Vice President Lasellia, Vice President Lasell Publishing Association; exempt from Law.

MARION COLE, *Chester, Ill.*   Entered in 1898.   S. D.   Junior year—Local Editor
LEAVES, 2d Sergeant Company C.   Senior year—Treasurer, Vice President, President,
S. D., Sergeant-major Drill, member of Christian Endeavor Society, Orphean Club, and
Lasell Instrumental Club.

EDITH DUSTIN, *Gloucester, Mass.*   Entered in 1898.   Lasellia.   Junior year—
Guard, Critic, Lasellia; Secretary, President, Christian Endeavor; Associate Editor of
LEAVES.   Senior year—Vice President, class; Secretary, President, Lasellia; Secretary,
Missionary Society; President, Lasell Publishing Association; exempt from Law.

MARGARET EDWINA FISHER, *Red Oak, Iowa.*   Entered in 1898.   Lasellia.   Junior year—Treasurer, class; Treasurer, Christian Endeavor.   Senior year—Secretary,
Christian Endeavor; member of Orphean Club and of Housekeeping Class in both Junior and Senior years; exempt from Law.

ETHEL LOUISE GALLAGHER, *Auburndale, Mass.*   Entered in 1897.   Junior year—
Secretary, Missionary Society; winner of Second Prize, Competition Drill.   Senior
year—Subscription agent, LEAVES; Captain, Company A; member of Orphean Club.

ZOE HILL, *Council Bluffs, Iowa.*   Entered in 1899.   S. D.   Junior year—Secretary, S. D.   Senior year—Historian, class; Vice President, President, S. D.; Star Actor,
Senior Play; Toast mistress, Washington Birthday Banquet; exempt from Law; member of Orphean Club and Lasell Instrumental Club.

BESSIE MARIE LUM, *Minneapolis, Minn.*   Entered in 1899.   Lasellia.   Junior
year—Editor-in-chief, LEAVES.   Senior year—Treasurer, class; Secretary, Lasellia;
President, Christian Endeavor; member of Executive Committee, Missionary Society;
member of Housekeeping Class both Junior and Senior years; Stage Manager, Senior
Entertainment; member of Orphean Club.

MABEL MARTIN, *Springfield, Ohio.*   Entered in 1898.   Lasellia.   Sophomore
year—Guard, Lasellia; Associate editor, LEAVES.   Junior year—Secretary, Lasellia;
President, Secretary, Christian Endeavor; President, Lasell Publishing Association; 3d

Sergeant Company A. Senior year—President, Lasellia; Exchange editor, LEAVES; Captain, Company C; exempt from Law; member of Lasell Instrumental Club.

FLORENCE GERTRUDE PLUM, *Indianapolis, Ind.* Entered in 1899. Lasellia. Junior year—Subscription agent, LEAVES. Senior year—Vice President, President, Lasellia; Vice President, Missionary Society; Captain, Company B; member of Christian Endeavor Society and Lasell Canoe Club.

FLORENCE POOLER, *Wellesley, Mass.* Entered in 1896. Lasellia. Sophomore year—Guard, Lasellia; Local editor, LEAVES. Senior year—Exempt from Law; member of Lasell Instrumental Club; took Drill one year; completed course in Cooking.

INA SCOTT, *Paris, Texas.* Entered in 1899. Lasellia. Junior year—Subscription agent, editor-in-chief, LEAVES. Senior year—Guard, Vice President, Lasellia; Vice President, Christian Endeavor; Lieutenant, Company C; exempt from Law; member of Orphean Club; completes course in Studio work.

LELIA AMY WALKER, *Milford, Mass.* Entered in 1898. Lasellia. Senior year—Secretary, Lasellia; Exchange editor, LEAVES; 3rd Sergeant, Company B; member of Orphean Club and Lasell Instrumental Club.

HARRIETTE SMITH WARD, *New Haven, Conn.* Entered in 1899. Lasellia. Junior year—Vice President, Christian Endeavor; Secretary, Lasell Publishing Company. Senior year—Vice President, Lasellia; Lieutenant, Company B; composer Lasell Song.

THE IDLE DREAMS OF AN IDLE JUNIOR.

ONE beautiful May afternoon, when everything outside was green and the sun was shining brightly, Helen came up from drill, hot and tired, and threw herself upon the bed. From without, through the half closed shutters, there came to her sounds of the girls playing golf and tennis, and of the chatter of others sitting upon the grass, enjoying the beautiful spring weather, and talking as only Lasell girls can. She heard one group talking of the coming Commencement, and this set her to wondering what original things the Seniors had planned for their Class Night.

She had taken a book from the shelf, before lying down, intending to study as she lay there near the open window, but how could one study with such fascinating thoughts of Commencement running through her head? Certainly, this lively Junior could not, and she was soon wondering upon what *she* would do when she became a grave and reverend Senior. Most of all she wondered whether it would be said of the Class of "1902" as it had been said of the Seniors, "It is strange that a class of sixteen girls should all be so kind and thoughtful of the comfort of other people." As she was dreaming in this way of the happy times to come she really fell asleep, and her mind being full of such things, it is not strange that she dreamed of the Commencement week of her own class, and that her new classmate, Dr. Henry van Dyke, whom she had met but a short time before, figured prominently in her dreams. In her dream he seemed to be the minister on Baccalaureate Sunday. She floated into church that morning with all the other Seniors, and could hardly understand how she was there. However, there is no doubt but that "their thoughts were lifting them up," and Mrs. Martin's teaching had been of real benefit to them on this occasion, for once they had, indeed, "put their souls into it." She noticed but few things in the church, for Dr. van Dyke was so interesting that she thought of nothing else until he had finished speaking. One of the things which did then attract her attention, was the fact that the entire church was a mass of white carnations, the class flower. This was due to the fact that the Juniors, the Class of 1903, had very kindly worked for a number of days to make beautiful wreaths and bouquets of this lovely flower, for the adornment of the church.

As she returned to Lasell, something was said about Class Night, and when she reached the Seminary, night seemed suddenly to have succeeded the day; and then she at once remembered that *she* belonged there, too. Hurrying to the Gymnasium stage, she found all the girls awaiting her, and much worried lest she would not be on time, for they knew that the reputation of the class, in Mr. Bragdon's eyes, at least, depended on their beginning at eight o'clock, sharp. They were not a second late, but appeared for the first number exactly on time. The prophecy was a great success, but my readers will have to return in 1902 in order to hear it, as well as the class song, and the other numbers of the program which Helen heard in her dream that night. I will mention what was presented to Lasell then, for if that should come true, I am sure you would be especially pleased at having known it all this time. When Ruth appeared for the presentation speech, the Faculty, and the Faculty, only, began to applaud. At first this seemed odd, but it presently appeared that, on account of the nature of the gift, they had known some time what it was to be, having been obliged to sign numberless papers regarding it. After the room became silent, there was presented to Lasell, the signed contract for Carpenter Hall, to be ready for occupancy the following September. The building was to be fitted out in the costliest manner, and was to exceed any college hall in America. In the curious manner in which dreams sometimes change from one place or time, to another, she was soon back in the church again, receiving her diploma from Mr. Bragdon. All the girls looked very much as if they wanted to cry, and she felt a tear on her own cheek. She thought it very strange, as she had always expected to be perfectly happy if she ever finished school. Walking back to the Seminary, she began to think of her many walks, in the past, to and from that church, and as she realized that this was her last walk over that ground, the tears began to roll down the cheeks, and when she reached her room, she threw herself on the bed and burst out crying at the thoughts of leaving dear old Lasell, and then—well, she awoke to find the pillow wet with tears, and the dinner gong ringing in approved Lasell fashion, and, behold! she was only a Junior still, and an idle one at that, and she had over a year more in which to enjoy all Lasell gives to its girls.

She hurried to get ready for dinner, a much wiser girl, and resolved, from that time forth to make it as pleasant as possible for all the Seniors, and especially for her especial "Senior," in view of the fact that they were going to lose so much in June.

Miss P. (as a dish of lettuce is brought on the table)—What's this?

Miss S.—Oh! merely another edition of the Lasell Leaves.

THE BELLS.

(With apologies to E. A. Poe).

Hear the roaring rising bell—
    Banging bell!
What a world of happv dreams its clanging notes
    dispel!
How it thunders, thunders, thunders,
    Through the halls at break of light
Quiet sleep so ruthlessly surprising,
Telling all 'tis time for rising
    With a sort of wild delight,
      Crying rise! rise! rise!
'Till you have to ope your eyes,
For the frantic driving, banging, as it ceaseless roars
    along
With its dong, dong, dong, dong,
      Din, din, dong.
O, the clanging and the banging of that gong!

Here the joyful dinner bell,
    Iron bell!
What a dash of sudden hurry its sounding notes com-
    pel!
Through the halls at dinner hour
How it rings with all its power,
And invitingly denotes
    What we love.
While a scent of goodies floats
To the hungry girls that listen for its notes
    Up above!
Then from out the sixty doors,
What a throng of eager girls immediately pours!
    What a flurry,
    How they hurry
Down the stairway!   Delay opposing
Or, mayhap, some grave excuse composing,
Lest that dreaded door be closing.
Loud we chatter at the clatter
    Of the bell, bell bell,
    Of the loud, loud bell.

Hear the shrill electric bells—
    Pealing bells!
Of what a round of duties here, their ceaseless ring-
    ing tells.
If to chapel, loud they call,
How we rush along the hall;
What a chatter—what a din,
Every voice is chiming in
With a racket never heard before,—
Till we pass inside the door
    All subdued.
Now perhaps these bells are pealing, just to kindly
    let us know
That our school life's not all play-time, but to les-
    sons we must go.

To the class of English Lit.,
Where our history is reviewed,
And gymnastics are subdued,
Or perhaps it may be some one
To the swimming tank they summon,
Where she goes with quaking fears
And the well-known order hears,
    "One, two, three!"
If the bell two-twenty rings
Quickly on we get our things,
For 't is walking hour, you know,
And we all must surely go—
If it is n't rainy weather—
"Always two, at least, together."
    No time for stopping!
    Do no shopping!
For we must be back at three,
When another bell there 'll be.
    Always ringing,
    Summons bringing
To some duty everywhere;
Till the last bell in the evening bids us sleep and
    drop all care.
    While we dream
    Of the bells, bells, bells, bells,
      Bells, bells, bells—
Of the ceaseless, constant ringing of the bells.

Hear the loud alarum bells—
    Brazen bells!
What a flood of terror wild their angry note impels.
Through the silent halls they scream,
And 't would almost surely seem
They would burst their iron throats
With the awful clanging notes,
    Wild and fierce!
Surely fire must be raging—madly, furiously blazing,
Such a din to startle—such confusion to be raising.
Do you hear the loud commotion
Of those girls who have no notion
What to save, and what let perish;
Whether hats or gowns to cherish?
Some fond heart 't will surely pierce
If those love notes burn.
Can 't she of some power learn
    To quench the fire?
If the flames are only small,
There is water in each hall.
Do not try to use those patent bottles there,
For a *girl* could break them ne'er.
    But why this quiet?
    I hear no riot!
Now the bells cease, all is still.

Did all the rest imagination fill?
Well, you see, 't is only Monday, so we have not
    aught to fear,
      Though we hear
All that clanging, all that banging
      Of those bells;
Of those wild, fierce fire-bells.

  Hear the little table bell—
      Silver bell!
How·it loves through all the room, its little voice to
    swell.
Out upon the din it rings,
And a sudden silence brings,
As we listen for the message that's to follow.
  With knife or fork in air,
  For to move we would not dare—
      E'en to swallow;
While the notice all are waiting.
Now it may be it is skating
      For tomorrow;
Or, if summer skies are shining,
  It will surely be canoeing
On the peaceful Charles reclining,
  Mr. Winslow's bark pursuing.
Or perhaps the bell was ringing
With a merry summons bringing

    To the Gym,
Where we went for frolic yearning
While the lights above were burning
    dim.
When Miss Austin's girls, one time,
Some cute verses did combine
With an act in pantomime.
Would some class a meeting hold,
  Should we like to know
On what train in town to go,
All would·by this bell be told.
    Busy bell!
Which each Tuesday night
Always rings with all its might.
  Merry, happy little bell!
  Little silver bell!

Thus we live—each hour a bell
Always of some work to tell.
  Thus we live at old Lasell!
So our minds will some day dwell
  On 'how we lived at dear Lasell!
Each task doing by some bell.
Then we'll miss their helpful call!
Then we'll want them one and all!
    Helpful bells!
Ever ringing—e'er to memory clinging bells!

A SUMMER SCENE.

THE doctor told me that I needed a good rest and some healthful exercise. If I could but make my Armstrong (which I was well Abell to do), I would be all right. "Great Scott!" I said, "are you Stark-mad? When you say I am run down you Ly-man." But he insisted, so I decided to take a sojourn in the North. Going to a Taylor and a Draper, I got the needful clothes and the next Day sought the peaceful Bowers of a Hill not far from there. Here I could either be a Fisher or Hunt and Chase the game over Peak and Krag to its Lair.

A Mann met me at the depot with his small son George and asked me if I was much of a Ryder, for he said he kept a Blackstock of horses. I told him though I was not as Greene as I looked, I was a much better Walker. So to my Dyer dismay he said if I was such a good Walker I might Carrie George. As we walked in the hot sun I got Dustin my eyes and I thought this mistake of mine in saying I could walk would be a Thorne in my flesh the rest of my stay. After dinner, however, I managed to Vail my wrath, and we started out for a walk of a few miles, and as I started I said to my escort, "Let her go, Gallagher." I picked a Plum on the way, and when I asked what to do with it, my host, in his peculiar way, said: "Wall, you might Skinner." As it was Albright and clear, we went through the village, passing the Brewer, the Barber, who was Cole-black, and the Miller, who was white with meal. It was even suggested that we visit a distant Palmer, but I concluded to Ward off such an attack of energy and decided not to go. However, as we were crossing one of the Brooks, I slipped on a Stone and fell in. "This walk is Fuller of mishaps than most," I said, as I pulled myself off of a Tarbox on which I had landed, hoping it would Rouse my host·to see my wet clothes. "Howes that," he said, then looking at me, he exclaimed, "Hew-son, how wet you are!" "Say no Mower," I replied, "my plight Shields me from further efforts at walking." I felt like one who has Beenett in tag, and, gazing at a Martin which was flying overhead, I said, "Thus do the Goodwin."

DRILL.

TO all who are interested in military drill, the exercise has always been a delight, not only to those who have learned the fundamental movements both in the setting up exercises, the manual of arms and the marching, but also to those who have gained the responsibility of holding an office. This work has been increasing for twelve years. It was founded in 1886, Major George H. Benyon being the commander for two years, and again taking command after two years' absence. He remained with the battalion until last year; at that time Lieutenant Charles A. Ranlett took command, and is now our instructor.

The whole battalion is composed of companies A, B, and C, with their commissioned and non-commissioned officers. The members are looking forward to the annual contest which occurs during the last of the spring term, when the work will be exhibited at its best, and a prize awarded to the company deserving the honor.

The following are the officers:

Lieutenant Adjutant, Edith A. Harris; Sergeant Major, Marion Cole; Color Sergeant, Sue Tee Lair.

Co. A.—Captain, Ethel Gallagher; Lieutenant, Georgie Duncan; 1st Sergeant, Ida Mallory; 2nd Sergeant, Anna Mae Pinkham; 3rd Sergeant, Emily Clemens.

Co. B.—Captain, Florence Plum; Lieutenant, Harriette Ward; 1st Sergeant, Ellen Chase; 2nd Sergeant, Florence Brewer; 3rd Sergeant, Lelia Walker.

Co. C.—Captain, Mabel Martin; Lieutenant, Ina Scott; 1st Sergeant, Bess Krag; 2nd Sergeant, Ethlyn Barber; 3rd Sergeant, Ruth Talcott.

SIDE TALK WITH GIRLS.

H-r-is, E.—It is usually customary to answer "Present" to roll call, and not "Come."

Sk-n-er—We usually celebrate Washington's Birthday on February 22d, and not in March.

Suggestion to Misses P. and H.—It is preferable in drill to give the commands right molinet and right forward, guide right, to right movement A and right forward, glide right.

Hel-n H-w-s—It is not customary to use profane language in literature class.

RETROSPECT.

September 11—"Auburndale!" cried the conductor as the train pulled up before a modest little vine covered station. The train stopped, and girls—girls of every description, size, age, complexion and disposition; girls with big hats, girls with little hats; girls with hand-satchels, girls with suit-cases; girls followed by fond relations, girls alone; girls with smiling faces, and, still more, girls with tears, came hurrying out of the cars into the station. Who could they be, and whence had they come? I heard some one say, "Does this carriage go to Lasell?" The problem is solved: *they are the new girls,* who have come to take their part in both the pleasures and the duties of a year at dear Lasell.

September 12—Today the new girls were awed to silence by the queenly looking girls who now began to arrive. It was soon evident that they were old girls from the greetings which flew through the halls, "Oh, you dear! so you really have come back!" "Say, have you seen so and so? She hasn't changed a bit! Has she?" "Isn't it dreadful without all the old girls?"

September 14—From the rooms of the new girls come strange sounds, which seem decidedly like moans, but surely that is impossible. The old girls decide that it is nothing fatal, only an attack of that disease so common at this time of year.

September 26—First called meeting of the Junior class.

October 1—"Fore!"   There goes a tiny golf ball, whirling off the tee under Miss Witherbee's window, while the golf enthusiast, hastily gathering up her clubs, madly rushes down the hill for fear the bell may ring before she makes the round.   The tennis court at this time is the field of many exciting contests, which Mr. Winslow and his parties of boaters would be unable to leave except that canoeing has so many more alluring attractions.

Today, October 3, the Juniors decided that Yale blue and gold should be the class colors, and the white carnation their flower.

October 12—Has Lasell become a school of oratory?   No, it is only that some of the girls, who saw Hamlet last night, seek to give an illustrated account to their less fortunate friends.

The thirteenth of October will long be remembered by the Juniors as the day on which the Seniors gave them the glorious "Golf Dance."

Where in the world have all these poor "raggety" children come from, who are pouring down the stairs and out into the gymnasium?   Can they be Lasell girls, or are they from some Mission school in Boston?   This question was not decided until, standing in the light of a grinning Jack-o-lantern, I saw a familiar form, a second glance enabled me to peep behind *his* mask and to discover the face of the Senior President. Then I remembered it was the twenty-seventh of October, and the evening of the Senior "Poverty Party."

October 31—Will some one kindly furnish the names of the lucky girls who ate the pieces of cake which contained rings?   It will be of much assistance in writing class prophecies.

When thinking of November days the thoughts of the upper classmates linger around the pleasant evening spent at the Juniors' "Salamagundi Party," for, this like all which the Juniors do, was a great success. Then, too, they with the rest of Lasell long for some of the good things which went a-begging in the bountiful supplies of Thanksgiving Day.

December—"All those wanting trunks please state whether they are marked 'Wanted' or 'Not wanted,' and also give number of room." These words caused our hearts to beat most wildly, for we knew vacation was here at last. What a hurry and scurry we were all in! The trunks are packed, good-byes and "Be sure you write to me's" are said, and then the girls are gone to the several chimneys where Santa Claus is most likely to find their stockings.

January 9—Once more we are all back at old Lasell, beginning with this new century another term; but do our thoughts never stray from our tasks, or, perhaps, as we sit before the fire in the library, dinner over and the time to study not yet come, do we never think of that last dance, or of all the theatre parties, or, yes, of certain of our *friends?*

January 24—"Hush, here they come!" "Company, attention! Present arms!" The battalion is ready to receive Charles Ward Post, 62, G. A. R., which now marches between the rows of excited girls. "Company, salute! Port arms. Disband!" A rush, introductions, a good time, and the evening is over. Some of us, who attended

Mr. Ranlett's exhibition of fencing, are trying to decide whether the duels described in modern novels are strictly in accordance with the rules.

February—It must be the beginning of the nineteenth century instead of the twenti-eth, or else I am dreaming, for I certainly see, clad in flowing robes, with bodices grace-fully draped with crossed fichus, stately white-haired ladies descending into the dining-room.   Looking out from under high puffs of powdered hair are bright, happy faces, whose rosy cheeks, with here and there pieces of black court plaster, are in striking con-trast to their blanched locks.   We all seated ourselves, an orchestra commenced to play, and, and—"Why, what is the matter! I have been asleep at the table, do you say?   It is impossible, for do I not still see those old fashioned ladies?"   "February twenty-second," you say, "and our girls are dressed up?   Well, I never!"

On the evening of February 9 the "Senior Play" was a grand success.   The advice now given to the Supes is, "Look well to your senior and prevent her from being forced, on account of her wonderful powers, into becoming an actress."

Let February 15 be forever a day of mourning, for it was then that Mr. James intro-

duced us to Joaquin Miller.   He little thought that "Columbus" would become a haunt-
ing dread to Lasell girls.

March—"Won't you come in?"   "No, I can't stop a minute, because I just must go
and finish my composition, and then there is all that French for tomorrow.   I do wish
Mademoiselle wouldn't give such long lessons just now, when everyone else does, too."
Now-a-days this is what is heard on all sides; for we are all busy, especially the Seniors
with their essays and Class Day affairs.   It is certainly useless to mention here the
French play.   We refer you to the last number of the LEAVES.

If April showers bring May flowers, then Auburndale ought to soon become a wilderness of color and beauty. We all feel like saying as a little boy did; "Mamma, will God have enough water left way up there to drink when He's thirsty?" Although the sun insisted in being angry and turned his back to us, still we all seemed to be able to enjoy vacation.

Miss C.—Where did you say your quotation was from?
Miss H.—Wordsworth's Ibid.

———————————

Dr. G.—You may tell us something, Miss C., about infant industries.
Miss C. (unhesitatingly)—It is a place where children are employed.

A LASELL GIRL'S ANSWER.

HE.

Pretty maid! Pretty maid! Will you be mine?
You shall not wash dishes, nor yet feed the swine,
But sit on a cushion and wear a gold ring,
And feast upon strawberries, sugar, and cream.

SHE.

Thank you, sir! Thank you, sir! Your offer is kind,
But I love to wash dishes, and soon I should find
That to sit on a cushion and not do a thing
To me great discomfort and sadness would bring.

"AND THE LAST SHALL BE FIRST."
—Blackstein.

When Gabriel blows the final trump,
    And all the dead arise,
And gather into happy homes,
    Awaiting in the skies;
When all the blest are gathered in,
    And Peter 's shut the gate;
At Heaven's door, as at Lasell,
    Will Marion Cole come late?

STRIKES.

"Two souls with but a single thought,
    Two hearts that beat as one."
Griffin and Martin.
George and Walker.
Ramsdell and Too Numerous to Mention.
"Jonie" and Ethlyn.
Leavitt and Kimball.
Harris E. and Foster G.
Hamilton and Smith.
L. Chase and Kendrick.
Jones and Dustin.
Chase E. and Pearson.
Stone C. and Crosby.
Hill and Lair.
Whitley and Taylor.

SENIOR STATISTICS.

"To those who know thee not, no words can paint!
And those who know thee, know all words are faint."—*Hannah More.*

NAMES	NOTED FOR	POSITION IN CLASS	AMBITION	ALWAYS FOUND	PET EXPRESSION	LACKS	MATRIMONIAL PROSPECTS
E. BARBER	Fondness for Maurice	President	To sing	With "Jonie"	"Oh dear"	Ability to make stump speeches	J. Deering
C. BROOKS	Neatness	The last member	To reread letters from Boston	In love	"I was 'hacked' to death	A pompadour	F. Hayden
I. CLEMENS . . .	Appetite	Secretary	To argue	Hunting "Kitty"	"Mighty nice"	Ability to fall in love	M. Goodwin
M. COLE	Forgetfulness	Youngest	To enjoy life	Behind time	"Ugh"	Energy	L. Hewson
E. DUSTIN . . .	Being a "dandy" girl	Vice President	To tease somebody	Up to some mischief	"My land"	Humor	E. Chase
M. FISHER . . .	Being a good cook	The "teaser"	To go to Boston		"Je ne know pas"	Favor of C. A. C.	B. Clokey
E. GALLAGHER .	Curly hair	Singer	To talk to Lieutenant	Singing	Very peculiar	Lasell spirit	M. Ramsdell
Z. HILL	Boisterousness	Historian	To run things	With C. C. B.	"Doozy"	Pretty hair	H. Howes
B. LUM	Ability	Favorite	To be President of Missionary Soc.	Where most needed	"You don't say"	Nothing much	A. M. Pinkham
K. McCOY	Smallness	"Baby"	To "parlez Français"	With a six-footer	"Don't be so persnickity"	Height	M. Mann
M. MARTIN . . .	Drill	Looks after its religious welfare	To be a deaconess	In "12"	"You're an anthropophagy"	Conceit	H. McGregor
F. PLUM	Good disposition	Prettiest girl	To have a caller	Playing jokes	"Superspas matatical"	Dignity	E. Harris
F. POOLER . . .	Quietness	Most experienced at Lasell	To graduate at Lasell	Listening to Bess	Doesn't use them	Conversational ability	B. Krag
I. SCOTT	Pleasing voice	Artist	To write a good Senior Essay	In the studio	"Is that so"	Vanity	M. Hollenbeck
L. WALKER . . .	Organ recital	Pianist	To see Carrie of tener	With Carrie	Never says it out loud	Several things	G. Duncan
H. WARD	Composing Lasell song	Organist	To be a Senior	Practicing	"Oh, no"	A good supe	S. T. Lair

'01.

"Augers bore holes, but these bores bore a whole community."—*Anon.*

E. B-rb-r—"Congratulate me, friends, for I am to marry."

C. Br- -ks—"People of a lively imagination are generally curious, and always when a little in love."

I. Cl-m-ns—"I was ever of an opinion.'

M. C-le—"One ear it heard, at the other out it went."

E. D-st-n—"She was made for happy thoughts, for singing and sweet laughter."

M. F-sh-r—"A bright, little, comely girl with large, dark eyes.'

E. G-ll-gh-r—"She had a great liking for show, and bright colors."

Z. H-ll—"Business managers, attention! I am a star player."

B. L-m—"Good, oh, so good! How do you endure this wicked world?"

M. M-rt-n—"I want to be a captain
And with my comp'ny stand.
Four stripes upon my drill suit
And a sword within my hand."

K. McC-y—"Little, but oh my!"

F. Pl-m—"Why should the evil one have all the good times?"

F. P- -l-r—"As silent as the pictures on the walls."

I. Sc-tt—"A manner so plain, grave, unaffected and sincere."

L. W-lk-r—"Bashfulness is an ornament to youth."

H. W-rd—"Wit now and then, struck smartly, shows a spark."

'02.

"Noble by birth, yet nobler by great deeds."—*Longfellow.*

E. Ch-s- —"Hang trouble, care will kill a cat."

L. Ch-s- —"Another tumble! That's her precious nose."

B. Cl-k-y—"Order is Heaven's first law."

J. D- -r-ng—"What she undertook to do, she did."

B. Dr-p-r—"I hear, yet say not much, but think the more."

B. F-ll-r
G. D-nc-n   } —"Two souls without a single thought."

M. G- -dw-n—"She thinks too much.   Such girls are dangerous."

E. H-rr-s—"Gude folk are scarce—tak' care o' me."

M. H-rr-s—"There's no art to find the mind's construction in the face."

F. H-yd-n—"He who has a superlative for everything wants a measure for the great or
    small."

L. H-ws-n—"Be not all sugar or the world will gulp thee down."

M. H-ll-nb-ck—"If you have tears prepare to shed them now."

H. H-w-s—"She tells you flatly what her mind is."

K. K-ndr-ck—"Where the tall nothing stood;
        A shapeless shape."

B. Kr-g—"When I first put this uniform on,
        I said as I looked in the glass,
        'There's one to a million
        That any civilian
        My figure and form could surpass.'"

S. T. L- -r—"She was not inclined to labor
        For herself or for her neighbor,
        For she dearly loved her ease."

C. McL- -n—"The worst I know, I would do good too."

M. M-nn—"So wise, so young, they say, do never live long."

H. McGr-g-r—"Sweet mercy is nobility's true badge."

A. M. P-nkh-m—"Neved idle a-moment, but thrifty and thoughtful of others."

M. R-msd-ll—"Her words do show her wit incomparable."

A. R- -s- —"Give thy thoughts no tongue."

M. Uph-m—"Every artist was first an amateur.

L. W-lt-rs—"Her head was bare but for her native ornament of hair, in which a simple
        bow was always tied."

B. Wh-t- —"So light of foot, so light of spirit."

'03.

"There is small choice in rotten apples."—*Anon.*

M. B-ddl- —"This incessant giggling must be stopped."

I. Bl-ckst-ck—"The fat, affectionate smile."

I. B-w-rs—"Impulsive, earnest, prompt to act."

G. B-ll-ck—"A geometrical line, length without breadth."

E. Cl-m-ns—"Whose sore task does not divide Sunday from the week."

C. D-Gr-ff—"She had a cool, collected look,
        As if her pulses beat by book."

C. D- -gl-ss—" Linked sweetness long drawn out."

C. G- -rg- —"My attachments are strong attachments, but often weaken."

L. H-rm-n—"She was made for happy thoughts."

B. H-yd-n—"With a clear and warbling voice, like a skylark singing."

J. H-tch-ns—"To see her is to love her and love but her forever."

J. L-P-wsk- —"Large she was in every way."

L. L-P-wsk- —"On their own merits modern men are dumb."

N. J-n-s—"A villian, a liar, a mean horse-thief,
All these and more make an editor-in-chief."

F. L- -v-tt—"Her sunny locks hang on her temple, like a golden fleece."

M. Lym-n—"I still see something to be done."

I. M-ll-ry—"Her voice was ever soft, gentle,
And low, an excellent thing in woman."

H. Orc-tt—"A maiden modest, yet self-possessed."

H. P-nd-xt-r—"Sober as a judge."

B. R-b-s-n—"Lips refusing out in words their mystic thoughts to dole."

E. R-z-lle—Prov. 16:18.

M. St-rk—"As good as a comedy."

Ca. St-n- —"I am nothing if not critical."

G. St-n- —"And still they gazed, and still the wonder grew,
That one small head could carry all (she thought) she knew."

E. Th-rn- —"A good child on the whole, meek, manageable."

M. Wh-tn-y—"Can any mortal mixture of earth's mould
Breathe such divine, enchanting ravishment?"

'04.

"Unthinking, idle, wild, and young."—*Anon.*

E. B-hn—"Nut-brown maiden, thou hast a slender waist to clasp."

E. Ch-ndl-r—"Known unto few, but prized as far as known."

P. D-v-s—"Pleased with a rattle, tickled with a straw."

F. Edw-rds—"Laugh and grow fat."

J. Gr-ff-n—"Seein' as a leopard can't change his spots,
I reckon you 'll allus be sorter Fresh."

E. H-nt—"I to myself am dearer than a friend.

E. W. K-mb-ll—(See below.)

G. McC-nn-ll—"Fresh as a flower."

E. L-ckw- -d—"That same face of yours looks like the title-page to a whole volume of
roguery."

G. Ordw-y—"Neat, not gaudy."

M. P-lm-r—"But what I want 's a perfect man,
Complete, and all alive."

M. P-rk-r—"And then came one of sweet and earnest looks."

D .R-g-rs—"Think of me as you please."

E. S-ss-n—"Thy locks uncombed, like a rough wind appear."

E. S-th-rl-nd—"The style is the girl."

R. T-vl-r—"The fairest rose is always the freshest."

L. Z-ll-r—"Thin as a shadow, short as a dream."

E. W. K-mb-ll—"She seemed a cherub, who had lost his way and wandered hither."

'05.

"Oh! Mirth and Innocence: Oh! Milk and Water."—*Byron.*

G. P-tt-rs-n—"Something quite out of the common."

V. T-bl-r—"So sad, so tender, and so true."

E. Wh-tl-y—"Modest she seems, not shy."

B. V- -l—"Little at the first, but mighty at the last."

L. W- -db-ry—"When there 's a man in the case,
           You know all other things give place."

SPECIALS.

"Satan finds some mischief still for idle hands to do."

M. Ab-l—"Something between a hindrance and a help."

M. Albr-ght—"If she will, she will,
          You may depend on 't;
          If she won't, she won't,
          And there 's an end on 't."

L. Al-x-nd-r—"A highly respectable young woman."

L. Armstr-ng—"In stature she was passing tall,
          And sparely formed and lean."

A. W. B-rk-r—"Upper rooms to rent she has,
          Without furniture, but with gas."

A. B-nn-tt—"She had the blithest little laugh you ever heard."

M. Bl-g- - —"None but herself can be her parellel."

S. B-wl-nd—"A heart that in her labor sings."

F. Br-w-r—"There 's little of the melancholy element in her."

M. B-ff-ngt-n—"Music hath charms to soothe the savage breast."

H. Ch-lds—"There is not such another."

D. Cl-rk—"She taketh most delight in musical instruments."

L. Cr-sby—"At every word a reputation dies."

C. C-rt-s—"She 'll grow up by and by."

A. Dw-n-ll—"Not beautiful in curve and line, but something more and better."

L. Dw-ght—"Too bright to live."

S. Dy-r—"Neat as a pin, and blooming as a rose."

B. F-lk—"Such a fresh, blooming, chubby, rosy-cosy, modest little bud."

M. Fr-nch—"Shy she was, and I thought her cold."

A. F-st-r
G. F-st-r }—"Same name, but yet how different."
L. F-st-r

A. G- -r—"My man 's as true as steel."

A. Gr- -n- —"Ah! when I see that smile appear,
          My heart again is filled with cheer."

F. H-m-lt-n—"She looks like the afternoon shadow of somebody else."

E. H-z-lt-n—"Talking she knew not why, nor cared not why."

E. H-wl-y—"I can guard my own."

F. Irw-n
M. Irw-n } "Put 'em in a bag and shake 'em,
        Yourself o' th' sudden would mistake 'em
       And not know which is which."

S. L-wr-n- - —"Light she was, and like a fairy."

G. L-th-n—"A mind not to be changed by place or time."

G. L-wr-n- -

M. M-w-r   } "We stand among them, but not of them,"

J. P-lm-r

C. LeS- -r—"A babe in a house is a well-spring of pleasure."

M. M-hl-r—"I am neither cross nor proud."

G. M-tth- -s—"Methought I heard a sound cry, 'Sleep no more.'"

M. M-ll-r—"Techy and wayward."

M. N-ls-n—"They say she knew much that she never told."

T. N-rth—"A lovely being, lithely formed and molded"(?)

E. P- -rs-n—"Every monkey will have his gambols."

A. Ph-lps—"Oh! rare the head piece, if but brains were there."

I. R-ss—"For my voice, I have lost it

With howling and singing of anthems."

R. Ryd-r—"Quick and fine-witted."

M. Sh- -lds—"What 's in a name?"

R. Sk-nn-r—"The earth has bubbles like the sea,

And this is of them."

F. Sm-th—"She wears the rose of youth upon her."

S- -thw-ck—"Why, how you stand, girl!"

C-r- St-n- —"She is so queer.   Is she a native?"

R. T-lc-tt—"But oh, my little golden head!"

J. T-rb-x—"She would not with premptory tone

Assert the nose upon her face her own."

F. T- -l- —"There are no men to conquer in this wood,

That makes my only woe."

T. Uhr-c—"Hast thy toil o'er books consumed the midnight oil?"

A. W-lls—"Be to her virtues very kind; be to her faults a little blind."

K. Wh-ld-n—"Bright gem, instinct with music—vocal spark."

SCATTERING.

Methodist Choir—"Swans sing before they die,

'T were no bad thing did certain

Persons die before they sing."

Shakespeare Class—"Time elaborately thrown away."

Annex Girls—"To mischief bent."

Chorus Classes—"Sentimentally they are disposed to harmony, but

Organically they are incapable of a tune."

Cooking Classes—"One may live without friends, one may live without books,

But civilized man cannot live without cooks."

Board of Editors—"Hush! don't disturb them,

They 're hunting for an idea."

Grinds—"Pains, reading, study, are their just pretence,

And all they want is spirit, taste, and sense."

BEFORE AND AFTER.

'Twas in the year of ninety-eight,
  One lovely Autumn day,
She left the home bequeathed by fate
  For Lasell far away.
Her trunks had all been neatly packed
  With dresses new, though plain.
There was n't a single thing she lacked,
  So thought this maiden vain.
Her hair was braided down her back
  And tied with ribbon bright.
Her dress—'t was made more like a sack
  For fear 't would be too tight.
Her walking skirt was rather short—
  Eight inches from the ground—
For well the Catalogue she 'd sought,
  That no flaws might be found.
She 'd said good-bye to every friend;
  She'd kissed her mother dear.
They little dreamed that ne'er again
  The same she 'd reappear.

        *   *   *   *   *

'T was in the spring of ninety-nine,
  One perfect day in June,

She left the school she thought so fine
  For home—'t was all too soon.
Her trunks were packed—though not
    first-rate;
  Her eyes were filled with tears.
She 'd said good-bye to all the girls
  Whom she 'd not see for years.
Her hair was coiled.   I can't tell how—
  Her dress—it fitted well—
She thought she was quite plain now,
  But really she looked swell.
Her skirt—it trailed three feet behind,
  Quite contrary to rule
The Guide had hung—Well, never mind,
  She 'd been one year at school.
She reached her home—How all did stare!
  But why, she could not guess.
Her mother knew.   This school so rare
  Does many parents bless.

    *   *   *   *   *

The moral of this little rhyme
  'T is wiser not to tell,
Lest maidens all, of every clime,
  Should heed, and seek Lasell.

LASELL LEAVES

"DUX FEMINA FACTI."

VOL. XXVI   LASELL SEMINARY, AUBURNDALE, MASS., JUNE, 1901.   NUMBER 9

Published monthly during the School year by the Lasell Publishing Association.

EDITOR-IN-CHIEF.
NELL DAVIS JONES, '03.

ASSOCIATE EDITORS.
MARINETTE RAMSDELL, '02.   FONNIE E. DAVIS.   EVA L. CHANDLER, 'o

LOCAL EDITOR.   SUBSCRIPTION AGENT.   EXCHANGE EDITOR.
LENA ARMSTRONG.   DORA E. CLARK.   M. BELL CLOKEY, '02.

BUSINESS MANAGER.   ASST. BUSINESS MANAGER.
ETHLYN F. BARBER 'o1.   JOANNA F. DEERING.

TERMS, in Advance: One copy, one year (including Postage), $1.00. Single copies, 15 cents.

Editorials.

AS the year draws to a close it is with a feeling mixed with sadness that we think of leaving. Even the thought of home does not quite make up for leaving the girls. For many weeks we have been so closely united, that we almost felt it would continue indefinitely; but the time has come to say good-bye. For those of us who are coming back next year, it will be hard not to find the Seniors, of whom we have been very proud during the past year. Never has there gone out from Lasell a class of nobler girls; and as they begin their new life we all join in wishing that their graduation day may be in truth the commencement of all success and happiness.

WE have been sorry to hear of changes in our faculty for the next year; as our Associate Principal leaves us for larger fields, we send with him all the good wishes of Lasell, but just as warmly welcome his successor.

THE announcement of the departure of our English teacher came with a great crash. She who has been such a support to Lasell for the past few years, takes a year—perhaps two—for study and rest. Our Latin teacher goes to a post in Wellesley College. Her place here will be hard to fill. We sincerely wish them both much success, and trust they will not forget Lasell and their old friends.

—Of the twelve members of the class of '57 there were present at the Semi-Centennial banquet on Commencement Day, NINE. This would be hard to beat, we think, considering the date of their graduation.

For some reason the editors of the May LEAVES overlooked the joint authorship of the latest Lasell song, and the one which we hope may touch the popular heart. In two places it gave Harriette Ward the credit of its making. We gladly make the correction, and give, as is due, to Zoe Hill the credit of the words, and to Harriette Ward that of the music.

Senior Reception.

THE class receptions at Lasell have always been among the most enjoyable of the entertainments of the year. From the opening of school they are greatly anticipated and are afterward remembered with much pleasure. But of all those of the year, none quite equals that to which favored ones are invited to meet the Senior class. This year the reception was one of the most pleasant ever held at Lasell.

The parlors were beautifully decorated with an abundance of smilax and the class flower, marguerites. The Juniors introduced the Seniors' friends to the reception committee, Mr. Bragdon, Miss Carpenter, and Miss Barber, the Senior president. Mr. Bragdon's cordial welcome at once put all at their ease, and the parlors were soon filled with a bright and happy company.

Owing to the limited space of the parlors, the gymnasium was made use of, and was uniquely decorated. Many little cosy corners covered with pillows of all descriptions completely transformed the gymnasium, and the dim light of the Japanese lanterns made one feel as if they were in fairy land.

The dining-room was also artistically arranged, and here refreshments were served by the Juniors.

Altogether, the evening was one of much enjoyment to all, and will be long remembered as one of the "events" of the year. It is to the Juniors that we owe much for the pleasant evening. Their earnest and faithful labor in a few hours transformed Lasell into a bower of beauty, and we feel that they deserve a very fine reception next year.

Junior Garden Party.

THE annual Junior Garden Party was held Saturday, June 1, but on account of the rain, the Juniors were obliged to re-sort to the gymnasium. This was decorated with the class colors and flowers; chairs, rugs, cushions and cosy corners were very artistically arranged around the room. Through the open door floated the lively music of the hurdy-gurdy, mingling with the gay conversation within.

When all were seated, the curtain was drawn, and Miss Anna Mae Pinkham rendered a beautiful solo, followed by a garden play written by Miss C. Austin and presented by eight of the Junior class. The stage was decorated with branches to represent a woodland bower, and the performers were all dressed in the garb representing some wild field flower. These were Miss Lotta Hewson as "Trailing Arbutus," Miss M. Hollenbeck as "Violet," Miss Florence Hayden as "Black-Eyed Susan, or Daisy," Miss K. Kendrick as "Golden Rod," Miss J. Deering as "Sweet William," Miss McGregor as "Forget-me-not," and the Misses Goodwin and Ellen Chase as "Quaker Ladies."

The play was very interesting and very well staged. These little flowers, after dancing and singing their fantastic songs, decided to go to the laboratory of the "giants," of whom they had heard so much. How surprised they were to find such things there as umbrellas, footballs, golf sticks, and other wonders, which they supposed were flowers of the "giants." After relating how Golden Rod had fallen in love with Violet, they ended their frolic with a song and dance, and tripped out, leaving the audience delighted with their charming ways.

A dainty repast of ice cream, cake and strawberries was served, and all left well pleased with their entertainment and the grand success of the Juniors.

Commencement Concert.

The Commencement concert, given in the gymnasium on the evening of June 6th, was, as might have been expected, the best musical entertainment of the year. The way in which the girls gave their selections showed both talent and perseverance, and reflected great credit upon their teachers. We surely have reason to be proud of Lasell's musical department.

Chorus. Hunting Chorus .... Hummel
    Hither Fairies Trip .... Tully
    Orphean Club.
Pianoforte Duo. Prelude and Fugue......... Vogt
    Miss Bowers and Mr. Hills.
Songs. q. Lieber Schatz, sei wieder gut mir..Franz
    b. My love is like a red, red rose..Hastings
    Miss Draper.
Pianoforte Polonaise .... Schumann
    Miss E. Chase.
Song. Lift thine eyes (Elijah). By request....
    Mendelssohn
    Misses Hill, Gallagher and Hamilton.
Organ Sonata in C Minor. (First three move-
    ments) .... Mendelssohn
    Miss Ward.
Song. The Throstle .... Maud Valerie White
    Miss Hill.
Pianoforte duo. Valse lente .... Lazarus
    Miss Clark and Mr. Hills.
        PART SECOND.
Violin. a. Prayer .... Weber
    b. Rondo .... David
    Misses Winn, Blackstock, Hawley, Biddle
    and Le Seure.
Song. He is kind, He is good (Hérodiade) Massenet
    Miss Gallagher.
Pianoforte. Caprice in A Major............. Hills
    Miss Cole.
Song. Vieille Chanson .... Bizet
    Miss Pinkham.
Organ. a. Intermezzo .... Dunham
    b. Fanfare .... Lemmens
    Miss Walker.
Songs. a. L'esclave .... Lalo
    b. The Quest .... Eleanor Smith
    Miss Hamilton.
Pianoforte Quartette. Symphony in C. Minor.
    (First Movement) .... Gade
    Misses G. Stone, Lum, Buffinton and Bennett.
Chorus. Down in the Dewey Dell........... Smart
    Orphean Club.

Society Banquet.

The banquet of the Lasellia Club and S. D. Society, on June seventh, was greatly enjoyed by all the guests, and was one of the most pleasant ever given at Lasell. It was a reunion of many old members who had come back for Commencement week. Early in the evening the guests met in the parlors and some minutes were spent in meeting old friends. Soon, attracted by gay music, the guests went down to the dining-room, which was decorated in the class flower, the daisy. The posts were twined with green, and daisies were heaped on the tables. The tables were arranged in the shape of a cross, At the ends of the arms sat the Lasellia president, Miss Smith, and the S. D. president, Miss Hill. At the two other ends, Miss Skinner, the toastmistress, presided, and opposite her Miss Barber, senior class president. The banquet itself was greatly enjoyed, but the best part of the evening was the toasts. As Miss Skinner rose, a pleased hush went around the room. After a clever introduction, the toastmistress announced the "Welcome," to be given by Miss Mower. The cordial words, delivered in a most charming way, made all feel at home. The response for the Seniors was given by Miss Barber, who with her graciousness won the admiration of all. Then Miss Hill gave a most interesting toast in verse on "The Scarcity of Men at Lasell," followed by a dainty little song by Miss Wheldon. The bounty of each season at Lasell was cleverly shown by Miss Brooks, and then our little trials were delightfully told of by Miss Dustin, whose merry words created much laughter. Miss Cole gave a striking picture of the future Lasell girl, and the Athletic Girl of Miss Ryder's creation captivated all. The "Farewell" was given by Miss Isabella Clemens in her usual witty manner. Before the banquet closed, impromptu toasts were given by Miss Katherine White and Miss Madora Marsh, two prominent members of last year. By all the girls and honorary members, the banquet was pronounced a decided success.

The menu was as follows:

Bouillon
Boiled Salmon and Green Peas
Cucumbers
Chicken Croquettes and Peas
Rolls
Lettuce and Tomato Salad
Olives
Frozen Pudding
Strawberries and Cream
Assorted Cake

Drill Day.

I N spite of our fears, and the rainy days preceding, Drill Day this year was just such a day as we would have chosen; clear, but not too warm. The lawn and crow's nest were gay with happy school girls and their friends on this first day of Commencement week. All through the trees and in the windows floated the red, yellow and blue bunting, no rivalry for place *this* year, but all prettily draped together, yellow for Co. A, red for Co. B, and blue for Co. C. At three the orchestra started to play, and soon the excited but well trained girl-soldiers of Co. A were told to "fall in." After First Sergeant Ida Mallory had brought the company to position and called the roll, the captain took command and with her clear, strong voice directed her company and took them through the manual of arms, amid the cheers of the onlookers. It was easy to see that the company had been in excellent training and had learned to work together as one under the direction of their competent and most faithful captain, Ethel Gallagher. When Co A was dismissed amid the cheers of all and the clashing of the many little souvenir swords, the orchestra played again. As they played two merry friends of Co. B. led across the drill ground a black goat, the mascot of Co. B. His majesty seemed not to mind his decoration of red bunting nor the beating of Co. B's small souvenir drums, but behaved in a true mascotly manner. Then

Co. B "fell in," all full of eagerness to do their well-trained best for the dearest captain that ever commanded a company; who could do otherwise than work to win under the guidance and faithful training of such a leader as Captain Floss Plum? After Co. B, the Junior prize squad showed how the well trained individual goes to make up the perfect company. Company C, under command of Captain Mabel Martin, showed a new course of training for second year work, a course in manual of arms instead of the bayonet drill, as in the past. The officers' sabre drill, next, was commanded by Captain Adjutant Harris and exhibited some excellent training, and also showed the great advantage of the new steel sabres over the wooden ones, which have been the trial of the officers in former years. The senior prize squad followed, commanded by Captain Martin. Then the prettiest feature of the day, the Battalion Parade, under command of Captain Gallagher, as acting major, closed the successful programme of the day. Then the girls seemed real soldiers, as marching in the three companies, commanded by their respective lieutenants, they passed in review before their captains and major, with the colors flying in the front rank of Co. B. The flag was carried by Standard Bearer Sue T. Lair. After much deliberation on the part of the judges, who had hard work to determine between the companies on account of their most excellent practice, the following prizes were awarded while the battalion stood at attention: Prize banner, Co. B, Captain Floss Plum, Indianapolis, Ind. Senior squad, first prize, Bessie Sanger Krag, Columbus, Ohio. Junior squad, first prize, Ethel Kile Rozelle, Concord, N. H.; second prize, Edith Eloise Sisson, Binghamton, N. Y. Sabre drill, first prize, Ida Minnie Mallory. Franklin, Pa.; second prize, Georgie Mayhew Duncan, Bath, Me. Honorable mention, senior squad, Ida Mallory; junior squad, Sarah Dyer; sabre drill, Bessie Krag.

· Baccalaureate · Sermon.

A more beautiful Baccalaureate Sunday could not have dawned than June ninth; and it was indeed a fitting ending for the helpful year which had passed. A happy procession walked from Lasell to the church preceded by the Faculty. The church was decorated with yellow and white bunting, the class colors, and marguerites, the flower. At the back of the pulpit hung the handsomely embroidered class banner. All this harmonized well with the service which followed. The sermon was given by Prof. S. F. Upham, D. D., LL. D., of Drew Theological Seminary, Madison, New Jersey. He was assisted in the service by Rev. Mr. Southgate, Rev. Mr. Worth and Bishop W. F. Mallalieu of Auburndale. The text was found in Psalms 61 : 1-2, "Hear my cry, O God; attend unto my prayer. From the end of the earth will I cry unto thee, when my heart is overwhelmed; lead me to the Rock that is higher than I."

The helpful thoughts might be summed up in the following: Once there was a castle and near it was a large rock. The owner of this castle had wires connect the two, thus making an Æolian harp. The winds played over them in the summer, however, and no music was produced; but when the storms of winter came, and heavy winds played upon the wires, wonderful music came therefrom. So it is with us. There are the human chords of sympathy and affection, and when the storms come into our lives, these chords sound.

A modern literary critic says that "the poets' finest works are productions in moments of sorrow." Everyone is acquainted with Milton's "Paradise Lost," and it is a liberal education for one to know it, and yet Milton's blindness was the cause of some of his finest passages. We all know that famous hymn of Cowper's, which was written when he knew an attack of insanity was about to come to him:

> "God moves in a mysterious way,
> His wonders to perform,
> He plants his footsteps in the sea,
>   And rides upon the storm."

So when David sang this Psalm, he was troubled. Absalom had planned a revolt. David had been compelled to leave his home and he knew not what was coming. A weight was upon him, but in all this great storm of life he was able to say, "Lead me to the Rock that is higher than I." When Paul and Silas were in prison, with nothing surrounding them but bare walls and the bars of the prison door, certainly the storm of life had come upon them, and yet I have no doubt but what they sang this Psalm of David's. The Psalms are today like so many speaking-tubes in every chamber of sorrow, through which we cry unto God.

"Life" is the instinctive cry of humanity. One time I was on a train and a man came and sat in the seat with me. I suppose he noticed by my dress that I was a clergyman, for very soon he began to talk on religious subjects. He said he was not an atheist, because he believed in God; but he did not believe in prayer, and he repeated several times that he did not believe in a hereafter. When the train reached its destination and we went to get off, I noticed a band of mourning on his hat. I turned to him and asked him if he had lost a friend. He turned to me, his lip quivered, and he said, "Yes, my wife died a few weeks ago and she is in heaven now." So I found a way to that man's heart and I found that, after all, 'way down deep in his heart he believed in a life eternal.

Every man has the instinct of prayer. He may not show it, but it is there and has only to be found. Let me take for an illustration Peter in prison. Not far from that prison is a little company gathered together to pray. They are *earnestly* and humbly praying to God that Peter might be taken from prison. They know not how, but leave it wholly in God's hands, and in the night an angel came and took Peter out, and their prayer was answered. For another illustration take a calm, bright morning, a little party going out for a day's outing. On the water all is peaceful and quiet. It is a very gay party and perhaps many things are said which are not pleasing to God. In the middle of the afternoon the wind begins to blow; a storm is coming on; peals of thunder are heard, and their little boat is tossing with the waves. The party sees there is danger and instinctively a prayer goes forth from each of those hearts.

David's cry was mysterious. He was alone and talking with One whose face he had never seen and whose voice he had never heard. It was mysterious. So is our talking with one another mysterious. I stand facing you and throw out words into the air, and they come to you. This is the finite talking with the finite. But when a man is in his closet *alone,* he knows there is no human voice to hear him, no human eye to see him. Then it is the finite talking with the Infinite. Prayer is the speaking to God at any time, in any place, on any subject.

How often you hear this objection to prayer: It is an interference with nature. How do you know? What ground have you for that statement? The law of nature is that rain will wet you, but you can have a roof between you and the rain. You do not consider the roof an interference with this law of nature. No more is prayer an interference with any law of nature.

Does God care for the individual? Let us see by this illustration: There is a ship, behind that ship is a small boat, and in the boat is a man holding an end of a rope in his hand. The other end of this rope is fastened to the ship, and no matter how hard the man pulls, he cannot make the ship come to him, but he can come to the ship. Man is not insignificant. He has but to reach out to God, and God will draw him near to Himself, and prayer is the connecting link between him and God, and is the rope to which the man can cling and thus pull himself to God. No place is so accessible as the throne of Grace.

Class Night.

A T last the long looked for Class Night, with all its pleasant surprises, has come and gone. The Seniors of '01 may well be proud of the success which was the result of patient and untiring energy. Long before seven o'clock the gymnasium began to fill up with expectant relatives, friends and classmates, and by eight all were in their places, awaiting the coming of the Seniors. In they came, a stately procession of sixteen noble girls, bearing on their shoulders daisy chains and singing as they went. On they marched until the front was reached, when the files parted, going to either side; there the Juniors received the daisy chains, and the two bands of Seniors united to form a semi-circle across the stage. After the song was finished and all had taken their places, Ethlyn Barber, their beloved president, stepped forward and gave us one and all a hearty welcome. Now that Class Night had truly begun, we were glad to hear Zoe Hill's "Roll Call." All were present and appeared when called for. Feeling it was necessary to give "A Word to the Wise," Isabella Clemens, our philosopher, gave her friends several good suggestions, such as: petitions should be drawn up with great tact; walks should be cut to obtain the privilege of gymnasium, and Roman History should not be neglected. For fear such sound advice might be lost if not allowed time to be absorbed, the Seniors sang, "Oh, We are Sixteen Seniors."

Now followed a solemn event, which solemnity we were all able to appreciate after our Law lectures, for it was nothing more or less than the drawing up of the "Last Will and Testament of 1901" by Edith Dustin, and signed by Harriette Ward, Lelia Walker and Katherine McCoy. It was thoughtful of the Seniors to think of us at a time of such importance, and we wish to thank them for the appropriate gifts, the Junior president receiving a cap and gown, Mollie Mower will not need to tramp around Boston after bargains, thanks to her *Bargain Columns*, and Edith Pearson was thoughtfully provided with *samples* and *hair-tonic*.

Ina Scott next gave the "Class Prophecy." We all enjoyed seeing Ethlyn as an old maid, Cleora as a Red Cross nurse and Edith Dustin looked like her own dear self. The three athletic girls, Zoe, the famous rider, Harriette, a crack sportsman, and Floss, whose husband is an admiral.

/ "*Non Nobis Solum*," the class motto, was, shall I say, well explained by Florence Plum. She ended her talk by presenting the school with an elegant silver loving-cup, which is to be used at all future Class Nights./ Then our Bessie Lum told us in such a dear manner the Seniors' "Farewell," which was followed by a song.

Hastening out to the lawn, which was brilliantly lighted by electric lights scattered among the dark foliage, along the banks of the drive, along the porch, and collected to form an "01" on the front bank, we saw the Seniors and their "supes" After marching around the lawn, Ethel Gallagher gave to the Juniors the bench near the front porch as the "Senior Seat." Her address, "You're Naughty Two," was given while the procession halted around this seat. Then came the "Last Rites and Ceremonies" around the bonfire. Margaret Fisher as speaker, called each girl by name to sacrifice some treasure of her school years. Many were the interesting and amusing gifts. Ina Scott has caused a loss to the world by burning her art studies, while Zoe Hill sacrificed all the Senior privileges which had been gained by a petition which was read and burned by Bessie Lum. But the greatest of all was that of Floss Plum, who as she threw her Roman History on the fire, exclaimed "Rome, Rome, thou hast been a tender nurse to me." After singing another song, the Seniors seated themselves around the fire and drank from the loving-cup. Lastly was sung a song, "We're Going," written for the music of "Old Black Joe." Thus ended the Class Night of '01.

Roll Call of the Class of '01.

I.

Listen, my children, and you shall hear
Of the wonderful class of this very year.
On the eleventh of June, in naughty-one,
The very smartest class under the sun,
Graduates from Lasell, their school so dear.

II.

I tell you, my friends, if this class would but start
To show you the wonderful members within it,
Your breath would come fast; so, the beats of your heart,
And your wonder would cease that I'm proud to be in it.
Our president grand will first stand before you.
I tell you, dear people, she's beaten by few.
Her name it is Barber, the locket she wears,
To open and look into, nobody dares.

III.

Next on our list is a girl, who by some
Is considered a maiden most wise and sedate.
Let me introduce to you Miss Betsy Ann Lum.
To taste of her cooking may it soon be your fate.

Tho' rainy the weather, a small Pooler, two
Won't keep her away when at class she is due.
In Bible especially she's a bright light,
She shines in her lessons, yet goes out at night.

IV.

No fisher of minnows, this naughty one, sure,
Who takes squelches so sweetly, she deserves a gold
　　badge.
With her line and her fly 't is big game she'll allure,
This heart-breaking, cake-making, squelch-taking
　　Madge.
Then a maiden from Texas; she paints for the class.
A gay poster printer, an artistic lass.
Who is she, pray tell you, this maiden much sought?
She's one of our number; here she comes, "O great
　　Scott."

V.

"Issy," the critic, debater so grand,
Her glasses and stature, her nature belie.
She laughs and she giggles behind her white hand,
This dignified Senior, our smart Clemens, I.
A kitten we have, who, although very small,
In the size of her brain she has beaten us all.
Kid McCoy, you have heard of that person, no doubt,
Best not quarrel with her, she's a champion stout.

VI.

Now comes Mabel Martin, a girl whom we all
Consider in physical culture a queen.
At all times of night she roams through the hall,
Yet no teacher this reckless young maiden has seen.
Next comes a maid fond of high stocks and curls,
Wise sayings fall from her mouth like rare pearls.
To her drill maidens all she's a joy and a spur,
Loud rings the shout, "Let her go, Gallagher."

VII.

A girl of pure gold is our true Lelia Walker,
If you want a rare treat, you should just hear her
　　play.
She's not much of a brag, nor yet a great talker,
Let the organ speak for her, by night or by day.
This maiden you see is the life of our table,
To get words in edgewise, no one else is e'er able.
With knowledge and secrets this maiden is bustin',
This wee little, queer little, dear little Dustin.

VIII.

This girl, my dear people, to join us was last.
Her name is Cleora Jane Peabody Brooks.
'T would have been a great grief to us had she not
　　passed.
We like her ambition, as well as her looks.
Here is a girl whom I know you'll agree
Is jolly as ever a maiden can be;
She smiles, and she smiles, and she never is glum,
Of this whole class she's our sweet sugar "Plum."

IX.

Here's another small maid who worked hard for our
　　class,
She's like a young bird, always bobbing her head.
She has one great failing, over which I can't pass,
Harriette Ward will be good, if on sugar she's fed.
Marian, Marian, why hasten so?
The bell only rang just an hour ago.
Don't worry, my dear, the teachers can wait;
For, you know, they know truly, Cole *never* is late.

X.

And now comes the last and the least of us girls,
In writing and speaking she has little skill,
Her audience quakes when her sweet voice she hurls,
This new Sarah Bernhardt, renowned Hamlet Hills.
Our class as a whole is a wondrous fine crowd.
We're neither too quiet, nor are we too loud.
There are some of us weighty, and some of us lean,
And taken together, we're just sweet sixteen.

The Following are the Songs Sung.

I.

At last this year has reached its close,
And we sad Seniors are,
For all is o'er nor as before
We'll work and study more.
But still as Seniors true we'll be,
And not forget our school.
We'll sing it here
With right good cheer,
We'll not forget Lasell.

Chorus.

Oh, dear Lasell,
We love thee well,
And e'er for thee our praise shall tell.
How dear thou art
To each girl's heart;
We wish we did not have to part.

II.

We wonder now what we shall do,
But yet we cannot tell.
Our school days here we've spent with cheer
And they will be most dear.
But now as we at last must part,
Though sad each heart must be,
We'll sing it here,
With right good cheer,
We'll not forget Lasell.

III.

We thank our teachers for their care,
For they have been most kind.
Our schoolmates whom we love so well
We hate to leave behind.
Within our hearts a love we find
For all that's in this school;

We 'll sing it here,
With right good cheer,
We 'll not forget Lasell.
Sung "To Charity" from "Miss Simplicity."

Oh, we are sixteen Seniors,
And we feel so very gay,
For Class night now has come at last,
And soon we 'll go away.
We carry here a daisy chain
Just for a pretty sight;
Our class flower is a marguerite,
Our colors gold and white.
Chorus.

Now at last we 'll graduate,
Diplomas we 'll have soon;
We thought so many times this year
We 'd surely meet our doom.
Our Roman History it was hard,
Our English, too, alack!
But if you said we would not win
You 'd better take it back.
Chorus.

Naughty Ones, they are all right,
You 'll find it ever true;
There only are sixteen of us,
But yet we are not so few.
The teachers tried to scare us—
Said for study we had no knack,
But if you said we would not win,
You 'd better take it back.
Chorus.

We 've studied Lit. and Logic,
Both Bible, French, and Art,
And now as we have learned so much,
We think we 'll make a start.
And then, besides, we learned to float,
And so you must n't talk;
We 'll sail on all the rest of life
And never have to walk.
Chorus.

We gave a little play one night,
Which really showed our knack.
It brought us fifty dollars,
And now we 'll give it back.
For in our will we 've left some things
We 've chosen with fine tact.
But if you do not like our gifts,
Why, you can give them back.
Sung to "You 'd Better Take It Back," from "Miss Simplicity."

Sung as the Class Marched Out.

We're the ones, the very Naughty Ones,
That have caused you so much trouble.

All the other classes had such lovely names;
Ours the only naughty one.
When next year we 're no longer here,
Naughty Ones will be forgotten.
All the other classes are so very good;
Ours the only naughty one.

Sung to "Old Black Joe," Around the Camp Fire.

Gone are the days when we first met here so gay;
Gone are the days with the end so far away.
Into the past they slip as on this night
We leave our Alma Mater for the world's great fight.
Chorus.

We 're going, we 're going,
From the school we love so well.
We 'll always have a memory sweet
Of dear Lasell.

Gone are the days of our jolly Junior year.
We suped and worked for the other Seniors dear.
What happy days looking forward to the goal,
So steadily advancing as the moments roll.
Chorus.

Gone are the days of our Senior year so bright,
How dear to us they are upon this night
We 've studied hard to learn our lessons well,
And as we leave, we 'll give a cheer for dear Lasell.
Chorus.

Commencement Day.

THE Commencement exercises were held at the Congregational church in the afternoon of Tuesday, June 11. After the opening prayer, Mrs. Thompson, an old Lasell girl (Sadie Hollingsworth) sang very sweetly several songs. Rev. S. Parkes Cadman, the speaker of the afternoon, a well-known clergyman of Brooklyn, gave us a most interesting talk. He spoke upon the Puritan's message to the twentieth century, and his words were most helpful and uplifting. He showed us the greatness of Puritanism, and the sterling qualities of the Puritan stock. We were made to realize that a country may have learning of the highest sort, may excel in all the fine arts, may be in advance of other nations in many of the things that tend to make a nation great, and still decline and fall. The reason of this is that such countries lack that faith which America had so strongly marked in her first settlers; and the message of these Puritans to us is, "Be true to yourself, be true to your fellowmen, be true to your God." In the special address to the graduating class, Dr. Cadman said, "Members of the graduating class of 1901, sixty-three years ago a young girl no older than you, and younger than many of you, was crowned at Westminster Abbey. . . . As this girl queen of eighteen received the crown she said, 'I will maintain, God being my help.' . . . . When this good Queen Victoria died the people said, "She has maintained." Can you maintain as she did?" After this the class came forward, and Mr. Bragdon presented the diplomas; the benediction was then pronounced.

/ At five o'clock came the banquet, given by the Seminary in celebration of the completion of its fiftieth year. Mr. George L. Briggs and Miss Lilla M. Briggs, children of former Principal Briggs, were present, as were also Miss Louise Lasell and Mrs. Ellen Lasell Gould, children of the founder, Edward Lasell. There were in attendance a large number of the alumnæ, the oldest being Mrs. Whitin, of the class of '55' and many of the friends and patrons of the school. /

An appetizing feast was provided, after which Miss Lillie Rose Potter, class of '80' acted as toastmistress. Mrs. Isabella Jennings Parker, class of '57' spoke of the "Lasell of Earlier Time," giving various pleasant reminiscences of the early days of the Seminary, dwelling especially upon the lovable characters of the two earliest principals. Mr. Edward F. Porter, one of the trustees at the time when Mr. Bragdon entered upon the principalship in '74' spoke about "The Old and the New," giving some account of the manner in which the school came to be

financially embarrassed, and how Mr. Bragdon became its principal and rescued it from its impending insolvency, establishing it on a firm foundation and carrying it on to its present successful condition. Mr. Alfred Hemenway, who was to speak upon the subject of "Law," was unexpectedly absent. Mrs. Ellen H. Richards, of the Institute of Technology, responded to the toast, "The Economic Woman—Her Future." The future of this woman (in none so well represented as in Mrs. Richards herself), the scientifically trained woman, she believed to be emphatically the woman of the future. To Mr. Bragdon she paid the fine compliment of saying that though she had herself often wavered in her belief that it is the best thing to bring the kitchen into the classroom, to make the ordinary work of the home the subject of scientific study, he never had. Rev. Dr. A. B. Kendig, in his speech on "How I Know It," told what splendid things Lasell did for his own daughters, who were educated here; and Rev. Dr. F. N. Peloubet amusingly remarked on Lasell's many excellences as a next-door neighbor. Bishop W. F. Mallalieu, responding to the toast, "Better to Come," emphasized the value of the good home to the indivdual, to the community, to the nation. Mrs. Whitin, being called upon for a few words, responded very briefly, her friend, Miss Louise Manning Hodgkins, supplementing her words in a short, bright speech. Mrs. Mary A. Livermore, speaking of present lacks, told with much interest certain experiences of hers in her youthful efforts to secure a liberal education; of her doubts, in earlier days, as to the wisdom of Lasell's ideas of making the study of cookery a part of the work to be done in school, and of her subsequent belief that it was really a good thing to do this.

Dr. Bragdon then made a short speech, in

LASELL LEAVES 221

which he paid a fine tribute to Miss Caroline A. Carpenter and Miss Angeline C. Blaisdell, both invaluable assistants ever since he first took charge of the school in 1874, and to Mrs. H. N. Noyes, of Andover, who had for years helped him by wise counsel and effective co-operation. He introduced Mr. George F. Jewett, of Youngstown, O., as Associate principal of Lasell. Mr. Jewett briefly responded, saying that he should endeavor to act in this capacity in accordance with the methods and principles so long recognized at Lasell.

An interesting feature of the celebration was the presentation by the alumnæ, to the school, of fine portraits of Edward Lasell, the founder, and of Mr. Briggs, the first principal. The widow of Mr. Josiah Lasell had presented a portrait of her husband, and Dr. Cushing lately sent his, so that the school has now fine pictures of four of its former principals.

Dr. Peloubet's Response to the Toast, "Lasell as a Next Door Neighbor."

THE old Greek is said to have placed a higher price upon his house because of its neighbors. And certainly if I were compelled to sell my house, the first inducement I would offer to a buyer would be that it is close to Lasell, which spreads before my windows its well kept lawn and noble trees, and its lighted windows brightening the evening view with its stars.

When I thought of buying the lot where my house stands, I was several times warned against it on account of the music lessons at Lasell. A piano in this room would be playing a sonata of Beethoven, and in that room a concerto of Chopin, and in a third, the anvil chorus; while overhead a soloist would be training her voice to vie with Patti, on the piazza below a group of girls would be singing college songs, with an occasional

hand organ thrown in for good measure—all going at one and the same time.

The fact is that one of the pleasantest things about being a neighbor to Lasell is connected with the sweet sounds that come through the trees. I have been told that somewhere in the upper air there is a certain point where all the sounds of earth; the cries of the beggars; the rattle of the wagons; the shouts of the boys; the whistle of the engines; the barking of dogs, and the singing of the birds, are in perfect harmony. That point so far as Lasell is concerned is exactly at my house.

Then in the early summer evenings, when the girls gather on the front lawn in beautiful dresses and gay ribbons, they make me think of the picturesque word by which St. Mark describes the crowds upon the grassy plain where Jesus fed the 5,000, as parterres of flowers. It is a very attractive display. And with the golf course, and the stories of the lost ball, and a free invitation to play, there is much that is charming. After eleven years' residence as a neighbor of Lasell, I think of the story of the little girl who asked her father, who was somewhat old and homely, "Did God make you?" "Yes." "And did he make mother?" (who was young and handsome). "Yes." "Well, how much he has improved!" I think it must have been the family to which the previous speaker referred. (Audience, "oh! oh!" Then I forgot that he was speaking of himself. I am like the man Frank Beard speaks of, "He never opens his mouth but he puts his foot in it.")

As I was coming from the services this afternoon I noticed one of the essays was entitled the "Gospel of the Quiet Hour." I know the essay must be as good as the subject. But if Miss Mabel Martin, the writer of it, will come to my house a week from tonight and note the deserted lawns and the dark windows and the stillness that can be felt, she will have some new impressions about the quiet hour. For my part, I sympathize with the reply of Dr. Tyng, of New York, to a gentleman who wanted to join his church in order to be at rest the remaining years of his life. The Dr. told him that he had better join the church of the Heavenly Rest, as his church was the church of the Earthly Activities. Give me the activities of my neighbor Lasell, rather than the quiet hours after Commencement.

"Oh! solitudes, where are the charms
That sages have found in thy face!
I'd rather dwell in the midst of alarms,
(From stray golf balls!)
Than look at that desolate place!"

In conclusion I will give a toast. Dr. Geo. Gordon began one of his Lowell lectures, not long ago, with the story of the prayer of a Presbyterian minister for the Queen of England in her presence at the church: "May our Queen, as she grows to be an old woman, become a new man, and in all works of righteousness may she go forth before her people like a he-goat upon the mountains." Such is the toast I would give to Lasell. And you will understand its meaning better if you will turn to Proverbs 30 : 31, and see that the he-goat is one of four things that have the strength and beauty of healthy activity, and are "comely in their going."

And of your beloved principal, may I say in the words of the Duke of Buckingham about his king:

"May he live
Longer than I have time to tell his years;
Ever beloved, and loving, may his rule be;
And when old Time shall lead him to his end,
Goodness and he fill up one monument."

At the Business meeting of the Alumnæ, the following officers were elected: President, Mrs. C. E. Parker, '57; vice presidents, Miss Edith Gale, '89, Mrs. G. D. Gilman, '67; secretary, Miss Grace Loud, '95;

treasurer, Miss Ruth Rishell, '99; executive committee, Miss Martha Lucas, '60, Miss Lillian Packard, '83, Miss Jessie Macmillan, '82, Mrs. F. D. Sampson, '57, Miss Lillie R. Potter, '80.

Former Pupils at Commencement.

Sarah Pratt Whitin, '55, Whitinsville; Mary P. Jones, '56, Newton; Fanny Gray Merrick, '56, Walpole; Mary Shaw Rogers, '56, St. Louis, Mo.; Martha E. Stone, '56, Newton Centre; Charl A. K. Bancroft, '57, Wellesley Hills; Fannie Sykes Davis, '57, Newton Centre; Adelaide Sears Gilman, '57, Newton; Emma Sears May, '57, Newton; Sarah Hills Hitchcock, '57, Newton; Abbie Hills Holbrook, '57, Newton; Isabel Jennings Parker, '57, Auburndale; Flora Drew Sampson, '57, Newton; Carrie Spear, '57, Newton, Susan Hall, Blount, '60, Wellesley; Lucy Rogers Gove '60, Minneapolis, Minn.; Martha B. Lucas, '60, Boston; Caroline Hills Leeds, '61, Newton; Rosaella Perkins Cook, '66, Natick; Angeline C. Blaisdell, '67, Auburndale; Sarah F. Boynton, '67, Allston; Ella Richardson Cushing, '73, Boston; Marion E. Gilmore, '76, Cambridge; Jennie Darling Folsom, '78, Lyndonville, Vt.; Carrie Kendig Kellogg, '79, Brookline; Irene G. Sanford, '79, Boston; Lucy E. Curtis, '80, Rockland; Lillie R. Potter, '80, Boston; Sophie Mason Dumas, '83, Lowell; Lillian M. Packard, '83, South Boston; Nellie Packard Draper, '84, Westford; Lillie Fuller Merriam, '85, South Framingham; Blanche Ford Hill, '86, Boston; Mosetta Stafford Vaughan, '86, Watertown; Annie M. Gwinnell, '88, Newark, N. J.; Elizabeth Eddy Holden, '88, Dorchester; Nettie F. Woodbury, '91, Beverly; Mary P. Witherbee, '92, Laurel, Del.; Jennie Arnold Felt, '93, Peabody; Nellie M. Richards, '93, Groton; Dasie A. Hartson, '94, Napa, Cal.; K. Belle Bragdon, '95, Auburndale; Grace E. Loud, '95, Everett; Mabel M. Lutes, '95, Indianapolis, Ind.; Mabel Sawyer Rogers, '95, Newton Centre; Josephine B. Chandler, '96, Malden; Annie F. Cushing, '96, Foxcroft, Me.; Bessie S. Hayward, '96, Temple, N. H.; Edith A. Dresser, '97, Charlotte, N. C.; Nellie J. Feagles, '97, Toledo, O.; Grace P. Washburn, '97, Melrose; Carrie Kendall, '98, Leominster; Alice A. Kimball, '98, Presque Isle, Me.; Ruth K. Merriam, '98, Meriden, Conn.; Emily A. Bissell, '99, Rockville, Conn.; Emma F. Cleaves, '99, Pigeon Cove; Mabel Currie Hill, '99, Norwalk, Conn.; Ethel Johnson, '99, Hallowell, Me.; Katherine S. Mason, '99, Boone, Ia.; Edith F. Moulton, '99, Salem; Helen Rishell, '99, Newtonville; Ruth Rishell, '99, Newtonville; Elise E. Scott, '99, Chestnut Hill; Mary B. Vance, '99, Cambridge; Gertrude Watson Linscott, '99, North Woburn; Alice Ashley, '00, Norwood, N. Y.; Ella B. Cotton,

'oo' Omaha, Neb.; Agnes Flaherty, 'oo, Massena, N.
Y.; Blanche E. Gardner, 'oo, Wilkes Barre, Pa.; An-
nie E. Ives, 'oo, Meriden, Conn.; Helen M. Ramsdell,
'oo, Woburn, Mass.; Eva S. Raymond, 'oo' Salem,
Mass.; Elsie Reynolds, 'oo' E. Haddam, Conn.;
Katherine V. White, 'oo' Parkersburg, W. Va.; Ed-
na Cooke, W. Winsted, Conn.; Elsie F. Clarke, Fair-
haven; Annie Clark, Cambridge; Nellie Chamber-
layne, Cazenovia, N. Y.; Elizabeth Cossar,
Manchester, N. H.; Helen Deering, Saco,
Me.; Myra Davis, Weston; Mabel Eager,
Auburndale; Mabelle Gamwell, Pittsfield;
Clarissa Hammond, Lyons, N. Y.; Marion Harrow-
er, Wilkes Barre, Pa.; Georgie Lord, Irvington-on-
Hudson, N. Y.; Bertha Metcalf, Plainville; Madora
Marsh, Glens Falls, N. Y.; Katherine Moses, Saco,
Me.; May E. Merrill, South Framingham; Mrs. Pliny
Nickerson, Newton Highlands; Alberta Peck, Col-
chester, Conn.; Alice Taylor Potter, New-
ton Centre; Bertha Sheldon, Providence, R.
I.; Edith Locke Slaten; Harriet Sawyer,
Brookline; Marion Safford, Sharon; Marion
Stafford, Fall River; Margaret Tarr, Gloucester;
Helen Wiedenmayer, Newark, N. J.; Eleanor Waite,
West Newton; Grace Wells, Kingston, R. I.; Elsie
Woodbury, Beverly; Frances Wood, Worcester;
Sade Hollingsworth Thompson, Evansville, Ind.;
Clara Robbins, Nashua, N. H.; Clementina Butler,
Newton Centre; Lina Maynard Bramhall, Lowell;
Nellie Briggs, Somerville.

Club Notes.

NEXT YEAR.

President .... Miss Marion Mann
Vice President............... Miss Frances Leavitt
Secretary .... Miss Mabel Goodwin
Treasurer .... Miss Bessie Draper
Executive Com.....Misses Howes, Hayden, Hewson
Critic .... Miss Edith Sisson

FOR NEXT YEAR.

President .... Miss Deering
Vice President .... Miss Kendrick

Secretary .... Miss McGregor
Business Manager .... Miss Lapowski
Executive Com....Misses Chase, Taylor, E. Clemens
Critic .... Miss Wheldon
Guard .... Isabelle Blackstock

CLUB SONG.

Who, oh, who, is the girl who is fair and bright?
Who, oh, who, is the girl that hates wrong, loves
  right?
Strong in muscle, firm in mind,
Happy in spirit, true and kind,
She is the girl with the monogram hat,
Heart-shaped pin with an owl in the middle of that,
Merry of face and air so gay,
Listen and you will hear her say:
Shout D. A. N.; here's to Lasellia,
Loud as you can, cheer for Lasellia.
Ever be true to the gold and blue,
Raise on high the banner of Lasellia.

April 17—The Lasell battalions were roy-
ally entertained at Newtonville by the
Charles Ward Post of the G. A. R. The
evening was very much enjoyed, and each
girl was presented, as a memento, an army-
button hatpin.

April 20—The Missionary Society invited
us into the gymnasium to hear the "Cradle
Songs of Different Nations, given in Costume." All the different peoples were represented, and the "lullabys" finished, the audience moved around the room to gaze and
laugh at the photographs of the Lasell girls
as they appear at the tender ages of between
two and five years.

On the evening of April 27 the Juniors
and Specials, with a few favored friends,
were received by the Faculty in the parlors
of Lasell. When all had assembled, there

was a short programme, followed by light refreshments. Then came the usual rush for trains, all the guests realizing that when the Faculty feels inclined to entertain, one is assured of a "good time."

Sunday evening, April 28, Frances Hamilton kindly agreed to give a song recital in the gymnasium, assisted by a selected quartette. The girls brought their cushions with them, in order to sit comfortably on the floor, and fully enjoyed Frances' ever-popular singing.

On May 1st, after much surmising on the nature of the entertainment, we were invited by the Sophomore class to come into the gymnasium for a May Day party, including a May Pole dance, in which the entire class of 1903 participated. The different features of the dance were well done and heartily applauded by the audience, from their reserved seats on the floor. The pole having been set aside, the girls danced to the inviting strains of an orchestra, until at a late hour duty, in the guise of Miss Carpenter, suggested our dispersion.

Thursday evening, May 2, Miss Frances Eaton gave us some of her humorous character sketches, which were truly delightful and unique.

On Sunday evening, May 5th, we had the pleasure of listening to another song recital, the solo parts being carried by Ethel Gallagher, while the girls present joined in on all the Gospel Hymns.

May 11 the girls assembled in the "gym" to listen to the wonderful melodies of the Claflin University Quintette. The boys sang well and were cordially invited to come again next year.

On the evenings of May 20, 21 and 22, Miss Mary A. Mullikin of Cincinnati, Ohio, gave a series of lectures, beginning Monday evening with the "Morning and Noon of Flemish Art." The subjects of the three other lectures were "A Treasure Hunt in the Spanish Peninsula" and "Raphael, the Decorator," and "Creeds in Stone." The subjects were very interesting and were rendered still more so by the sketched and photographed illustrations.

Thursday evening, May 23, Mr. William J. Mann lectured on "Art in History."

Est Il Possible !

She was a little polyglot,
 Was sweet Clorinda Belle;
And puzzled much her precious brain
 To learn her "language" well.
And how she practiced on them,
 The patient folk at home!
They sometimes wished to boarding school
 They had not let her roam.
When they of some small thing would tell.
 "*Est il possible!*" cried Clorinda Belle.

With Brother Will a-bicycling
 Clorinda rode one day,
And as they wheeled they chatted of
 The beauties of the way.
Clorinda tucked in German
 As often as she could,
To prove to him her accent was
 Unusually good.
And once, when from his wheel Will fell,
 "*Eheu! quid agis?*" shrieked Clorinda Belle.

But most in exclamations
 She spoke, this learned maid,
And had a favorite phrase or two,
 Which she full oft displayed.
Her country cousin, come to town
 To visit her one day,
Had on, it chanced, a brand-new gown,
 A marvel—*in its way.*
And when fair Susan of its cost did tell,
 "*Est il possible!*" said Clorinda Belle.

Her mother sent Clorinda down
 To ask the old black cook
To teach her how to make a cake
 From Mrs. Lincoln's book.
The cook explained the process,
 The novice standing by,
And then she got materials,
 And told her she might try.
That cake—like Babylon, it fell!
 "*Est il possible!*" sighed Clorinda Belle.

One time too oft she used this phrase,
 And worked herself much woe,
As you'll acknowledge when I tell

What 't was that grieved her so.
John Jack came wooing her one day—
She loved the lad full fain,
But all unwittingly she caused
Him woful grief and pain.
"My darling girl," he said, "I love you well!"
"*Est il possible!*" gasped Clorinda Belle.

The startled youth, who could not know
How fast her heart was beating,
Thought only, "She is making game!"
And lost no time retreating.
Poor Clo was left alone. She gazed—
In tears her brown eyes swimming—
Down street, where fast the manly form
Of her John Jack was dimming.
And as he rushed along pell-mell,
"*Est il possible!*" wept Clorinda Belle.

Moral: Study your French and escape the toils of matrimony.

Query: (from the standpoint of Clorinda Belle's father): Does boarding school pay?

From Fair Freshman to Sedate Senior.

DRAMATIS PERSONAE.

CHARLES .... King of Lasell
LADY CAROLINE ....Lady of Lasell Palace
FRIAR CHARLES .... The King's Assistant
GUY .... Prince of the House of Hur
MISTRESS MARY .... Tutor to the Sophomores
MARTHA .... Mistress of Artillery Room
Freshmen   Sophomores
     Juniors   Seniors

THE COMEDY OF ERRORS.
Scene—Lasell Palace.
PROLOGUE.
Enter Chorus.
Chorus—
"In fair Lasell, where we lay our scene,
All has been quiet, calm, serene;
But now there bursts through its spacious halls,
Laughing shouts and merry calls.
Girls old and new alike are here,
All united to bring good cheer.
The old—familiar with everything seem;
The new—how solemn! fresh! and green!
ACT I.
Scene 1—Court Room (office) Lasell Palace.
Enter King Charles, Lady Caroline, Freshmen.
King—Ah! here come the freshmen fair,
In this comedy they're to share.
See! in fright how they do shake,
And many "errors" will they make.
Lady Caroline—I think it a very good plan to have

a code of laws for the freshmen. They seem a little wild and need to be brought under some restriction.
King—I agree with you, but would advise to have the laws just as "few" as possible.
Lady Car.—I was also thinking it a good plan for the older and "wiser" girls to give a little reception to the freshmen. They can get acquainted much easier and perhaps they after that will feel more at home with the older girls.
King—Indeed, I think that a very good plan.
First Freshman—O! I think this is the worst place I ever saw!
Second Fresh.—This morning I met the King and he frightened me so! I thought he was "bluebeard."
Fresh. in chor.—O, does he look like that!
First Fresh.—Look! there is the king. Do you suppose he has heard all we have said?
(Exit all the frightened freshmen.)

Scene 2—Artillery Room (Gym.).
Enter Freshmen, Sophomores and Seniors.
First Fresh.—Did you ever see such rules as are laid down for us. It is so hard to keep them.
Second Fresh.—O, they are awful! Last night I was in the blue room and did not leave until after the nine-ten bell had rung. I started down "Swell Headed Row," when suddenly I came face to face with Lady Caroline. I wished I had been in my own room. She wanted to know why I was not, and I had to tell her that a "senior" had told me that I was foolish to start just as soon as the bell rings, for I would not get caught if I did not leave for five minutes later.
First Senior—It is "preposterous" how the freshmen get into so much trouble.
Second Senior—
When I was a freshman fair,
To break a rule I ne'er did dare;
But now that I am a senior bright,
I can do what I think right.
Seniors, in chorus—
For we are dignified seniors,
And we're not afraid to tell
That we are jolly good seniors,
And that we are from Lasell.
Sophs.—O, those freshmen will be the bother of our lives. We can never plan to go anywhere or do anything without them. You know the "freshmen always want to go to everything that comes along for fear of missing something."
Freshmen, in chorus—
As freshmen we've done very well,
And been a credit to Lasell.
We leave this year without a sigh,
To be in one where we're not shy.

MUCH TO DO ABOUT NOTHING.

ACT I.

Scene 1—Assembly Room (hall).

Enter King Charles, Sophomores.

King—Look you yonder in the hall,
      Hear the "Sophies" loudly call,
      Only last year "Freshies" they;
      Now they're "sophs" in every way,
      Much about nothing they're to do,
      And look to being juniors true.

Scene 2—Intelligence Room Number 4.

Enter Mistress Mary and Sophomores.

Mis. Mary—We are assembled here to learn about "force emphasis, and life, which all come under the main head of 'force.'" Have you all studied your lesson?

Sophs.—Yes, Mistress Mary.

Mis. Mary—Can you tell me in what way we gain force?

Sophs.—"By the choice of words."

Class excused.

Sophs.—Happy juniors soon we'll be,
      Merry, joyous, full of glee.
      Soph'more year we'll ne'er forget,
      All the girls that we have met,
      All the fun that we have had,
      How oft' the teachers we've made sad!

AS YOU LIKE IT.

ACT I.

Scene 1—Artillery Room.

Enter Juniors.

Juniors, in chorus—
      Now as senior's "supes" we're true,
      Just as juniors ought to do.
      In "As You Like It" we can play,
      And when we've finished who can say
      That we have not been juniors bright,
      And always done just what was right.

First Junior—How do you like Shakespeare?

Second Junior—O, I think it is wild, but our teacher is "Wilder."

Enter King.

King—When we have a good speaker here on Commencement day, it is not one time out of ten'that the girls remember half of what he says. Why not have a five dollar speaker then? What is the use of having a good one?

Smart Jun.—If we have a good speaker, that will be the one time out of ten that we will remember what he says.

Scene 2—Banquet Room.

Enter Friar Charles.

Fri. Chas.—There will be an "opportunity" to go walking with the "prince" this afternoon. Do not fail to take advantage of this "opportunity."

Juniors, in chorus—
      This year is past, much work we've done,
      Some studies finished; some new friends won.
      And now we have one aspiration,
      Which is to leave our present station,
      And don the senior cap and gown,
      And then we'll be of some renown.

ALL IS WELL THAT ENDS WELL.

ACT I.

Scene 1—Banquet Room.

Enter King Charles, and Seniors.

King—See our seniors in cap and gown,
      Compared to them none can be found.
      Let's give three cheers for our seniors bright,
      Who are so loyal to the "blue and white."
      In these cheers let voices swell,
      For "all is well that ends so well."

Seniors—We're marching to a steady tune,
      Into the royal banquet room;
      To our table in the middle aisle,
      We are marching in a double file.

Scene 2—Artillery Room.

Enter Mistress Martha and Seniors.

Mis. Martha—You do not go walking every day, therefore, you must take gymnasium.

Seniors—We go to "gym." with smiling faces (but such a heavy heart). We are very happy that we have the privilege of trying the dear old machines again; but we would rather leave them for the other fair maidens. We may wear them out, "using them so much." (However, we will give the impression that we enjoy it very much.)

Scene 3—Intelligence Room, Number 4.

Enter Mistress Mary; Seniors.

Mis. Mary—We will have a primary lesson in spelling. First senior, please spell *Angel*.

First Senior—A-N-G-L-E.

Mis. Mary—You certainly deserve to wear the cap and gown.

Seniors, in chorus—
      Thus our senior year is done,
      And Lasell for us has won
      Many crowns for which we praise her,
      Loyal to our "Alma Mater."

Marriages.

—Jamie Louise Watson to John Lowry Wagner, Wednesday, April 24, at 9 o'clock, at the Normandie, Columbus, Ohio. After May 29, at home at Fairmont, W. Va.

—Maude Mayo ('98) to Harry Bentz, on

Tuesday, April 9, at Foxcroft, Me. Address: Larchmont Manor, New York.

—Helen Thayer Turner to Harold Hallowell Werner, on Tuesday, April 30, Auburndale, Mass. Address, after October 1: No. 332 Rich Avenue, Mt. Vernon, N. Y.

—Mary Dana to Frederick Herbert Baird, on Wednesday, April 17, at Auburndale, Mass. Mrs. Baird is a sister of our Bessie Dana.

—Alice Pauline Conant to Charles Franklin Sisson, Jr., on Wednesday, May 8, at Camden, N. Y. Address, after August 15, 39 Oak street, Binghamton, N. Y.

—Julia Elizabeth Hammond to George Joseph McBride, on Thursday, May 16, at Chicago. Address, after October 1, No. 4598 Oakenwald Avenue.

—May Louise Gurley to Edgar Hayes Betts, on Monday, May 27, at Troy, N. Y. Address, after November 1, No. 1914 Fifth Avenue, Troy, N. Y.

—Mary Abbie Thomas to William Darre Walker, on Thursday, May 29, at Peabody, Mass. Address, after October 15, No. 64 Willow Avenue, West Somerville, Mass.

—M. Corinne Salisbury to J. Edmund C. Fisher, on Saturday, June 1, at Beatrice, Nebraska.

—Mary Fuller Lothrop to Benjamin Fessenden, on Thursday, June 4, at Stafford Springs, Connecticut.

—Charlotte White to Sterling Frederick Higley, on Tuesday, June 4, at Glens Falls, N. Y.

—Lorena M. Fellows to Frank Drummond Hight, on Tuesday, June 11, at Bangor, Me.

—Ada Cadmus ('98) to Edward Alexander McCoy, on Monday evening, June 17, at East Orange, N. J.

—Lois Mabel Sawyer to Franklin T. Miller, on Tuesday, June 4, at Brookline, Mass.

—Ida Frances Trowbridge to Dr. Louis D. H. Fuller, on Wednesday, June 19, at South Framingham, Mass. Address after August, Saxonville, Mass.

PERSONALS.

—From Edith Gale we learn that she has had a pleasant visit with Ada Dunaway Caldwell and Mary Roberts Ogden. Ada has two nice children, Edgar, a boy of five, and little Virginia, a year and a half. Mary, too, has two fine youngsters, both bright, sturdy boys. Edith spent the month of May, moreover, with Lou Sargeant Warren, in her pleasant St. Louis home, 5535 Von Versen avenue, which she has purchased.

—Grace Allen saw Julia Hammond McBride and her husband on their way to Salt Lake, on their wedding trip. Elizabeth Stephenson Morgan is now settled in her new home in Oshkosh. Grace regrets not having been able to be with us at our fiftieth anniversary celebration. So do we.

—Mabel Taylor spent the winter in Washington with Mr. Gannett's parents, and in March, while she was still there, the elder Mr. Gannett died. She saw Anna Warner in Washington, and also Blanche Swope; and in New York, Florence Raymond. Martha Stone Adams and her husband have visited, she says, the Buffalo Exposition, and planned to visit Lasell before returning home.

—Sara Hitchcock expresses her appreciation of the LEAVES, a copy of which she has recently received. We should be glad to add her name to the subscription list, and send the paper regularly.

—At a violin recital given in Boston, April 25, by the pupils of Miss Edith Linwood Winn, our popular violin teacher this year, several of her Lasell pupils were present, and enjoyed the evening greatly.

—At an organ recital given April 8, in the Asylum Hill Congregational church, Hartford, Conn., the organist of the evening was S. Clarke Lord, who was assisted by Harriette S. Ward, of the seminary class of graduates this year.

—Elise Scott is visiting Avila Grubbs, at her pleasant home in Harrodsburg, Kentucky, and writes of having delightful times there.

—Ruth Sankey Ripley, 2008 E. Union street, Seattle, Washington, informs us that she is the proud possessor of a very small boy, named Bradford Sankey; and that her father and mother have gone to Seattle to live next door to the Ripleys. Both are to build new homes, and, to quote Ruth, "live happy ever after."

—Emma Goll Dacy has a wee baby girl, Marion Adéle, born on Thursday, May 2nd, and a treasure.

—Lulu Wells Brannen writes appreciatively of her visit here some time ago, and admiringly of Mr. and Mrs. Nordsick, who think of sending their daughter to Lasell next year. Clara Creswell Blakeney, she says, has another lovely boy, and Gertrude Seiberling, "the same strong, placid soul as of old," recently wrote her. For themselves she says they are thinking of a trip East this summer, or, possibly, Europe again.

—Nellie M. Richards writes, concerning the spring trip to Washington: "I was charmed with the girls, and think that if they are a fair sample, you must have a splendid lot this year. They were lovely to me, so that I enjoyed every moment of the trip."

She was hoping when she wrote to be with us at Commencement.

—Margie Schuberth speaks of having exchanged visits with Dorothy, recently, and of Daisy Hartson's spring visit to Helen Cooke, on which occasion Greta Stearns Kinsey had "quite a little Lasell party at her home one day for luncheon, to meet Daisy." Margie was there, of course.

—Ida Trowbridge, whose own reception on the occasion of the announcement of her engagement occurred but a short time ago, was present at the senior reception here, and looked to be in the best of health and spirits.

—Caroline Baldwin has been studying music in New York this year with Miss Bissell, and appeared as one of the performers at a public rehearsal given May 10, in Mendelssohn Glee Club Hall.

—Alice Linscott Hall has news to tell us; her husband has accepted the Greek professorship in Washington University, St. Louis, to which city the family will move next September. Her "boy" she tells us, is six feet tall, and a freshman; and Elinor is already well into her sixteenth year. It seems hardly possible! Mrs. Hall plans to attend Lasell's Commencement on the twenty-fifth anniversary of her graduation, but stipulates that Mr. Bragdon shall be there, *sine qua non.*

—Mattie Baker, when last heard from by letter, was planning to sail with her mother, father, and brother, for America May 21, and expected to be with us at Commencement, though we did not see her at that time. Rev. Dr. G. D. Watson and his wife have been in Jamaica, she says, pursuing their evangelistic work. She met them and was pleased with them. Her brother and his wife live at Port Antonio. Mattie and her mother paid them a visit in May. Their baby boy, she says, is now eight months old, and "a real *Baker.*" His Aunt Mattie is as proud of him as she can be, and threatens to bring him to Lasell to show him off.

—Sade Hollingsworth Thompson, whose sweet voice delighted us in other years, when she was a student here at Lasell, came back with her husband to see us this June, to be present at the Semi-Centennial celebration, and while here sang for us on the evening of Baccalaureate Sunday, and again on Commencement Day. We wish her old friends and schoolmates who have not seen her since they were here together might have been with us then, to hear for themselves what a splendid voice she has—full, rich, powerful, and in perfect control. She has, too, that rare accomplishment in a singer, perfect enunciation. It was a memorable treat that she gave us. She is looking well. Mr. Thompson is a pleasant and agreeable gentleman.

—Fräulein Adéle Roth, now connected with the Classical School for Girls, in Pasadena, Cal., sends an interesting letter, in which she gives sundry items of information, some about herself, others about some of our old girls. She met in Los Angeles the other day Sue Stearns that was, who has a fine little boy, and whose husband, now in England, is to return to America soon. Zoe Lowe Brown's little girl is a beautiful child. Katharine Watson, now Mrs. Jas. Pugh, is living in a charming bungalow on Lockhaven street, Pasadena. Fannie Watson is studying art at Pittsburg. Mabel Falley's husband is a Methodist now, and has a church at Detroit. Emma Roth was graduated from Stanford this month. About herself she says that she is enjoying her present situation very much, and gives us a hint of the delights of California in Maytime—such gorgeousness and luxuriance of flowers, and such sunshiny days.

—In the *Advance-Journal* of Camden, N. Y., a copy of which was kindly sent us, we find a very interesting account of Alice Conant's wedding early in May. Her beautiful home, Grove Cottage, was made even more lovely by the profusion of flowers used to decorate it for the occasion, and the ceremony was the impressive one of the Episcopal church. Bridesmaids, maids of honor, beautiful costumes—nothing dear to the heart of a bride was wanting. May we not, though late, cast our handful of rice also after the pair, and wish them much happiness?

—The friends of Lucy Ames and Elsie Burdick will be grieved to learn of the bereavement that has visited these two of our girls, and those who knew bright-eyed Bertha Wilson will also be saddened to learn of her untimely death.

—If you want to know *what maple syrup* really is you must have the good fortune of the Principal, and taste the product of a well-bred Vermont sugar maple, raised and trained by Miriam Nelson's grandfather. This pleasure the Principal has had by Miss Nelson's kindness, and is ready to say "Vixi." He has reveled in maple syrups before, but declares this of rare flavor and great consistency, and wishes he could share it with all of you.

—On his visit to New York to see his brother and family off for Europe, on the Hohenzollern, sailing May 18, Mr. Bragdon met Mrs. Fanny Barker Coffin, '68, who with her two sisters, were passengers, and our own Lou Barker, here in his early years, who was there to see Mrs. Coffin off. A very pleasant meeting and good wishes.

—Nellie Feagles, ('97) who has just returned from a two years' stay in Europe, made a brilliant record in Berlin, taking her degree second in a large class; and Nellie didn't pay much attention to German here usually, either.

—One of the pleasant surprises of April

was the appearance of Kittie Seiberling Firey and her husband, who are "taking their wedding trip" in rather an extensive fashion throughout the East.   As noted in the last LEAVES, they have been living in Indianapolis, but are soon to go to take charge of the Coates House, the best hotel in Kansas City.   Mr. Firey is following the usual custom of the genial Boniface.   Kittie doesn't seem to me to have changed a bit.   They took them for bride and groom in Washington, which rather amused them, since they have been married seven years.   She reports all well in Akron.

—John Cassidy and his wife, principals of the National Park Seminary, Forest Glen, Maryland, made us a welcome call the last of February.   They wore good clothes, and in every way looked prosperous.   One could hardly believe their statement that Mrs. Cassidy had been ill several months of the present year.   They both looked as if they had never known sickness, or want, or trouble. They were searching for good New England teachers for their popular school, in which they have been abundantly successful.   To see them and to hear them was a rare pleasure, making a red-letter day of that Monday.

—Mary. Hathaway Farnham ('88) "mothers" five boys of the Roxbury Latin School, in which Mr. Farnham is a teacher, living in the old Admiral Winslow house.

—Mr. Herbert Ingalls Gannett, of Omaha, Nebraska, to whom Mabel Taylor has announced her engagement, called on Mr. Bragdon early in May.   He is a manly fellow.

—Emilie Kothe sends post card from Rome, expressing her desire that she might have been with us during Commencement, not even the charms of the Eternal City being able to efface those of Lasell.

—Miss Grace Huntington, ('89), called June 20.   She is living in Brooklyn now,

and looks just the same as ever.   She says Blanche Pruyne has changed into a physical condition more suitable for active service; that Sue Hackett has lost her second child.

Mr. and Mrs. Frederic Aldin Hall
request the pleasure of your company
at their
Twentieth Wedding Anniversary,
Monday evening, June the seventeenth,
eight until eleven o'clock,
958 Benton Avenue,
Springfield, Missouri.

This was our Alice Linscott of '78·

—A late paper from Wheeling has the following: "Anna Chamberlin, wife of William P. Hubbard, who entered into rest Friday night, June 7, was a woman of remarkable character.   While not widely known, she impressed all who came within her circle by the strength of her religion and the sweetness of her charity.   The daughter of a Presbyterian minister, the Rev. Nelson P. Chamberlin, she was always devoted to that church.   Her life was in her home, where she welcomed all who came, and charmed by her kindly hospitality.   She was for many years a great invalid, and the attention of her daughters was beautiful." This is the mother of our Julia, Alma, and Louise.   Our sympathy is theirs, and their father's.

OVERHEARD.

Why was Room 22 so dark and gloomy the last term of school?   Because there was no Day there.

Dr. G.—When Briggs is with the girls he should dispense with his other canine friends.

We had always thought we saw out of our eyes until Mr. B., in chapel, one day said, "Now open your ears and look."

Teacher (in trigonometry class)—What are the great circles of the earth?

Pupil—I do not know, unless they are the hemispheres.

A Senior (standing on the veranda, watching the girls playing hop-scotch, exclaimed)—Oh, see! the girls are playing butter-scotch.

What is E. D.'s favorite vegetable?   Onion.

GYMNASIUM STATISTICS.

AVERAGE.	SEPT., 1900.	MAY, 1901.
Weight,	119.18 lbs.	124.92 lbs.
Height,	5 ft. 4.54 in.	5 ft. 4.78 in.
Lung Capacity,	149.53 cu. in.	162.19 cu. in.
Strength of Back,	87.35 kilos.	120.76 kilos.
of Chest,	27.4 kilos.	31.96 kilos.
of R. Forearm,	23.53 kilos.	25.61 kilos.
of L. Forearm,	19.62 kilos.	22.2 kilos.

Number of pupils incapacitated for gymnastic work
during the school year, 3
Number of pupils in the gymnasium during the
school year, 141

STRONGEST PUPIL (MAY, 1901).

Age,	18 years.
Weight,	127½ pounds.
Lung Capacity.	230 cu. inches.
Strength of Back,	160 kilos.
Strength of Chest,	38 kilos.
Strength of Right Forearm,	33 kilos.
Strength of Left Forearm,	30 kilos.
Height,	5 ft. 7.6 in.

SENIOR CLASS MEMBERS (16).

Average.		Average Gain.
Age,	19 yrs. 9 mos.	
Weight,	123.3 lbs.	5.77 lbs.
Height,	5 ft. 4.176 in.	.724 in.
Lung Capacity,	159.69 kilos.	20 cu. inches.
Strength of Back,	118.125 kilos.	33.75 kilos.
of Chest,	30.5 kilos.	4.25 kilos.
of R. Forearm,	25.69 kilos.	2.19 kilos.
of L. Forearm,	21.875 kilos.	3.19 kilos.
Tallest pupil (Miss Kendrick),	5 ft. 9.3 in.	
Heaviest weight,	195.5 lbs.	
Lightest weight,	80.5 lbs.	
Greatest gain in weight,	29.5 lbs.	
Greatest gain in strength,	123 kilos.	
Next greatest gain in strength,	111 kilos.	

Number pupils gained in all strength tests, 49

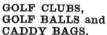

Lightning Source UK Ltd.
Milton Keynes UK
UKHW011139281118

333023UK00014B/1825/P